BAROQUE REASON

Theory, Culture & Society

Theory, Culture & Society caters for the resurgence of interest in culture within contemporary social science and the humanities. Building on the heritage of classical social theory, the book series examines ways in which this tradition has been reshaped by a new generation of theorists. It will also publish theoretically informed analyses of everyday life, popular culture, and new intellectual movements.

EDITOR: Mike Featherstone, *University of Teesside*

SERIES EDITORIAL BOARD
Roy Boyne, *University of Northumbria at Newcastle*
Mike Hepworth, *University of Aberdeen*
Scott Lash, *University of Lancaster*
Roland Robertson, *University of Pittsburgh*
Bryan S. Turner, *Deakin University*

Recent volumes include:

Risk Society
Towards a New Modernity
Ulrich Beck

Max Weber and the Sociology of Culture
Ralph Schroeder

Postmodernity USA
The Crisis of Social Modernism in Postwar America
Anthony Woodiwiss

The New Politics of Class
Social Movements and Cultural Dynamics in Advanced Societies
Klaus Eder

The Body and Social Theory
Chris Shilling

Symbolic Exchange and Death
Jean Baudrillard

Sociology in Question
Pierre Bourdieu

Economies of Signs and Space
Scott Lash and John Urry

Religion and Globalization
Peter Beyer

BAROQUE REASON

The Aesthetics of Modernity

Christine Buci-Glucksmann

Translated by Patrick Camiller

With an Introduction by
Bryan S. Turner

SAGE Publications
London • Thousand Oaks • New Delhi

Originally published as *La Raison baroque* by Éditions
Galilée, Paris, © Éditions Galilée, 1984

Translation © Sage Publications, 1994

Introduction © Bryan S. Turner, 1994

First published 1994

Published in association with *Theory, Culture & Society*,
School of Human Studies, University of Teesside

SAGE Publications Ltd
6 Bonhill Street
London EC2A 4PU

SAGE Publications Inc
2455 Teller Road
Thousand Oaks, California 91320

SAGE Publications India Pvt Ltd
32, M-Block Market
Greater Kailash – I
New Delhi 110 048

British Library Cataloguing in Publication data

A catalogue record for this book is available from the
British Library.

Library of Congress catalog card number 93–086832

Typeset by Photoprint, Torquay, Devon
Printed in Great Britain by Biddles Ltd, Guildford, Surrey

CONTENTS

INTRODUCTION

Bryan S. Turner

Aesthetic theory

Christine Buci-Glucksmann's brilliant study of modern social theory
is concerned with the ways in which social realities can be represented, and in particular with the possible means of representing
'modernity'. More specifically still, she wants to understand the
aesthetic systems of modernity. Representation concerns the multiple ways in which realities can be encoded in a system of signs,
typically through what we regard as art, religion and language, that
is through symbolic orders. Aesthetics is narrowly defined as the
philosophy of art, or more broadly as a theory of beauty. It has both
a theoretical wing (what are the discursive systems by which a work
of art is defined?) and a practical dimension (how is art produced?).
Aesthetics as a discipline arose in the late eighteenth century when
philosophers like Alexander Gottlieb recognized that the sciences
were incomplete, given the absence of a science of beauty. (We need
to remember that the German notion of science or *Wissenschaft* is
much broader than the narrow positivist understanding of science
which typically characterizes the English-speaking world.) Early
aesthetic theories were concerned not so much with sensory apprehension of reality as with the theory of poetry, whose topic was
thought to be the meaning of beauty. Aesthetics was subsequently
developed by Kant in *Critique of Pure Reason* in 1781 and in
Critique of Judgment in 1790 to include both a science of perception
and a judgement about taste. In the nineteenth century, aesthetics
was concerned with the philosophy of art (its most common
meaning) and with sensory perception of beauty. The idea of
decadence in that century was summarized in the idea of 'art for
art's sake'. In fact Benjamin (1983: 106), in the 'Addendum' to 'The
Paris of the Second Empire in Baudelaire', dates this development
from 1852 when the bourgeoisie withdrew from any political
involvement in the cause of writers and artists. Art began to lose
any social role, especially in relation to politics.

In recent decades, classical aesthetics has been criticized for its allegedly superior claims to universalism. This challenge to universalism can be traced back to Nietzsche's critique of the Kantian notion that the aesthetic judgement of taste is neutral, passionless and disinterested. In his idea of the physiology of art, Nietzsche claimed that rapture and dream rather than rational inspection were the basis of the aesthetic state. These Nietzschean ideas on emotion, discourse and aesthetics had their impact on modern thought partly through the work of Martin Heidegger (1979). Thus the impact of modern language philosophy has been to challenge the notion that 'art' is a universal, immutable phenomenon. Instead 'art' has to be seen in a sociological and historical context, and thus the aesthetic question becomes a sociological one: what set of cultural and social circumstances produces 'taste' (Bourdieu, 1984)?

Aesthetics (as a theory of beauty) in the twentieth century has been called into question by the destructive power of war and the violence of the modern state. In particular the concentration camps and mass genocide of the Holocaust have placed a fundamental doubt in the modern mind about the very possibility of the beautiful and the sublime. The Frankfurt School, especially in the aesthetic theory of Theodor Adorno, adopted the view that, as a consequence of the Holocaust, poetry was impossible; the production of beauty was a mere mockery of true values in a world of total violence. Thus, the destruction of classical confidence in the universality of beauty is connected with the erosion of religious values and the relativization of morality.

These problems lie at the centre of the aesthetic concerns of Walter Benjamin, whose writings on art, art history and politics have dominated much of the late twentieth-century debate about aesthetics (in the broad sense). Benjamin (1892–1940) failed to obtain an academic post in Germany after his thesis on German tragic drama (*The Origin of German Tragic Drama* [1977]) was rejected at Frankfurt in 1925. He subsequently became attached to the Marxist social theorists of the Frankfurt School as one of their most promising aesthetic theorists (although his relations with Adorno remained highly problematic). He studied the poetry of Charles Baudelaire during his exile in Paris in 1933, a study which produced *Charles Baudelaire: A Lyric Poet in the Era of High Capitalism* (1983), which was published posthumously in 1969. He committed suicide in 1940 during a forlorn attempt to escape fascism by migrating from southern France to Spain. Benjamin's work was neglected, until the original German publication of *The Origin of German Tragic Drama* in 1955, since when there has been a major revival of interest. There have been major reviews of

Benjamin's work in German, French and English (Eagleton, 1981; Fuld, 1979; Gaines, 1993; Roberts, 1982; Wolin, 1993). Buci-Glucksmann's interpretation of Benjamin is in many respects one of the most sophisticated and original. Her text, which is fully translated here in English for the first time, is a powerfully imaginative recovery of the world of Benjamin's own imagination, giving full play as it does to the Jewish mystical perspective on the unfolding of religious history, to the importance of both language and aesthetic philosophy in Benjamin, his fascination for Parisian consumerism, the problems of Baudelaire's poetic imagination and nihilism, and the historical connections between otherness, women and Judaism. Buci-Glucksmann's special concern with the function of allegory, particularly baroque allegory/reason, precisely captures one of the core issues in both Benjamin's aesthetics and his social theory.

Language, truth and beauty

The Romantic idea that 'truth is beauty, beauty, truth' had an ancient origin. It asserts an intimate relationship between what we value in aesthetic terms, and what we perceive to be truth. That which we value as true also has aesthetic authority. We might also add: what carries moral conviction also has an aesthetic authority. In traditional societies, there was relatively little differentiation between the realms or orders of religion, morality, regimes of truth and representations of beauty. The break-up of the integrated world of traditional societies brought about a fragmentation between language, truth and religio-moral orders. This break-up has been given various formulations: the transition from community to association, the modernization process, or the secularization and disenchantment of reality. For example, under the impact of Romanticism, these connections between morality and aesthetics were given a strongly subjective and individualistic resonance, because beauty was given an emotive and privatized content. The coherence of this relationship between aesthetics and morality was broken in the modern world by the differentiation of the aesthetic as a separate domain with its own autonomy and logic. The aesthet-icization of the everyday world was yet a further development in the evaluation of representations of beauty which occurred with the development of capitalism and the commodification of the life-world. Many social critics came to see this development as part of the alienation of human beings under the commodification of life and the evolution of a fetishism of consciousness. That which could be exchanged was true; that which could be bought was valued. The traditional equations of morality, aesthetics and truth were over-turned by these revolutionary developments in the social organiz-ation of the economy. The impact on religion and art – arenas in which divine values had been traditionally embedded – was equally profound. Traditional religious values were marginalized; art lost much of its conventional religious aura, just as its uniqueness was lost as mechanical means of reproduction, especially photography, became dominant. Benjamin (1986), in his article on 'Surrealism', claimed that the movement had finally broken the ritualistic and religious context which had separated art from life. As a result the way in which the world could be represented (or pictured) was also revolutionized (Lash, 1990). The picture of the world became a mere convention, not a divinely ordered regime. Buci-Glucksmann's study of baroque reason/representation and modern aesthetics/modes of capturing beauty can be seen as an extended reflection on these transformations at three critical or catastrophic points in the historical eruption of modernity: the seventeenth-century baroque, the world of Baudelaire's Paris, and the avant-garde artistic movements of the twentieth century. In literary or cultural terms, these crises have had a strong connection with problems of representation, and thereby with language and sym-bolism. At the centre of these debates, we can locate the diverse and complex social philosophy of Benjamin, a key figure in twentieth-century aesthetic theory and a core theme in Buci-Glucksmann's analysis.

In contemporary philosophy these traditional views of truth and beauty have thus been challenged by changes in the theory of language and in particular by structuralist approaches to language as a system of differences. Theories of language have dominated many of the major shifts and developments in philosophy, art and social practice in the twentieth century. In fact structuralism has trans-formed every branch of the humanities and social sciences because cultural phenomena are now seen as texts which can only be approached by the critical methods of literary studies (Vattimo, 1988). Epistemological questions (how is truth produced?) have always in the history of philosophy interacted closely with ontologi-cal questions (what can exist?) and with aesthetic notions (what is beautiful?). In the contemporary world, this traditional problematic has been given a new and decisive direction: what can be known, what can exist and what can be experienced is made possible (and impossible) by the structure of the language which is available to a social system. One interpretation of such grammatical determinism is that reality is a function of a regime of words, that is, a government of words. In seventeenth-century positivism, we can trace the origins of the correspondence theory of truth, which asserts that there is a direct and relatively simple relationship between language and reality such that the function of language is to register in a neutral fashion elements of the factual world. Language provides, as it were, a mirror of nature (Rorty, 1979). In the twentieth century, there has been a radical shift in how we think about language. In modern structuralism, language is interpreted as either producing reality through construction, or making possible an always partial apprehension of reality. In particular, the impact of Ferdinand de Saussure's *Course in General Linguistics* of 1916 (1959) has radically transformed understanding of the relationship between words and things, or more generally between reality and discourse.

Briefly, Saussure had argued a number of fundamental propositions: we must distinguish between language (*langue*) and speech (*parole*), that is, between language as a social resource of everyday practice and language as a system of elements which are structured by trans-social rules and logics; we must further distinguish between the synchronic study of language as a system of a historical relations which is a collective construct of a social group, and the diachronic study of the unplanned and unconscious changes which take place in language in use; and finally there is the study of the double-nature of the linguistic sign which comprises the concept and the sound or acoustic image. The relationship between these two is arbitrary; there is no internal or necessary relationship between the concept of dog and the various sounds ('dog', 'der Hund' or 'de hond'). More technically, the relationship between signifiers, signifieds and referents is arbitrary. This idea became the basis of a radical challenge to the correspondence theory of truth, because it uncoupled any simple relation of reflection between language and nature. Saussure focused primarily on language as a system of signs rather than on speech as a performative activity. He therefore attempted to show that meaning in language was not an indigenous feature of words but the product of differences between juxtaposed sets of dichotomies: up/down, wet/dry or good/bad. The meaning of reality, according to structuralist interpretations of Saussure's theory of language, is sustained by the effect of differences between orders of words. At best, language discloses reality through a system of differences.

This relatively simple set of notions has produced extraordinarily radical consequences. It is wrong to assume that Saussure has had a direct effect on all versions of structuralist and post-structuralist thought: there are various 'tight' and 'loose' versions of structuralistic linguistics (Megill, 1985). Although Michel Foucault's views on language owe more to literary criticism than to Saussure, his approach to language and reality had a distinctively anti-humanist and anti-anthropological direction which was highly compatible with post-Saussurian developments: the order of things is in fact an order of words (Foucault, 1991). One might almost add: an order of things is merely an order of words. Another possibility is that reality exists independently of the languages by which it is made available, but its real nature remains ineffable and hidden. This hidden quality of reality can only be grasped by prophetic insight, by imagination and possession; it can only be expressed by symbol, by allegory or parable. It is the poetic/religious imagination which has insight into inner reality; language as a system of formal differences has paradoxically relatively little capacity for authentic communication. This problem is fundamental to the work of Benjamin, whose theory of language has often been neglected in favour of exegesis of his aesthetic theories (Gaines, 1993).

While this radical analysis of language is appropriately associated with Saussure's linguistic philosophy, it had in fact many diverse sources. It was anticipated in Nietzsche's analysis of the will to power in which, as a consequence of the 'death of God', there is no hegemonic arrangement of truth: everything is a product of perspectives. Saussure's analysis also depended on the work of Émile Durkheim and Marcel Mauss (1963) who attempted to show that the dominant patterns of thought (collective representations) were produced and sustained by the dominant patterns of social organization. The notion of 'god' was an effect of collective rituals and collective sentiment. In contemporary applications of structuralism, the analysis of truth has been approached via an understanding of the prevailing patterns of power in that truth is seen to be a function of power: hierarchical, patriarchal, racist and despotic. The aim of such linguistic radicalism has been to penetrate the veil of representation to expose not a regime of veracity but an order of power. This critical function has been one feature of the method of deconstruction. Such an approach has been used as a means of understanding how, historically, transformations in the regime of representation have been associated with revolutions in the nature of power. For example, how did the emergence of the modern world out of a traditional and relatively stable order impact upon the sovereignty of regimes of representation? How did the origins of capitalism influence the methods by which truth and beauty were presented? How did baroque mentality or baroque reason allow people to see beauty/truth? In short, how did the baroque order of representation use allegory, symbol and sound to indicate an order of shimmering reality?

Linguistic philosophers and historians of ideas have been quick to detect a strange correspondence between modern structuralistic radicalism and the theology of ancient Judaism. Primitive Jewish culture placed an extraordinary weight upon knowing the Word, interpreting religious discourses and following the letter of the law. Unlike Christianity, Judaism had no sacerdotal priesthood, precisely because the main emphasis of religious activity centred on the word of God: in the beginning was the Word, and the Word was God. In fact the Abrahamic faiths generally shared this fascination with God's prophetic declaration of truth. In Christianity, Word was incarnate in the body of Christ; in Islam, the Qur'an is the unadultered, pure Word of God, delivered to Muhammad as the Last Word to the Last Prophet. Islam is the final religion of mankind as the completion of the work of Abraham, Moses, Christ and the prophets. The debate in the Abrahamic religions about how God discloses Himself to human beings has been parallel in many respects to the general philosophical question: does language cover up or uncover truth/reality, and how can we discover this reality? By philosophy, by poetry, by spirit possession? The great promise of the Enlightenment and rationalism was to recover reality/truth by disposing of religion, the great mystification of nature. Marxism in the nineteenth century can be seen as a continuation of this rationalist legacy: dialectical materialism would disclose the world, free from both the illusions of religion and the mystifications of bourgeois culture. Marxism was 'critical criticism' which would start with the deconstruction of religion and finish with the uncovering of the laws of the economy. It would expose and uncover the fetishization of commodities which was the basis of illusions (such as reification) in bourgeois capitalism.

Buci-Glucksmann's account of Baudelaire's nihilism and Benjamin's political theology is a reflection on the failures of this humanistic adventure and it is within this context of structuralist theories of language that we can best appreciate her analysis of orders of representation from the baroque to modern times via a study of the work of Baudelaire and Benjamin. The core of Benjamin's argument is that allegory, especially allegories about fate, death and melancholy, is the principal element in the aesthetic of modernity and has its archaeological origins in the forgotten and obscured past of modernity – the baroque. Let us say that the modern world, unlike the traditional medieval world of the hegemonic Church, its God and its symbols, is a fragmented, diversified, playful, incoherent flux. Its real nature is superbly illustrated by the passing, artificial, simulated, self-referential world of fashion, with its ever-changing styles, signs, sexual games, heroes, cultures, clichés, locations, and fashionable body-images. Madonna, simulation of the mother of Christ, sex-object and falsifier of sex, perhaps in the best of all possible worlds, is the central symbol of this modern hyperreality. What are the cultural or grammatical devices by which this world could be summarized, encapsulated? The leading candidates are montage, pastiche, allegory, irony and parody. What might provide the metaphors of this complexity? The ruin, the library, the labyrinth and the artifice. The literary or philosophical devices which might capture the fragmented, fractured, ruined nature of modernity also happen to be the dominant philosophical devices of the baroque period which, above all, was acutely aware of two things: the artificial, socially constructed nature of reality (its hyperreality) and the precarious, catastrophic, uncertain and hazardous nature of all human existence. The fantastic world of baroque theatre beautifully expressed this precarious fragility, just as Disneyland expresses the inner reality of modern consumerism. In order to prepare the basis for an appreciation of Buci-Glucksmann's account of these allegorical devices and the peculiar nature of modern consumerism, we need to pause briefly to consider Benjamin's theory of language.

Benjamin's views on language were deeply influenced by Jewish thought, especially by the mystical writings of the *kabbalah*, a spiritual orientation which was particularly influential in Germany. Benjamin's work is consequently characterized by its respect for reading and saying, namely the Word. This was evident in his study of the *Ursprung* (fount, origin, primal leap) origins of German tragic drama (1977), written between 1924 and 1925, but neglected until its initial publication in 1955. The main point of this work was to demonstrate that German baroque tragic drama, as distinct from tragedy, had its origins not in the classical Greek tradition but in medieval mystery plays and in the Christian themes of the mortification of the flesh. In particular, baroque drama was emblematic, hyperbolic and allegorical, reflecting on the tragedies of human embodiment, and hence on the dual life of humans (both animal and divine, fleshly and spiritual). Tragic feelings, within the Aristotelian paradigm, have little connection with the torrid emotions of the tragic drama. *Trauerspiel* (tragedy: literally 'sorrow-play') involved an audience in displays of palpable lament and ceremonies of public grief. Tragedy involves an educational process which is internal and often silent (Steiner, 1977). The *Trauerspiel* depends profoundly on allegory, at whose heart lies melancholy – a major theme not only for Benjamin, but also for the Frankfurt

School, the modern mind, and hence for Buci-Glucksmann's interpretation of modern aesthetics. These themes have been consistently inspired by the etchings of Dürer, especially the representations of death and melancholy. Throughout these interpretations of baroque *Trauerspiele*, Benjamin wanted to understand baroque language as a method of allegorically conveying meaning. Utterances, such as curses, have a direct impact on baroque personality.

Benjamin's theory of language might be called a naming theory, because the peculiar capacity of humans as rational and religious creatures is to name their environment. Adam's act of naming the creatures of the Garden of Paradise was the paradigmatic case. This naming process is not the external imposition of an arbitrary name to an object, but rather the sympathetic union of subject and object, producing an irreducible communion of sound, name and object. Benjamin, who rejected any mechanical correspondence between words and objects, developed a theory of language which was related to the symbolism of the circle around Stefan George (Roberts, 1982). In the George Circle, Ludwig Klages and Friedrich Gundolf proposed that the primal experiences of life had been obscured by civilizational processes and by language: it was only in art that these fundamental experiences could be approached. Although Benjamin was critical of the symbolists of the George Circle, he shared a common understanding with them of the importance and function of symbols. In particular, the symbolic significance of the ruin was a major feature of his understanding of the language of the baroque. The ruin, a sign of the transient character of human endeavour, was a primary allegory of the melancholy mentality of the baroque; the ruin was a statement of the inevitable passage of time, of our inability to escape from it. Truth and beauty were both circumscribed by death. Hence, the preoccupation with fictions, fantasies and fate. Because the contingencies of history and time were woven into the fabric of life, melancholy was a dominant component of the *Trauerspiel*.

Theories of modernity and postmodernity

Buci-Glucksmann's analysis of the origins of modern aesthetics via Baudelaire and Benjamin is also an account of theories of history. Is the process of history a radical leap from the sacred to the profane? Is it a revolutionary sequence of transformations of the modes of production by which social groups survive and reproduce themselves? Is it a moral history from lost solidarity to individualism and back to ethical collectivism? It is important to realize that Benjamin's view of history was saturated by a Judaic messianism: the present (exile) always reveals and holds the promise of a dramatic restoration through catastrophe to the land of justice. Periodization and its markers – exiles, holocausts, angels of destruction, prophets of gloom, the Lord of Hosts – play a central role in Benjamin's thought as they did, in a secular version, for Marx. Benjamin's view of history, although often expressed in the secular language of Marxism, was in fact a radical Jewish and messianic view of the unfolding of history. Like his contemporary Georg Lukács, Benjamin radicalized the Jewish notion of total redemption via an incorporation of Marxist revolutionary discourse, itself a secularized version of revolutionary Judaic historicism.

What then is traditionalism? What is modernism? What is posthistory? These are crucial questions for Benjamin and for Buci-Glucksmann. The latter's study of the three crucial turning-points in the origins of the modern aesthetics in fact problematizes history as a division between tradition and modernity. In order to grasp this problem in the philosophy of history, let us start with a monumental contemporary issue. What is this modernity which has destroyed everything behind it and threatens to destroy everything before it? In the following discussion, I am primarily concerned with the sociological notion of modernity, a notion which is often rather remote from the literary meaning of modernism and modernity. Baudelaire, whose ideas are clearly important for both Benjamin and Buci-Glucksmann, had an idea of the modern as the fleeting and trivial. Thus in 1863 he wrote 'By "modernity" I mean the ephemeral, the fugitive, the contingent, the half of the art whose other half is the eternal and the immutable' (Baudelaire, 1964: 13). This view of the modern as the fleeting has much in common with the sociological view of Georg Simmel, but it is less common in social science than in the humanities.

The problem of historical periodization in contemporary social theory is concentrated on whether the modern has come to an end. Indeed much of the intellectual debate in the humanities and the social sciences over the last decade has been dominated by the contrast between the modern and postmodern. Although this debate is fundamental and intellectually serious, the issue has often been dominated by a somewhat trivial pursuit of precise definitions. In order to understand Buci-Glucksmann's analysis of baroque reason, we have to grasp the social and cultural dimensions of modernity, modernization and modernism. If the core of Buci-Glucksmann's superb analysis of Baudelaire and Benjamin is the aesthetic character of modernity and its hidden archaeological roots in seventeenth-century absolutism, then it is appropriate to approach her argument via a comment on the struggles and contradictions which exist between modernism and postmodernism. It is important to emphasize the point that Buci-Glucksmann is not concerned with the analysis of the modern and the postmodern; this contrast is employed here as a device to understand her argument. The substantive reason for introducing a discussion of postmodernism in this Introduction is to indicate some unusual parallels between postmodern themes and baroque reason. In particular, both perspectives are held together by a fascination with artifice, especially montage and allegory, and both are inclined towards a profound melancholy mentality. I hope this digression will, therefore, provide the reader with even further evidence of the extraordinary range of Buci-Glucksmann's analysis.

We should not clutter this analysis by an inconsequential digression into the definitional problems which have bedevilled the debate. I therefore propose to give a summary account of the argument. First, it is appropriate to distinguish the intellectual debate around modernism and postmodernism from the sociological analysis of the social, political and cultural phenomena of contemporary societies which are best described in terms of modernity and postmodernity. Thus, postmodernism is a form of analysis or expression, while postmodernity refers to the sociological dimensions of a postmodern society. The analysis of postmodernism in art and aesthetic theory is well established, but it is only relatively recently that the social sciences have turned to the analysis of postmodernity as a form of social organization. In sociology, therefore, the study of postmodernity can be associated through the writings of Daniel Bell (1973) to an earlier discussion of the idea of a post-industrial society. In sociology, postmodernity is closely associated with the dominance of knowledge and information in late capitalist society, with the expansion of the mass media, and the globalization of communication through new electronic technologies. This view of postmodernity in terms of information technology and its impact on society dominates much of Jean-François Lyotard's *The Postmodern Condition* (1984) and more specifically the recent writing of Jean Baudrillard (Gane, 1991). The attempt to produce a sociology of postmodernity has, of course, inevitably run into a number of serious analytical difficulties, among which the attempt to form a coherent periodization of modernity and postmodernity has been dominant.

The second major issue in the definitional problems surrounding the distinction between modernity and postmodernity is the problematical nature of the 'post'-prefix. Analysis of postmodernity is characterized by a basic confusion concerning the nature of the concept itself: is it *after* or *against* modernity? If postmodernity simply means historically after modernity, then the debate is not particularly interesting in political or moral terms. It simply suggests a stage in the historical evolution of capitalism in which postmodern phenomena enjoy a certain continuity over historical time. Postmodernity might therefore be simply an elaboration of the fundamental features of an industrial capitalist system. As a consequence the idea of postmodernity as a critique of modernity has attracted much more sympathy and interest from the major commentators on this debate. Postmodernity is more typically associated with the idea of the 'end of history', that is with *posthistoire* (Niethammer, 1992). Postmodernity has developed, particularly in critical theory and feminism, as a major alternative to the assumptions of modernist thought and organization. If modernity stands for the tradition of the Enlightenment and liberal democracy, then postmodern thought has sought allies in the forces of de-colonization, cultural critique and feminist opposition. Insofar as modernism has become associated with instrumental reason, patriarchy and the domination of nature, then postmodernism has embraced play, irony and parody as sources for an oppositional critique. The non-rational and the irrational are drawn upon as resources for an anti-modern agenda and in this critical struggle desire is opposed to discipline, folly to reason, and play to labour.

From a social-scientific point of view, the most convenient approach to the analysis of postmodernity is to provide a coherent account of what we might mean by the conventional notions of modernization, modern society and modernity. For the sake of brevity and clarity, one could simply suggest that modernity as a sociological phenomenon is the social and historical product of the process of modernization, which we can associate closely with the development of capitalist societies in western Europe from the early part of the seventeenth century. Furthermore, we might argue that Max Weber's sociology of capitalism provides us with our most precise historical characterization of the major dimensions of modernity (Turner, 1992a). In order to understand postmodernity as anti-modernity we might simply turn to Weber's *The Protestant Ethic and the Spirit of Capitalism* (1930) as the most famous analysis in classical sociology of what is meant by social modernity. For Weber, modern industrial capitalist society was the historical product of instrumental reason and this instrumental rationality had its cultural and psychological origins in the Protestant asceticism of the early Calvinistic sects which developed a specific calling in the world, a calling which involved discipline, self-restraint and world mastery.

Calvinism emphasized self-regulation, the denial of luxurious consumption, the commitment to a vocation in the world, and an ascetic discipline of everyday life, whereas the cultures of the oriental world were dominated by religious systems which encouraged and sustained contemplative orientations to the world, or mystical withdrawal, or hedonistic appropriation of reality. In particular Buddhism, Hinduism and Confucianism were essentially passive approaches to reality in which the human spirit merely adapted itself to the brute facts of human nature and external reality. Weber regarded Judaism and Islam as merely failed or flawed versions of the dynamic asceticism and discipline of the Abrahamic tradition. Within the Protestant Reformation, Lutheranism, Wesleyanism and the various pietistic movements were weaker versions of the central trend towards ascetic domination of reality which was only embraced in its fullness by Calvinistic Christianity. From this sociology of religion, Weber developed a distinctive view of the cultural dynamics of rational capitalism, in which discipline, the calling, the ethic of world mastery and the self-restraint of personality all lead to a dynamic and radicalized culture. In sociological terms, this ethic of world mastery resulted in a social system in which instrumental rationality dominated all spheres of social existence. Thus, the bureaucratic organization of entrepreneurship, the rational application of technology to production, the differentiation of social institutions, the destruction of magic and religion, and the rational organization of the State to achieve collective goals were all simply manifestations of the inner logic of worldly asceticism. The 'iron cage' of modernity was the unintended consequence of the ethic of Protestant asceticism. It was a distinctive alternative to the glittering worldliness of many baroque themes of representation, drama and music. Baroque churches overflow with the frolics of bucolic, chubby cherubim; Protestant churches are stripped to their white walls. The unaccompanied human voice itself was often regarded as the only appropriate, modest instrument for the worship of God in Protestant circles.

In the conventional sociology of modernization, therefore, the social and historical processes which have produced modern society have been seen in terms of an evolutionary progression from traditional forms of organization to rational, modern social systems. Modern society in consequence has been characterized by industrialization, the urbanization of human populations, the dominance of factory production and technology, the increasing dependence upon literacy and the production of information and knowledge, and the social differentiation of institutions in order to achieve a more effective and efficient social organization of resources. It has been thought that modern society is essentially secular, demystified, rationally organized and hostile to superstition and traditional modes of thought and organization. The sociology of religion has typically supported such an interpretation, since it is felt that the process of rationalization brought about a disenchantment of reality whereby religious and magical modes of thought were gradually replaced by more scientific views and secular perspectives.

In the conventional sociological debate about modernization, it has been common for sociologists to develop a series of dichotomies by which to express this process of rationalization. For example, in the work of Ferdinand Tönnies, the secular, anonymous and neutral organization of the modern world was described in terms of a series of associations rather than as – and in marked contrast to – a collection of communities. Much of this was subsequently developed by American sociology, particularly by Talcott Parsons (1991), whose famous 'pattern variables' sought to describe modernity in terms of its universalism, its specificity, its individualism and secular neturality. These ideal-typical contrasts between community and association, tradition and modernity, and secular and sacred often disguised another, more implicit contrast between the modern West and the traditional East, one which was clearly elaborated in the whole tradition of orientalism in which the oriental world was seen to be hostile to the forces of progress and social change (Said, 1978). This implicit celebration of the West came in many circumstances to provide a normative legitimation for colonization. This view of the development of Western capitalism often had a triumphalist dimension, in which the erosion and disappearance of the Orient would be brought about by the inevitable and ineluctable dominance of Western traditions and institutions. It is for this reason that postmodern criticism of rational modernity had often been embraced by both feminism and social movements for decolonization.

This modernist world view has, of course, always had its critics. Opposition to this triumphalist view of Western reason has centred primarily on the notion that Western reason has a self-destructive aspect which negates the progressive aspects of secularization and ultimately threatens human life itself as a consequence of the remorseless logic of industrialization. In the late nineteenth century, the sharpest criticisms of capitalist rationalization came from the Marxist tradition of social theory which claimed that capitalism was based upon a system of alienation and exploitation which destroyed human life in the interests of egoistical accumulation of wealth. As we know, Karl Marx's vision of history suggested that the inevitable contradictions and conflicts within the capitalist system would, through the endless struggle of social classes, bring about the final destruction of a capitalist world, leading eventually to socialism and communism as social organizations which were neither contradictory nor self-destructive. In the late twentieth century, this communist alternative to capitalist domination and exploitation appears to be fundamentally flawed and historically problematic and the collapse of the Soviet Union and the retreat of communism as a political system has left many social critics with the conclusion that Marxism is not a viable alternative to capitalist systems of production.

The political alternative to capitalism is currently more closely associated with the ecological critique of capitalism as a system of industrial exploitation of nature which ultimately undermines human happiness and security by bringing about the inevitable destruction of the planet earth. Late capitalism has become a risk society (Beck, 1992) in which the very process of modernization itself results in new forms of hazard and uncertainty. This Green critique of industrial capitalism has often been associated with feminist opposition to patriarchal versions of instrumental reason, and both feminism and the Green movement are typically associated with anti-imperialism, since many third world societies see their economic plight as a direct consequence of first world, northern, industrial capitalist progress.

Both the Marxist and the ecological critique of industrial capitalism and instrumental reason suggest either implicitly or explicitly that the allegedly rational characteristics of capitalism are in fact substantively irrational. Capitalism is substantively irrational because its very development threatens the conditions of existence of humankind as such, and it appears to be impossible to create the political conditions by which this destructive force of capitalism could be contained. The exploitation of labour is merely one dimension of the exploitation of nature by a minority whose wealth and dominance come to threaten the happiness and security of the majority of the earth's population. The remorseless rational logic of capital accumulation is in fact an irrational logic which, from a moral point of view, is a substantive threat to humanity. The postmodern critique of capitalism as a unifying, colonizing and hierarchical system of dominance based upon a unitary theory of reason can be seen as one aspect of the current critique of patriarchal, instrumental reason as the inner core of capitalist modernity. Postmodernism as a theory argues that difference and pluralism stand in opposition to this unitary nature of capitalism as a system of domination based upon a notion of sameness (Boyne,

1989). Thus, postmodernity can be seen as a celebration of hetero-geneity against Western homogenization.

Buci-Glucksmann's analysis of baroque reason, feminism, the depravity and nihilism of Baudelaire's poetry and Benjamin's celebration of allegory is best understood within this broad analysis of capitalism and reason as forms of domination and exploitation. Buci-Glucksmann's *La Raison baroque* (1984a) and her equally influential *La Folie du voir: De l'esthétique baroque* (1986) are not therefore departures from her early political philosophy, such as her studies of Antonio Gramsci, especially on the questions of state hegemony and violence, for which she is probably best known to date in the English-speaking world. These early studies in the Gramscian critique of the state and capitalism (Buci-Glucksmann, 1981) were concerned with a socialist analysis of the nature of power and economics in modern capitalism. Her more recent analyses of the baroque and feminism are also situated within a profoundly critical response to modern society, which is of course very much within the tradition of writers like Adorno, Benjamin and the Frankfurt School. Her studies of the seventeenth-century baroque imagination, the emergence of feminist theories, and the avant-garde of the twentieth century are inquiries into an alternative cultural resource as a system of opposition to the dominance of patriarchal (capitalist) reason. Her research into the baroque feminist theory and the cultural analyses of Benjamin is now well established. For example her path-breaking *Walter Benjamin und die Utopie des Weiblichen* (1984b), an analysis of utopian mentality and political critique, is clearly influential in this study of baroque reason.

The critique of reason

My argument has been that we can best appreciate Buci-Glucksmann's analysis of the aesthetics of modernity within two domains: as a contribution to aesthetic theory, especially in the context of the relativization of discourse by language theory, and as a critique of instrumental reason. We can best understand instru-mental reason via a study of Weber's sociology of modernity. It is appropriate to place Weber within a discussion of Benjamin because the former belonged to an intellectual circle which included or was related to Stefan George, Georg Lukács, Georg Simmel and Karl Mannheim, all of whom are important in the development of aesthetic, literary and social theory.

Weber is typically seen therefore as the principal sociologist of rational capitalism and as a social theorist who appeared explicitly to justify capitalist development in terms of its destruction of magical world views. However, this conventional view of Weber has in recent years been challenged by a number of major commentators on Weberian sociology such as Wilhelm Hennis, Laurence Scaff, Harvey Goldman and Charles Turner. A close examination of Weber's two lectures on the vocation in science and the vocation in politics, the intermediary reflections on his sociology of religion and his preface to *The Protestant Ethic and the Spirit of Capitalism* suggests a rather different view of Weber's analysis of rationality and reason as the foundations of a modern capitalist system. Weber was in fact profoundly ambiguous about the nature and outcome of capitalist civilization, because the march of reason could not ultimately answer the question: what is the meaning and purpose of life? Instrumental rationality is essentially an effective system for the achieving of known ends, but Weber consistently argued that the appropriate ends of action could never be derived from reason itself. A rational system of medicine could never answer the question: what is the moral purpose of health? A rational system of scientific inquiry can never tell us what the purpose of nature is. These absolute values are ultimately derived from cultural systems, in particular from religious culture, which, as we know, falls outside the boundaries of reason. Religion is a system of values and practices which is concerned with the non-rational.

In fact modern systems of rationality continuously attack, erode and undermine systems of morality, religion and ethics. The secularizing impact of industrial capitalism destroys the cultural foundations of society and therefore undermines our capacity to live meaningfully within the modern world. There is in this respect a certain convergence between Marx and Weber as critics of capitalism, since both recognized that capitalist rationality would destroy the religious aura of existence by producing an alienating and reified reality. Weber's analysis of the disenchantment of reality has an important parallel with Marx's study of human alienation and estrangement (Löwith, 1993). In Marx's philosophical anthropology, the development of a capitalist economy brings about a fetishism of commodities which has the consequence of mystifying and alienating human existence. Human beings live in a social and economic reality, in which they are consistently estranged from themselves and from their material reality. In Marxism, capitalism is a radical and revolutionary system which brings about a fantastic reality of commodities in which 'all that is solid melts into air' (Berman, 1982). Weber's analysis of the disenchantment of human existence through the progressive secularization of reality also leaves human beings in a state of self-alienation, since the world becomes systematically meaningless as it is stripped of its religious aura. For Weber, the paradox of modernity is that rationalization merely shows that existence is pointless and lacking in purpose. This critical view of the paradoxical irony of capitalist rationalism was shared by a variety of social philosophers who were influenced by Marx and by Weber, such as Georg Simmel, Georg Lukács and Ernst Bloch, who in various ways also influenced the critical work of Benjamin (Bolz and van Reijen, 1991; Roberts, 1982).

However, Weber was also ambiguous about the rational character of capitalist modernization since the historical origins of capitalist instrumental reason in fact lay in the irrational quest for salvation in the melancholic theology of Calvin. Although Weber deeply admired the heroic saints of Protestantism (just as he admired the prophets of ancient Judaism), he also recognized that the bleak and frightening message of Calvin's soteriology had profoundly negative effects in terms of human psychological security. Calvin's attack on magical means of grace meant that the Calvinist believer could not depend on such intermediaries as priests, could not rely upon the institutional means of grace, which the Church made available through its collective rites and rituals, and could not rely upon institutionalized forms of Christian knowledge in order to achieve any inner certainty as to his or her salvation. The Calvinist believer was alone before God, and given this total uncertainty of salvation, the quest for certainty in Calvinist Protestantism could never be secured. Hence, the Calvinist quest for salvation was ultimately re-directed within Calvinist practice and theory towards the more comforting view that those who were successful on earth (in business or the professions) could take this as a sign of their celestial security in the next world. It was on this basis that Weber, using an expression from Goethe, argued that there was an elective affinity between the Calvinistic spirit of asceticism and the capitalist drive for discipline, order and profit. Within Weber's reconstruction of the history of capitalism, therefore, the origins of capitalist rationality lay not in a rational world view, but, on the contrary, in the deeply irrational impulse of salvation within the terrifying theology of Calvin. In short, the roots of modern rationality lay in religious irrationality.

This theme of the irrational within the rational was derived by Weber from a reading of the philosophy of Nietzsche. The impact of Nietzsche's critical philosophy on contemporary social theory (Freud, Weber, Adorno, Foucault and Heidegger) has only in recent years been adequately recognized. For example, the Nietzschean influence on Weber was manifest at various levels of his analysis of capitalism: in superficial terms, we can see it in his study of charisma, the religious origins of morality, the endless struggle over the will to power, the multiplicity of world views, and in what he called the polytheistic struggle between world systems. However, there are more interesting ways of viewing this relationship, particularly if we look at Nietzsche's account of the relationship between Apollo and Dionysus in his analysis of the historical impact of Greek civilization on Western societies. In Nietzsche's cultural critique, Apollo stands for order, law, form and rationality, while Dionysus represents sexuality, irrationality, energy and formless passion. Western history is a constant oscillation between these contradictory principles, but Nietzsche's argument was that it was only through the reconciliation of these two dimensions that personal and social health could be achieved. The idea that Apollo controls Dionysus became the basis of Sigmund Freud's theory of neurosis in which the demands of civilization require the suppression and final destruction of the instinctual sexual drive. Nietzsche used this argument about sexuality to criticize the existing view of Greek culture which dominated the romanticized German appropriation of Greek drama. In his *The Birth of Tragedy* (first published in 1872), Nietzsche argued that Hellenism was not based upon a rational culture which celebrated reason, the life of the mind and orderliness, but, on the contrary, had its historical origins in the rawer emotions and frenzied passions of the Dionysian cults. Although this view of Greek tragedy has often been challenged, for example by Benjamin in *The Origin of German Tragic Drama*, the thesis allowed Nietzsche to argue that behind many of the concepts of Western civilization, such as the soul, God, morality, culture and so forth, there lurked darker and more irrational forms of passion and desire. Thus, the morality of Christianity was really a psychological smoke-screen for the sense of envy and bitterness which characterizes a subordinate social group. In the work of Freud, this argument was redeployed in terms of the unconscious forces of sexuality which lie behind many of our moral systems. It was this view of the relationship between Dionysus and Apollo which formed the basis of Nietzsche's critique of the nihilism of modern societies, particularly the Prussian society which was the legacy of Bismarck. In Freud, this Nietzschean legacy led to the view that religion was a form of neurotic behaviour in which desire had been suppressed by the artificial outer cloak of civilized reason.

This theme of desire versus reason in the works of Nietzsche, Weber and Freud can also be found in the Marxist sociology of writers like Adorno and Horkheimer, particularly in their famous analysis of the *Dialectic of Enlightenment* (1972) in which the suppression of the life of the body by the mind was seen to be one source of the alienation of human beings in a rational capitalist system. One can argue therefore that the attempt by critical theorists such as Herbert Marcuse to develop a psychoanalysis of capitalism in order to supplement Marx's analysis of capitalist alienation had its origins in the work of Nietzsche and other romantic critics of capitalism, such as Lugwig Klages and Stefan George (Stauth and Turner, 1988).

Male reason/female unreason

If in these nineteenth-century and early twentieth-century debates there is an association between patriarchy and rationalization then there is clearly a problem about the relationship of women to the public realm of instrumental reason and political practice. It is clear that both orthodox Jewish and Christian theology developed a negative view of women. For example, in medieval theology, women were often regarded as monstrous because they were a second-order creation from Adam in the Garden of Eden. Within this patriarchal theology, it was Eve who brought about the seduction of Adam by listening to the (reasonable) arguments of the Serpent and it was Eve and the Serpent who brought knowledge into Paradise, thereby undermining the naive innocence of mankind. In early Christian theology, women were associated with sin, while the male characters of the Christian story were identified with virtue and grace. The essential weakness of human beings lies in the irrational vulnerability brought about by their sexuality. These themes were endlessly reproduced in the theology of St Paul and St Augustine, and in the Protestant theology of Luther, Calvin and Wesley. Women subvert the divine order of things by being creatures of their own sexuality and it was for these reasons that writers like Paul argued that marriage was a necessary evil, if men were to be protected from the endless pressures of human desire. There have been numerous counter-movements to such a bleak view of human sexuality and in Roman Catholicism Mariology attempted to produce a somewhat different view of women through the figure of the mother of Christ, whose virtue was eventually celebrated in the doctrine of the immaculate conception which simultaneously removed Christ and Mary from any taint of sexuality and sin (Warner, 1976). The dominant view, however, has been that of Pauline theology, which regards human sexuality as the primary location of human frailty and sinfulness, and regards women as the weaker sex.

Criticism of capitalism in the nineteenth century often sided with a feminist perspective on reason and reality in order to oppose the essentially patriarchal nature of reason which underpinned the public sphere. For example, Mary Shelley's feminist critique of patriarchal views of instrumental reason in the novel *Frankenstein* (1818) clearly expressed the association between a Romantic rejection of urban capitalism and an emerging feminist analysis of patriarchal authority. The Gothic novel showed how an obsessive idea (such as scientific rationalism) could destroy a whole society. The Gothic was an allegory of revolution.

A more pertinent example, from the point of view of my introductory argument, would be the work of Johann Jacob Bachofen (1815–87), whose writing promoted the idea of the matriarchal origin of civilization and was critical of nineteenth-century views of culture and authority in Europe. Bachofen's analysis of *Mutterrecht* ('mother-right') was influential in the development of German feminism, for example in the work of Max Weber's wife Marianne. In the theory of *Mutterrecht*, Bachofen developed a critique of Theodore Mommsen's *History of Rome to the Death of Caesar*, which had celebrated the Roman State in terms of law and power as the unifying aspect of ancient Italy. In Mommsen's study of Caesarism, Bachofen saw a celebration of the new Prussia in which masculine state power was triumphant. Against this political background, Bachofen developed a theory of matriarchal power based upon the creative ability of the female. It was this matriarchal principle which lay at the roots of religious culture and social life; matriarchal society had elevated the erotic to become the spiritual culture of the ancient world. Although Bachofen recognized that this *Mutterrecht* principle had eventually been overthrown, he nevertheless saw in the feminine the foundation of human cultural refinement, as opposed to the masculine whose basis is political dominance through the State. In this matriarchal system he saw a nurturing of the community through an erotic bond over and against the irrational regulations of male society. Although *Mutterrecht* as a theory of the origins of social existence has been thoroughly discarded, it played an important part in the feminist opposition to patriarchal institutions.

Capitalism and the Other

The point of this introductory commentary has been to raise a question about the rational origins of modernity, which I have associated necessarily with the development of an industrial urban capitalist society. The reason for taking Weber's sociology of capitalism as a paradigm case is that his name is inevitably associated in social science with the debate about modernity and his analysis of the cultural origins of capitalism has become a central feature of contemporary analysis. Recent interpretations of Weber have drawn attention to the role of Nietzsche's critique of culture, the problematic nature of Protestant salvational teaching and the importance of desire in relation to an ethic of responsibility. Buci-Glucksmann's book can be seen as yet a further probing of the irrational roots of modern society; in particular, she is concerned to explore the 'irrational' archaeology of modern aesthetics. Her argument is divided into three sections in which she considers the specific characteristics of the baroque, the poetry of Baudelaire and the writings of Benjamin. Throughout her analysis, she seeks to identify the key elements of the modern aesthetic through an inquiry into the nature of allegory, the baroque imagination and the nature of the feminine as a symbol of the Other. These inquiries are pursued through an examination of the importance of Paul Klee's *Angelus Novus* in the imagination and writing of Benjamin, in which the Angel stands for and is estrangement. In the second section of her thesis, she considers the female as an allegory of modernity via the poetry of Baudelaire. The book concludes with a discussion of baroque reason in the alternative aesthetic of the figure of Salome. Baroque reason is thus a challenge to reason, the subject, linear time, Apollonian organization, regularized space and positivist science. Baroque reason is essentially a 'theatricization of existence' which mobilizes the notions of ambivalence and difference to provide what Buci-Glucksmann calls the 'Reason of the Other' which permits us to see the modern world from within.

Buci-Glucksmann's argument is radical and, from the point of view of conventional historiography, somewhat perverse. It is indeed odd to suggest that the baroque might provide us with an archaeology of the modern from within, since surely baroque culture, as the culture of the crisis of seventeenth-century absolutism, was diametrically opposed to the forces of liberalism and Protestantism which writers like Weber, Mannheim and Parsons have identified with the origins of modern society, modern ideologies and industrial capitalism. Protestant religion, liberal politics and the culture of the seventeenth-century merchants were counterposed to the centralizing politics of absolutism, with its attachment to the Counter-Reformation and its identification with baroque cultural themes. Whereas liberal Protestantism was identified through the works of Hobbes, Spinoza and Locke with the idea of individual rights, the social contract and the responsibility of parliamentary government, absolutism championed the rights of divine kings to rule absolutely and arbitrarily. The culture of the baroque was a culture of spectacle which sought to mobilize the human senses to bring about a commitment of the masses to absolute monarchies (Maravall, 1986). Baroque culture was a conservative culture which manipulated the masses through fantastic images, colour and elaborate music. 'Baroque palaces, gardens, theatres and allées constituted extended spaces for the processions and receptions of courtly, aristocratic society; they served the self-display of sovereign authority as its symbols and decorations' (Vierhaus, 1988: 65). The baroque culture of the seventeenth century has been regarded as a culture industry which produced an artificial public arena by combining elements of high and low culture. Baroque culture was based upon 'reiteration, sentimentalism, easy passions that valorize the self, sub-ordination to a recipe book of known solutions and literary poverty' (Maravall, 1986: 90). It has been claimed that baroque works even of the highest quality, such as Bernini's *Santa Teresa* or Poussin's *Pastoral*, were in fact touched by elements of popular kitsch. The baroque music of Monteverdi was a form of musical alchemy which produced gold. The primary images of the baroque were in fact the ruin, the labyrinth and the library; all of these phenomena are based upon deception, complexity and artificiality. A fascination with ruins was an important feature of the baroque sense of the artificiality and the constructive nature of social reality, but it also expressed the deep sense of melancholy, spleen and anxiety of the period (Turner, 1992b). Robert Burton's *The Anatomy of Melancholy* (1621) is also fundamental to the baroque imagination, since melancholy, allegory and ruin all suggested a mentality of decadence and corruption, for which the medical interventions of Burton and others were seen to be a cure. Thus, the profound sense of social change and decadence which surrounded the political culture of the baroque found its expression in a set of images and themes which expressed a deep sense of alienation from society, self and nature. The melancholy personality contemplating ruin and death was one of the dominant topics of baroque literature and art.

The fact the baroque culture dwelt upon the image of Saturn, the ruin, the academic library and the labyrinth was a consequence of the pervasive sense of political catastrophe, the collapse of tradition and the emergence of an uncertain and destructive present. In classical drama, the chorus was composed of the strophe and the anti-strophe, the catastrophe being the climax of a dramatic narrative which brings about a profound reorganization or destruction of the characters of the main sequence. Catastrophe, risk and hazard were concepts which have a profound relationship to the origins of absolutism and capitalism. The idea of risk in economic terms grew out of early trading problems, particularly those concerned with long-distance trade and exchange. It is therefore not surprising that reflection upon catastrophe should constitute such a significant element of the baroque. The philosophy of Gottfried Leibniz (1646–1716) has often been closely associated with the development of the baroque in this respect and is interesting for two reasons. First, in his *Monadology* (1714) he argued that the world is made up of irreducible monads which perfectly express all other monads, and exist in complete harmony with each other. This work was an attempt to lead us out of what he called the 'two famous labyrinths' in which our reason is often trapped, namely the questions of liberty and necessity. Secondly, Leibniz, in his celebrated *Theodicy* (1710), elaborated the doctrine that we live in the best of all possible worlds. A theodicy is any system of thought which attempts to reconcile God's goodness with the existence of evil in the world. Liebniz's doctrine of the nature of monads and his view of theodicy have often been received by other philosophers as a cynical justification of absolutism and arbitrary government. Leibniz's manuscript on theodicy was orginally conceived as a consequence of conversations with Queen Sophia Charlotte of Prussia, who had on various occasions induced him to write professional philosophical essays. Leibniz's doctrine of the best of all possible worlds can be seen as philosophical legitimization of centralized absolute power under the cloak of a theodicy of evil, but it also expressed a baroque view of the universe as a perfect labyrinth of 'windowless monads'.

What, one might ask, does this discussion about absolutism, baroque culture and theodicy have to do with modern society or modern culture? The answer to this question is probably best located in Buci-Glucksmann's notion of the theatricization of social reality. Just as baroque culture created the spectacle as a means of suborning mass populations in order to induce them into conformity through pleasure, so the modern world of consumerism can also be seen as a spectacle. The idea that the modern world is based upon spectacle and that the masses are seduced by the spectacular nature of modern popular culture was developed by a group of social theorists in France in the 1950s and 1960s. Known as the Situationist International they expounded in their journal *Internationale Situationiste*. The Situationists employed a Marxist paradigm of capitalism but combined this with avant-garde artistic ideas from both Dada and Surrealism (Plant, 1992). In 1977, one of the leading theorists, Guy Debord, published *The Society of the Spectacle* (1977), which provided a general theory of the role of spectacle in contemporary society. Unlike the Marxists within the working-class movement in France, the Situationists believed that capitalism was faced with an imminent collapse through violent revolutionary struggle. The Situationists' view of capitalism seemed implausible at the time, but with the student revolt of 1968 their ideas gained greater acceptance in France and elsewhere and many of their followers, such as Jean Baudrillard and Jean-François Lyotard, subsequently became closely associated with the postmodern movement.

Debord argued that modern capitalism was based upon a large, alienated, mass working class which was kept subordinated to the hegemony of capitalism through the manipulation of pleasure by television, cinema and spectacle. In particular, leisure, tourism and consumption provided a series of seductive images of power which undermined the possibility of conventional political struggle. The pleasures of modern consumption perfectly complemented the passive, contemplative characteristics of modern urban life in which working-class boredom, *ennui* and apathy were dominant. Mass pleasure, mass consumption and the endless reproduction of life-style functioned as a modern form of religious illusion and the fetishism of commodities was precisely the modern religion of the masses in which a new sacred aura surrounded everyday commodities. The culture industry of modern society is thus a new version of the culture industry of the baroque in which absolutism in government and the superficialities of everyday consumption are perfectly combined to produce a passive mass audience.

In contemporary sociology, these ideas have been further developed by Baudrillard in various analyses of the role of consumption and the masses. For example, in his *In the Shadow of the Silent Majorities* (1983) Baudrillard has argued that capitalism is impervious to political change and philosophical critique, since the mass acts as a black hole which absorbs and destroys all the attacks directed at it. The creation of the mass by modern technologies of communication means that modern society is a kaleidoscope of whirling symbols and values, a simulated world of signs which are divorced from, and no longer connected with, any sense of social reality. Baudrillard has put this form of analysis to brilliant effect in *America* (1988), in which he suggests that America, as the leading edge of hyperreality, transforms the social universe into a system of simulated cultures. Even political reality can no longer be distinguished from TV reality, since the masses consume news reports of political violence, street warfare and gangsterism in the same way as they consume fictions and fantasies about simulated violence.

Many of these arguments in contemporary postmodernism, Situationist theory and avant-garde social analysis depend heavily on the image of the city as the fulcrum of modern social change. The baroque city provided the image of the endless labyrinth within which the new masses could hide and threaten authority through their very proximity. Throughout the nineteenth century, the development of the city, particularly Paris and Berlin, provided many of the themes, images and metaphors of social change and in the twentieth century the image of the urban masses rising against authority has been a consistent theme of social inquiry. The organization of the metropolis and the artificial character of urban culture provided an important topic for much of classical sociology, particularly in the writing of Simmel on the mentality of metropolitan existence. Moreover, the theme of fantasy and city life plays in important part in Buci-Glucksmann's account of modern aesthetics which she develops from the writings of Baudelaire and Benjamin.

Paris, capital of the nineteenth century

The nature of imagination, fantasy and desire in relation to modern systems of consumption plays an important part in Baudelaire's poetry and Benjamin's analysis of modern society. Buci-Glucksmann's reflections on these themes in Baudelaire and Benjamin depend significantly upon the role of the city in the formation of modern aesthetic appreciation. Clearly the question of the city, especially Berlin and Paris, constantly engaged Benjamin's world view and dominated much of his writing and analysis. In the hauntingly evocative *A Berlin Chronicle* (1986) Benjamin wonderfully captures the beauty and danger of Berlin from his own childhood. In addition his incomplete project on Paris which he began during his association with the Institute for Social Research was an examination of the development of arcades and new shopping districts in the city. These studies have been published as *Das Passagen-Werk* (Benjamin, 1982–3). There are in addition a number of important essays on Moscow, Marseilles and Naples which have been collected together in *Reflections* (Benjamin, 1986). Finally, Benjamin's volume on Charles Baudelaire (1983) was also a study of the problem of lyric poetry in the context of Paris, which he regarded as the capital of nineteenth-century Europe. Benjamin, like many sociologists in the period 1890–1920, was fascinated by the new forms of existence made possible by large capital cities such as London, New York, Paris and Berlin. The city provided sociologists with a natural urban experiment within which social observers could study crime and delinquency, the differentiation of

social institutions, the problems of bureaucracy in large, compli-
cated, urban environments, and the problems of social control,
disease and affluence in a rapidly changing social environment.

The major social theories of this classical age of sociology were all
concerned in one way or another with the new problems generated
by the mass society of large cities. This observation is as true of
Simmel as it is of Marx, Durkheim, Weber and Mannheim. While
Benjamin falls within this group of commentators on urban civilization, he was primarily concerned with the cultural forms of urban
life and its manifestation within an underworld of social existence to
which writers like Baudelaire had turned their attention. It was this
underworld of the large city which captured Benjamin's imagination
just as it had captured T.S. Eliot's in *The Waste Land*. In particular,
Benjamin, in his analysis of Baudelaire's poetry, focuses on two
figures which are seen to be essential to the urban landscape,
namely the bohemian and the *flâneur*.

Benjamin's analysis of Baudelaire starts with a commentary on
the *bohème*. Bejamin notes that the *bohème* had appeared in the
writings of Marx on capitalism as part of the development of
proletarian political consciousness, especially in conspiracies against
governments. Hence, Benjamin sees Baudelaire's poetry as part of
what he calls a 'metaphysic of the *provocateur*'. The bohemian was
part of the café society of Paris, a social world in which the cocktail
hour was the centrepiece for the distribution of political gossip and
literary analysis. Alongside the *bohème*, Baudelaire and Benjamin
were both fascinated by the figure of the *flâneur*, a creation of the
new industry of luxury and consumption, at home strolling around
the façades and arcades. The new capitalism promoted the
hegemony of the eye over the ear, providing fresh vehicles for
gazing and consuming – gas-lighting, trams, walkways, railroads,
buses, arcades and shopping empires – the natural habitus of the
flâneur (Buck-Morss, 1989). This new actor epitomizes the detached,
nihilistic observer of society, a mere strolling figure, the externally
observing eye, gazing at the novel luxuries and consumption items
of a modern capital; and the phenomenon of 'flâneurism' can be
regarded as an essential feature of modern alienation, indicating as
it does our estrangement from the social in a world of commodity
fetishism.

Within this social world, Benjamin was also fascinated by the
growth of the detective story, a form of literary creation which he
felt perfectly matched the anonymous obliteration of individual
differences within the large city crowd. The detective story was
parallel to the culture of the *flâneur* since the detective is an
individual whose observations of humanity within the new urban

spaces of the capital are an essential basis for this trade. These new forms of crime were the incentive for innovative developments in social control including finger-printing, the photography of criminals, the new sciences of criminology and penology. Mass society gave protection to the criminal, requiring the detective to be a furtive, seeking, gazing individual depending on creative technology for detection and control. Within this context, it was the crowd that became the subject of Baudelaire's lyric poetry. Hence, the modern city produced a new scenario of social actors: the *flâneur*, the *bohème*, the detective, the policeman, the crowd and indeed the sociologist. (For many writers, Simmel was the sociological *flâneur* of Berlin [Frisby, 1992].)

Walter Benjamin and political theology

Benjamin has been clearly associated with the Institute for Social Research, commonly called the Frankfurt School, in the mainstream literature on twentieth-century Marxism. The Frankfurt School which flourished in Germany in the 1920s can be seen as an attempt by Marxist theory to come to terms with major changes in capitalism as a consequence of the transformation of Western societies in the late nineteenth and early twentieth centuries. In particular, the Frankfurt School theorists attempted to draw upon psychoanalysis in order to provide Marxism with a better understanding of the dynamic relationship between the self and society, but they also drew upon Weberian and neo-Kantian sociology to develop a more sophisticated epistemology to deal with the problem of meaning and understanding in the interpretation of social action. The School also took up new areas of research which had been somewhat neglected by classical Marxism, and in particular through Adorno and Benjamin it addressed the question of art and culture in capitalism. Adorno and Benjamin are considered the principal source of aesthetic theory in Marxism. The Frankfurt School, through the work of writers like Marcuse, began to examine alternative sources of rebellion and revolution in late capitalism, particularly by studying the social role of such groups as students, women and blacks. Unlike classical Marxists, the critical theorists had to confront the growing dangers of fascism and racism in Germany which, since they were virtually all Jewish by cultural and ethnic background, affected them as individuals. While the critical theorists were a product of Jewish intellectual culture in Germany, their Jewish background has often been understated in the conventional histories of the Institute for Social Research. One major feature of Buci-Glucksmann's analysis of contemporary theory and the work of Benjamin is to bring to our attention the theological roots of Benjamin's work in Jewish religious tradition. This aspect of Benjamin's intellectual career has been much debated (Niethammer, 1992), but Buci-Glucksmann's analysis of the political theology of his work has both depth and sympathy, rarely achieved by many existing interpretations.

Benjamin is seen as a member of the Institute for Social Research by the major historian of the Frankfurt School, namely Martin Jay in his deservedly famous *The Dialectical Imagination* (1973). In addition, Marshall Berman in *All That Is Solid Melts into Air* perceives Benjamin, with regard to the temptations of the modern city, as a writer caught between a fascination with the superficial attractions of urban life and his socialist conscience which suggests that the modern world is 'decadent, hollow, vicious, spiritually empty, oppressive to the proletariat, condemned by history' (1982: 146). The alternative interpretation of Benjamin is that he was caught between his Jewish consciousness and a secular Marxist one, that is, it is possible to see Benjamin's implicit critique of capitalist cultural superficiality as a product not so much of Marxism as of traditional Jewish thought. This alternative interpretation of Benjamin depends heavily upon evidence presented by one of Benjamin's closest friends, namely Gershom Scholem in *Walter Benjamin: The Story of a Friendship* (1981). Scholem repeatedly shows that Benjamin was primarily influenced by Jewish theology, but in particular by kabbalistic mysticism. Benjamin's critique of capitalism was in this framework driven by a religious hostility to the world of money and secular power and not by a secular social science such as sociology or Marxism. In a similar vein, Perry Anderson in his *Considerations on Western Marxism* (1976) argued that writers like Benjamin, Adorno and Marcuse were far removed from the original concerns of classical Marxism, because they had for various reasons become divorced from working-class struggle. In particular, Anderson argued that the 'Frankfurt School's constant perception of history was best expressed by Benjamin in a language that would have been virtually incomprehensible to Marx or Engels' (1976: 89–90). It is difficult to place Benjamin in any convenient or simple category. Jürgen Habermas (1987: 9–16), for example, regarded 'now-time' (*Jetztzeit*) in Benjamin's work as a manifestation of Jewish mysticism and messianic theories of history. Benjamin's 'Theses on the Philosophy of History' (1973) were a reflection on the radicalization of time-consciousness in modernity.

We can therefore attempt to analysis Benjamin's writing as a theological discourse of modern times and it was this set of theological premises that provided the framework through which Benjamin interpreted Marx's theories of history and social justice. Historical materialism was reinterpreted through the paradigm of messianism. Many of Benjamin's later works certainly reveal this increasing concern with theological inquiry, such as the 'critique of violence' and his 'Theologico-Political Fragments' (1986). Benjamin's thoughts about history in the context of the growing shadow of fascism in Germany increasingly assumed the messianic language of mystical Judaism in which the unfolding of history is necessarily tied to the unfolding of the divine plan. Many of the images and metaphors which Benjamin used are well known to the Jewish tradition, and this is particularly evident in the debate about angelology. Buci-Glucksmann's concentration on the Angelus Novus in her study of Benjamin highlights this Jewish legacy. The allegory of the Angel of history and Angel of revenge played an important part in Benjamin's imagination and the strength of Buci-Glucksmann's interpretation of Benjamin depends heavily on her perception of this allegorical figure in his work.

Benjamin's theological views were often seen to be an embarrassment to the Institute for Social Research. Thus, Scholem comments that

> it became very plain to me in Paris that Benjamin's relations to his fellow Marxists were marked by something like constant embarrassment, which of course was connected with his attachment to theological categories. This was true of Brecht as much as it was to the circle around the Institute. Benjamin's painstaking alertness and his emphasis on the identity of views could not conceal the fact that something had to be excluded. Brecht was visibly disturbed by the theological element in Benjamin.
>
> Adorno himself had no real theological interests, but he noted that it had a central significance for Benjamin. (1981: 206)

Benjamin was in fact much influenced via Scholem by the work of Franz Rosenzweig who published *The Star of Redemption* in 1921. Rosenzweig was an important figure in the Judische Lehrhaus, which was in close contact with members of the Institute (Lowenthal, 1987: 219). It was during this time that Benjamin bought Paul Klee's water-colour called the *Angelus Novus* for around 1000 marks. Klee's painting hung in Scholem's Munich apartment where Benjamin stayed during his period at Munich. Scholem told Benjamin about the importance of the Talmud and the mystical writers of Judaism concerning the hymn of angels, and clearly this commentary on the role of angels in mystical Judaism had an important impact on the latter's thought. The significance of the painting of the Angel is fully explored by Buci-Glucksmann, who locates it within the problem of allegory, which is of central interest to Benjamin. Buci-Glucksmann's commentary on the importance of the *kabbalah*, allegory and the Angelus Novus does not require further elaboration here. However, it is important to note the fact that the theme of messianic deliverance was of acute importance to the Jewish community of Europe in the period leading up to the national socialist take-over of Germany and the subsequent horror of the Holocaust. Of course, the Jewish community of Europe had been the victim of many onslaughts from the Middle Ages to the early twentieth century, but the horrors of fascism within Germany were particularly acute.

A variety of Marxist and other social theorists turned to the theme of religious hope and messianic movements in this period. In the late 1920s Mannheim published his famous essays *Ideology and Utopia* (1991) in which he claimed that, without a utopian vision of the future, humanity could not survive, and that indeed what defined the human spirit was this capacity for utopian hope against all possible odds. Mannheim was particularly concerned with the Anabaptist movements, but he was also profoundly conscious of the legacy of prophetic Judaism and the theme of messianic hope within the Jewish community. Without the collective mythology of the idea of the end of history and the return of justice, the collective identity of marginal groups such as the Jews could not be sustained. Against the disillusionment which these authors felt for their times, the theme of hope and messianic return was an important motif in their analysis. For example, Ernst Bloch (1885–1977), who was not only a victim of fascism but also became severely disillusioned with the communist regimes of the twentieth century, developed the theme of the principle of hope as an essential characteristic of human history; indeed this theme provided the title of his major work (1986). Bloch, rather like Mannheim, saw in the revolutionary theories of Thomas Müntzer and the development of seventeenth-century Anabaptists an anticipation of the Bolshevik Revolution.

Conclusion: the feminization of the divine

The problem of patriarchal authority and repressive culture has been central to nineteenth- and twentieth-century social theory. The absolutist patriarchal tradition of the seventeenth century had been challenged by liberal theory from Hobbes and Locke through to the nineteenth-century liberal theorists such as T.H. Green and J.S. Mill. However, the problem of patriarchal structures and authority has remained as the social underpinning of capitalist and industrial relations. In this Introduction and throughout Buci-Glucksmann's analysis of the aesthetics of modernity, the feminine arises consistently as a challenge to existing social theory and practice when the male principle dominates to the exclusion of the female principle. For example, Mill's rational utilitarian view of society was undermined by his own emotional and psychological breakdown, for which the therapy was located in art and the company of women (Lepenies, 1988). Nietzsche's overtly rugged and masculine evaluation of moral failure in the nineteenth century in fact disguised a fundamental problem about the status of women in society, the feminine and social theory. His personal life was punctuated by endless frustrations, failure and unhappiness in terms of his relationship to women, and he experienced frequent illness and feelings of isolation and depression for which there was no obvious cure or remedy. Weber's marriage was unfulfilled and he constantly suffered in the 1890s from mental depression and from a sense of being overwhelmed by devils. Benjamin was distressed by the major problems of European civilization in relation to Judaism, but also his relationship with women was relatively painful and problematic. Therefore, the Freudian problems of the libido and the Ego, that is, the relation between nature and culture, have remained persistent themes in nineteenth- and twentieth-century consciousness and their impact on social theory, while recognized, has probably been underrated. The representation of the female as the Other has been a significant feature of modern social theory and was not originated by Buci-Glucksmann; however, she picks up this theme brilliantly in the final sections of her overview of the aesthetics of modernity in which otherness, Jewishness and femininity come into focus.

We have already noted the influence of the theory of *Mutterrecht* on social theory from the works of Bachofen, but the dominant theme of Judaeo-Christian culture has been that of the supremacy of the male and subordination of the female. The feminization of opposition and the idea of the feminine Other are inevitably a feature of opposition to this patriarchal, hegemonic culture which has shaped the contours of social theory for the last three or four centuries. Buci-Glucksmann correctly notes the constant inter-relationship and interweaving of the themes of Jewish opposition, the female Other, bisexuality and the danger of sexual deviation from the perspective of an ethic of world mastery, asceticism and domination. From the point of view of an English reader approaching either Benjamin or Buci-Glucksmann, the linguistic relationship between power, violence and masculinity is obscured by the nature of the English language. In the German, *Herrschaft* is derived from *Herr*, meaning master or lord, and *Herrschaft* means domination, sovereignty, rulership or power. *Herrlich* stands for magnificent or delightful, whereas the female is associated with the stupid or ineffectual. In German, therefore, the male gender is interlinked with the ideas of dominion, rulership, power and beauty, whereas the female gender is associated with weakness and stupidity. In his reflections on Benjamin's essay on the 'Critique of Violence' (1986), Jacques Derrida (1991) has commented in a similar fashion on the word for violence in German, namely the concept of *Gewalt*, which means force, power and might, but is also associated with the concept of valuation, the sacred, and has connotations of strength, might and immensity. Many of these attributes can be traced back to the Judaeo-Christian tradition in which God is simultaneously the male, the almighty and the source of all values, but also the origin of violence, retribution and jealousy (against other gods and powers). Benjamin and Buci-Glucksmann can interweave these themes of power and violence with terror, the abnormal and the unearthly. Again in many respects the German is of more use to us than the English. *Unheimlich*, literally the 'unhomely', conveys the sense of the uncanny, the weird and the sinister. Human life, from the perspective of Benjamin and social theology, is alienated, that is, characterized by a strangeness and the sense that human beings are in an unfriendly environment. However, the notion of being alienated and unhomely is also associated with the weird, uncanny and the strange. Here again we are taken back to Benjamin's fascination with the Angel, which in French has a double meaning: As Buci-Glucksmann notes in her discussion of the Angel as allegory, one can play upon the meaning of the uncanny (*l'étrange*) and the angelic (*l'être-ange*). The bisexual character of the Angel is also a feature of its weirdness: the Angel of revenge, the Angel of history, and the Angel of destruction combine the male and the female principle uncannily into a unified presence. In Judaeo-Christian monotheism, angels occupied an ambiguous place in the divine plan; in fact they were given substance primarily within an ecclesiastical context, namely within the hierarchy of the Church. This had important implications for the artistic representation of angels where writers like Milton in *Paradise Lost* cast them in the role of intermediaries, as Schelling (1989) noted in his *Philosophy of Art* of 1859.

These reflections suggest that the origins of the modern and modernism may be derived less from the male principles of universalism, rationality and coherence than from the uncanny, weird principles of otherness, contradiction, ambivalence and catastrophe which can be expressed only through the literary methods and devices of allegory, pastiche, parody, irony, and ambivalence. These literary devices, according to Buci-Glucksmann's interpretation of Benjamin and Baudelaire, are derived archaeologically from the themes of allegory and parody in the baroque period in which the strange metaphors of the library, the labyrinth and the ruin were central themes. From the point of view of writers like Benjamin, Simmel and Adorno, the fact that the rationalist systems of capitalism found their ultimate expression in the Holocaust, in the terrors of fascism and in the absolutist systems of communism, came as no surprise. From the point of view of an alternative history of capitalism it is the irrational violence of passions and the destructive energies of human sexuality which are important and not the rational systems of bureaucracy and organization. This perversity of human rationalism is probably best captured by the ambivalent figures of Benjamin's Angel and Baudelaire's prostitute, by the *flâneur* and the bohemian, rather than the penny-pinching, rationally organized, capitalist entrepreneur. The sources of capitalist rationality and modernity are in literary terms probably better expressed by the decaying and decadent world of Thomas Mann in *Death in Venice, Doctor Faustus* and *Buddenbrooks* rather than through the rational world of the Protestant ethic (Goldman, 1992). The ascetic spirit of modernity in this scenario is the product of evil, demonic forces operating on the souls of men and women. Benjamin's importance therefore lies with his presentation of not a sociology, but a theology of modernity.

References

Adorno, T. and Horkheimer, M. (1972) *Dialectic of Enlightenment*. New York: Herder & Herder.

Anderson, P. (1976) *Considerations on Western Marxism*. London: New Left Books.

Baudelaire, C. (1964) 'The Painter of Modern Life', in Jonathon Mayne, ed., *The Painter of Modern Life and Other Essays*. Oxford: Phaidon.

Baudrillard, J. (1983) *In the Shadow of the Silent Majorities*. New York: Semiotext(e).

Baudrillard, J. (1988) *America*. London: Verso.

Beck, U. (1992) *Risk Society: On the Way to a New Modernity*. London: Sage.

Bell, D. (1973) *The Coming of Post-industrial Society*. New York: Basic Books.

Benjamin, W. (1970) *Berliner Chronik*. Frankfurt: Suhrkamp.

Benjamin, W. (1973) *Illuminations*. London: Fontana.

Benjamin, W. (1977) *The Origin of German Tragic Drama*. London: New Left Books.

Benjamin, W. (1982–3) *Das Passagen-Werk* (2 vols). Frankfurt: Suhrkamp.

Benjamin, W. (1983) *Charles Baudelaire: A Lyric Poet in the Era of High Capitalism*. London: Verso.

Benjamin, W. (1986) *Reflections: Essays, Aphorisms, Autobiographical Writings*. New York: Schocken.

Berman, M. (1982) *All That Is Solid Melts into Air: The Experience of Modernity*. New York: Simon & Schuster.

Bloch, E. (1986) *The Principle of Hope*. Oxford: Basil Blackwell.

Bolz, N. and van Reijen, W. (1991) *Walter Benjamin*. Frankfurt: Campus Verlag.

Bourdieu, P. (1984) *Distinction: A Social Critique of the Judgement of Taste*. London: Routledge & Kegan Paul.

Boyne, R. (1989) *Foucault and Derrida*. London: Unwin Hyman.

Buci-Glucksmann, C. (1981) *Gramsci and the State*. London: Lawrence & Wishart.

Buci-Glucksmann, C. (1984a) *La Raison baroque: De Baudelaire à Benjamin*: Paris: Éditions Galilée.

Buci-Glucksmann, C. (1984b) *Walter Benjamin und die Utopie des Weiblichen*. Hamburg: VSA.

Buci-Glucksmann, C. (1986) *La Folie du voir: De l'esthétique baroque*. Paris: Éditions Galilée.

Debord, G. (1977) *Society of the Spectacle*. Detroit: Black and Red.

Derrida, J. (1991) Unpublished Lecture, Essex, 1991.

Durkheim, É. and Mauss, M. (1963) *Primitive Classification*. Chicago: University of Chicago Press.

Eagleton, T. (1981) *Walter Benjamin, or Towards a Revolutionary Criticism*. London: Verso.

Foucault, M. (1991) *The Order of Things*. London: Routledge.

Frisby, D. (1992) *Sociological Impressionism: A Reassessment of Georg Simmel's Social Theory*. London: Routledge.

Fuld, W. (1979) *Walter Benjamin zwischen den Stuhlen*. Munich: Hanser.

Gaines, J. (1993) 'Research on Walter Benjamin', *Theory, Culture & Society*, 10(2): 149–67.

Gane, M. (1991) *Baudrillard's Bestiary*. London: Routledge.

Goldman, H. (1992) *Politics, Death and the Devil: Self and Power in Max Weber and Thomas Mann*. Berkeley: University of California Press.

Habermas, J. (1987) *The Philosophical Discourse of Modernity*. Cambridge: Polity Press.

Heidegger, M. (1979) *Nietzsche: The Will to Power as Art and the Eternal Recurrence of the Same* (2 vols). San Franscisco: Harper.

Jay, M. (1973) *The Dialectical Imagination: The History of the Frankfurt Scool and the Institute for Social Research 1923–1950*. London: Heinemann Educational Books.

Lash, S. (1990) *Sociology of Postmodernism*. London: Routledge.

Lepenies, W. (1988) *Between Literature and Science: The Rise of Sociology*. Cambridge: Cambridge University Press.

Löwenthal, L. (1987) *An Unmastered Past: The Autobiographical Reflections of Leo Löwenthal*. Berkeley: University of California Press.

Löwith, K. (1993) *Max Weber and Karl Marx*. London: Routledge.

Lyotard, J.-F. (1984) *The Postmodern Condition: A Report on Knowledge*. Manchester: Manchester University Press.

Mannheim, K. (1991) *Ideology and Utopia: An Introduction to the Sociology of Knowledge*. London: Routledge.

Maravall, J.A. (1986) *Culture of Baroque: Analysis of a Historical Structure*. London: Macmillan.

Megill, A. (1985) *Prophets of Extremity. Nietzsche, Heidegger, Foucault, Derrida.* Berkeley: University of California Press.

Niethammer, L (1992) *Posthistoire: Has History Come to an End?* London: Verso.

Nietzsche, F. (1993) *The Birth of Tragedy.* Harmondsworth: Penguin.

Parsons, T. (1991) *The Social System.* London: Routledge.

Plant, S. (1992) *The Most Radical Gesture: The Situationist International in a Postmodern Age.* London: Routledge.

Roberts, J. (1982) *Walter Benjamin.* London: Macmillan.

Rorty, R. (1979) *Philosophy and the Mirror of Nature.* Princeton: Princeton University Press.

Said, E. (1978) *Orientalism.* London: Routledge & Kegan Paul.

Saussure, F. de (1959) *Course in General Linguistics.* New York: Philosophical Library.

Schelling, F.W.J. (1989) *The Philosophy of Art.* Minneapolis: University of · Minnesota Press.

Scholem, G. (1981) *Walter Benjamin: The Story of a Friendship.* Philadelphia: The Jewish Publication Society.

Stauth, G. and Turner, B.S. (1988) *Nietzsche's Dance: Resentment, Reciprocity and Resistance in Social Life.* Oxford: Basil Blackwell.

Steiner, G. (1977) 'Introduction' to W. Benjamin, *The Origin of German Tragic Drama.* London: New Left Books. pp. 7–24.

Turner, B.S. (1992a) *Max Weber: From History to Modernity.* London: Routledge.

Turner, B.S. (1992b) 'Ruine und Fragment: Anmerkungen zum Barockstil', in W. van Reijen, ed., *Allegorie und Melancholie.* Frankfurt: Suhrkamp. pp. 202–23.

Vattimo, G. (1988) *The End of Modernity.* Cambridge: Polity Press.

Vierhaus, R. (1988) *Germany in the Age of Absolutism.* Cambridge: Cambridge University Press.

Warner, M. (1976) *Alone of All Her Sex: The Myth and Cult of the Virgin Mary.* New York: Alfred A. Knopf.

Weber, M. (1930) *The Protestant Ethic and the Spirit of Capitalism.* London: Allen & Unwin.

Wolin, R. (1993) 'Aestheticism and Social Theory: The Case of Walter Benjamin's *Passagen-Werk*', *Theory, Culture & Society*, 10(2): 169–80.

BAROQUE REASON
The Aesthetics of Modernity

I kneaded mud and made of it gold. To glorify the cult of images (my great, my only, my original passion).

Baudelaire

Nothing for me is disenchanting.
The world has cast a spell on me.

Quevedo

Imagine a city with several entrances, a labyrinthine proliferation of squares, crossroads, thoroughfares and side streets, a kind of multibody of the past and memory. In short a baroque town: Rome, Vienna, perhaps Mexico City. Here a *flâneur* is eagerly seeking out the new and the strange scale-games played with reality and unreality. In this theatre the traveller with no homeland and no source of rest meets a venerable old man. 'Who are you?' he asks. 'I am disillusion' (*Yo soy el desengaño*) comes the reply. The man takes him on a tour of this phantasmal city with a thousand faces. They come to a main street, nameless and without end, inhabited by a thousand figures: the Street of Hypocrisy. And there they find a beautiful woman who leaves hearts filled with sighing and desire, a gentle face of snow and roses wrapped in her own aura – the very object of love. The master of disillusion then reveals all: her teeth have been artifically whitened, her hair dyed, her face skilfully made up, and behind the appearances age and death are doing their work. Everywhere in this street of the mighty and beautiful, the world is upside down. Madame Fashion and Madame Death are on the prowl. It must be turned the right side up again: to baffle all the frontiers of the real and unreal, belief and knowledge, world and theatre; to see the world from within.

Such is the great allegory that Quevedo deploys in one of his *Sueños*: *El mundo por de dentro* ('The World from Within').[1] Such too might be the thoroughly Baudelairean city-allegory, woman-allegory of this book on baroque reason. Several entrances, several facets, several layers of writing:[2] but always the same stage, the same voyage of modernity in its paradoxes and ambivalences. Our voyage is mainly devoted to the work of Walter Benjamin, which continually refers us elsewhere: to the nineteenth century of Baudelaire and Salome, to the great crisis cultures of Musil, Weininger or Klee, to that baroque region, particularly evident in Barthes or · Lacan, which has never ceased to haunt our present age. For baroque reason, with its theatricization of existence and its logic of ambivalence, is not merely another reason within modernity. Above all it is the *Reason of the Other*, of its overbrimming excess. With its help we may perhaps try to see the world *por de dentro*.

Notes

1. For an English translation, by Wallace Woolsey, see *Dreams*, New York: Barron's Educational Series 1976.

2 A first version of Part One appeared as 'Une archéologie du moderne: *Angelus*

Novus' in *L'Écrit du temps*, 2, 1982; and of Chapter 8 as 'Féminité et Judaïté', in the special issue 'Questions de judaïsme' of *L'Écrit du temps*, 5, 1983. Some of the material concerning the relationship between Baudelaire and Benjamin was first presented at a seminar held in February–June 1984 at the Collège International de Philosophie: *Archéologie de la modernité: De Baudelaire à Benjamin.*

PART ONE

AN ARCHAEOLOGY OF MODERNITY

Angelus Novus

The considerate kindness of the Angel mollified me in no little measure; and, aided by the water with which he diluted my port more than once, I at length regained sufficient temper to listen to his very extraordinary discourse. I cannot pretend to recount all that he told me, but I gleaned from what he said that he was *the genius who presided over the contretemps* of mankind, and whose business it was to bring about the *odd accidents* which are continually astonishing the sceptic.

Edgar Allen Poe, 'The Angel of the Odd'

Who, if I cried, would hear me among the angelic
orders? And even if one of them suddenly
pressed me against his heart, I should fade in the strength of his
stronger existence. For Beauty's nothing
but beginning of *Terror. . .*
Every angel is terrible [schrecklich].

Rainer Maria Rilke, *Duino Elegies*

A Klee painting named 'Angelus Novus' shows an angel looking as though he is about to move away from something he is fixedly contemplating. His eyes are staring, his mouth is open, his wings are spread. This is how one pictures *the angel of history*. His face is turned toward the past. Where we perceive a chain of events, he sees *one single catastrophe* which keeps piling wreckage upon wreckage and hurls it in front of his feet. The angel would like to stay, awaken the dead, and make whole what has been smashed. But a storm is blowing from Paradise; it has got caught in his wings with such violence that the angel can no longer close them. This storm irresistibly propels him into the future to which his back is turned, while the pile of debris before him grows skyward. This storm is what we call progress.

Walter Benjamin, 'Theses on the Philosophy of History'

Within literary modernity the allegorical figure of the Angel describes strange networks which all have to do with that 'something' terrible, frightening and bizarre, that fundamental *contretemps* where humanity meets its own destruction 'by chance' (Poe), where history as the storm of progress becomes 'one single catastrophe' (Benjamin), where beauty is so terrible that it kills (Rilke). These, we might say, are the motifs of our juxtaposition of texts in which Freud's analysis of 'the uncanny' (*das Unheimliche*) reverberates again and again.[1] On a close rereading of Freud's article, one cannot fail to be struck by a peculiar censorship or asymmetry. The uncanny, with its well-known ambivalence of the 'familiar and terrifying', of the 'repressed which manifests itself anew', certainly appears in a constitutive relationship to seeing – to the double, to death, to all the processes of ego-duplication that are present in concentrated form in literature, telepathy or animism. And yet, the uncanny is never glimpsed in anything other than demonological terms. Dismembered limbs, severed heads, gouged eyes, people buried alive, animated puppets: all these phantasms and fabrications should, in Freud's view, be traced back to a primal terror, to that forbidden, limitless and truly dizzying abyss which is the mother's womb/genitals.

To be sure, in relation to the Father and castration anxiety, the uncanny is thoroughly enmeshed in violence. But there is never any question of that other violence, more female than paternal, more androgynous than phallic, more seraphic than Luciferian: the violence of the Angel. Not, that is, unless we follow Lacan's suggestion of 'another side' to sexual pleasure [*jouissance*], a more female side in which the uncanny [*l'étrange*] merges with the angelic [*l'être-ange*]. 'On the other hand, can something be grasped which would tell us how what has hitherto been only a yawning fault in *jouissance* could become real? . . . Curiously enough, this can be suggested only by *very uncanny* sightings. *Étrange* is a word that can be broken down into *l'être-ange*.'[2]

This other side, this beauty coming from the abyss which, strictly speaking, cannot be represented except through the excess of the twofold metaphor of femininity and theology, never ceased to haunt Walter Benjamin. The theme – and the allegory of the Angel – actually constituted his personal cipher after he had acquired Klee's famous picture *Angelus Novus*. It shaped all his thinking on the philosophy of the avant-garde and modernity (Baudelaire, Kafka, Klee. . .), in a world without aura doomed to generalization of the commodity form and endless reproducibility of artworks. And finally it marked the 'Theses on the Philosophy of History' that he composed at the end of his life. This allegory organized the most private circulation of his obsessions, where Baudelaire's satanic language links together sexuality and feminine archetypes, a rather androgynous seraphic element and the element of fetishism. 'Impotence is the basis of the calvary trodden by male sexuality. Historical index of such impotence. From this impotence comes also his attachment to the seraphic image of woman as his fetish.'[3]

In the major text on the Angel that Benjamin wrote in a semi-delirious state in Ibiza in 1933, he stated: 'The angel, however, resembles all from which I have had to part: persons and above all things.'[4] And at a more conceptual level, the 'Angel of history' melancholically shatters the temporal continuum (social-democratic faith in progress), replacing it with a catastrophist, messianic instance that will release the future buried in the past and build it with the present. Here the political and epistemological overturning of the victors' historicism culminates in a new concept of the present – the *Jetztzeit* or 'now-time' of genuine actuality. To the empty linear time of the cumulative succession of events, Benjamin opposes the necessity of a temporal break, an interruption in time disclosed by the imaginaries of history. *Jetztzeit* is an intensive, qualitative time which becomes visible in 'states of emergency', the moments when 'culture engenders barbarism' and the infinitely repressed memory of 'those without a name' (*Namenlosen*) finally reappropriates a history dominated by the historicism of the rulers.[5]

In the interpretation of these theses, an antinomy is usually drawn up between the Marxist Benjamin, friend of Brecht and anti-fascist militant, and the Jewish-messianic Benjamin. However, the metaphor of the Angel – its repeated and ever reinvested scene – roots the text in a *border zone beyond and beneath the human*. This places Benjamin close to Kafka, of whom he says: 'The legitimate mystical interpretation should be understood as indicating his folly and not his wisdom.'[6] Besides, Benjamin himself states that he has made his own 'Kafka's formulation of the categorical imperative: "act in such a way that the Angel has something to do"'.[7] As to the mystical folly, it falls in with history, because Kafka, like Klee, 'lives in a *complementary world*'.

> Kafka's world, frequently of such playfulness and interlaced with angels, is the exact complement of his era which is preparing to do away with the inhabitants of this planet on a considerable scale. The experience which corresponds to that of Kafka, the private individual, will probably not become accessible to the masses until such time as they are being done away with.[8]

This premonitory judgement, reaching the highest point of radical critique, announces a *destructive principle* at work in history as in literary modernity, an experience of violence infinitely repressed in the aseptic, codified world of market society, big cities and a technology of power that brings about the 'atrophy of experience' evoked in 1933 in Benjamin's 'Erfahrung und Armut'.[9]

This focus on the radical character of violence – on a different violence, not just that of the 'rulers' – is a constant feature in Benjamin's work. It governed his passage from a metaphysical, nihilistic anarchism influenced by Sorel to a torn Marxism radical- ized by the paradoxical polarity of materialism and messianism, atheism and theology. Violence is always there: 'The tradition of the oppressed teaches us that the "state of emergency" in which we · live is not the exception but the rule. We must attain to a conception of history that is in keeping with this insight.'[10]

The fact that something like Nazism is still possible, at the heart of the 'West' in the mid-twentieth century, should not surprise us if we have understood, 'by brushing history against the grain', that the history of the West has always offered such violence *to be seen*.[11] Thus the Angel – *l'être-ange* and *l'étrange* – might well represent the extreme psychic and historical risk in its ambivalent polarities: human/inhuman, ephemeral/eternal, Angel/Satan, female/male, real/unreal. This 'conception of history' would then be paradox- ically inscribed within literature, in the shock element which obsesses the writing of modernity, by destroying the assurances of an all-too-male humanist subject. And as a constellation of multiple temporalities (family novel, scene of writing and history of class struggles), the Angel would allegorize that conflictual meeting-point between the 'familiar' everyday and the 'uncanny' which so intrigued Freud and defined dialectics for Benjamin. 'We penetrate the mystery only to the degree that we recognize it in the everyday world, by virtue of a dialectical optic that perceives the everyday as impenetrable, the impenetrable as everyday.'[12]

The familiar that Benjamin saw coming to the surface in Baude- laire ('A remark of Leiris: the word *familier* (familiar) in Baudelaire is full of mystery and unrest'[13]) could not be the object of direct, total and totalizing knowledge. Fragmented and repressed in history, it occupied all those incomplete territories overflowing classical rationality (childhood, female culture, the world of the defeated, the experiences of limits) and belonged to an interpre- tative truth 'which is the death of intention'. This is why philosophy, in order to be 'materialist',[14] can only practise a veritable exodus outside philosophy, a style of work on its frontiers and 'margins' which dedicates it to ever critical analysis of a reality which, since Nietzsche and Marx, has become enigmatic, hieroglyphic, non- 'rational'. The 'rebus is the model of his philosophy', as Adorno very acutely observed.[15]

This 'conception of history', appropriate to states of emergency, therefore played not so much on the presence of a continuous conceptual framework – a meaning – as on the critical, micrological and 'analytic' excavation of an imaginary of history. It was this imaginary that had to be located and defined, including in 'the most inconspicuous crystallizations of existence, in its waste material'.[16] Benjamin would track down all the modes of this philosophical struggle for an oppressed past, visible and invisible like the Freudian unconscious, of this construction of an *image* of history in which each epoch dreams the one that follows it and any naive vision of progress falls away. He would find them in painting, allegory, parable and then – in the unfinished book of his life, the *Passagen-Werk* – in the dialectical image bearing a temporal constellation in which the archaic and the modern are woven together. At that point Benjamin's interpretative methodology, the gaze of the historian, becomes more 'Freudian' than ever:

> In the dialectical image the past of a given epoch is always 'the past of always'. But it presents itself as such only in the eyes of a particular epoch – the one in which humanity, rubbing its eyes, recognizes precisely this dream image for what it is. At that moment the historian's task is the interpretation of dreams.[17]

However, the visibility of such an image depends upon an acute awareness of crisis in its catastrophic dimensions. Faced with the fine totalities of classicism, or with a Marxist *Weltanschauung* aesthetic, Benjamin therefore emphasizes quite a different scanning of history to bring out an archaeology of modernity at its crucial turning-points: the seventeenth-century baroque, the nineteenth century of Baudelaire (and not Balzac), the literary avant-garde of the twentieth century. At those junctures allegory testifies to a seat of resistance in Western history, to a different, Saturnian history in which 'the observer is confronted with the *facies hippocratica* of history as a petrified, *primordial* landscape [*erstarrte Urlandschaft*]'.[18] Representation prior to representation, pictogram merging life and death like 'an amorphous fragment', it is the 'armature of modernity'.[19] In this 'image of petrified disquiet' (*Bild der erstarrten Unruhe*), 'the dreams of an epoch are immobilized'.[20]

Against the stream of the aesthetics of Goethe, Hegel and even Schopenhauer or Nietzsche, Benjamin revalues allegory as a mode of writing, the principle of an aesthetic of modernity, the rising up of a misunderstood past. Through an archaeological detour attentive to detail and the plurality of languages, the critical gesture calls forth the polyrhythmic profundity of time, the oblivion characteristic of the history of the nameless. Allegories are always 'allegories of oblivion', for through them is expressed the unfreedom of men and women, and no writing which sides with the victors' history, or which, even from the Left, postulates an evolutionary continuity, has ever been able to reveal that infinite servitude. 'By its very essence classicism was not permitted to behold the lack of freedom, the imperfection, the collapse of the physical, beautiful, nature.'[21]

It was thus only through a work on origins (the *Ursprung* of German baroque drama), then another on the pre- or proto-history (*Urgeschichte*) of modernity, that a new project announced itself. In this veritable archaeology of modernity, that which is forgotten by the 'philosophies of history' is always an *Ur*, a primal; it has to be integrated into Marxism, which is thereby itself radicalized and transformed. As Fabrizio Desideri remarks, *Urgeschichte* is much more than simple 'prehistory': it is *primal history*, which connects it with *Ursprung*, with a reality that alludes to '*Vor- und Nachgeschichte*' (pre- and post-history) and even to Goethe's concept of 'primal phenomenon', the *Urphänomen* cited by Benjamin himself.[22]

This primal history of the nineteenth century – the archaeology of a modernity understood as 'mass art' and 'mass dimension' of every process – bears precisely upon 'primal historical forms' (*urgeschichtliche Formen*). As Benjamin puts it: 'The "*Urgeschichte*" of the nineteenth century would be of no interest if it was not understood in such a way that primal historical forms could be found at the root of the nineteenth century.'[23] Such forms are not prior to history in the sense of *epistemes*; nor are they ideological reflections of an economic base, as they appear in a certain Marxist topography that Benjamin considered to be nominalist and mechanistic. Rather, they are imaginary expressions (*Ausdruck*), at once semantic and visual, of the rebus-scenes or '*dialectical images*' that accompany all social processes. But they emerge and become susceptible to interpretation only at moments of crisis when 'the new and the old interpenetrate'. In these wish-images of the future 'the fantasy, which gains its initial stimulus from the new', is turned back upon 'the primal past'. This is why, 'in the dream in which every epoch sees in images the epoch which is to succeed it, the latter appears coupled with elements of prehistory – that is to say of a classless society'.[24] Hence the utopias that flourished with industrialization in the nineteenth century; hence too the resurgence of myths, of an *irratio*, in the crisis of the twenties and thirties.

In these hollows of modernity, the dialectical images of a historical epoch obey a kind of dream logic governed by social ambiguity and historical ambivalence:

> Ambiguity is the figurative appearance of the dialectic, the law of the dialectic at a standstill [*Dialektik im Stillstand*]. This standstill is Utopia,

and the dialectical image therefore a dream image. The commodity clearly provides such an image: as fetish. The arcades, which are both house and stars, provide such an image. And such an image is provided by the whore, who is seller and commodity in one.[25]

If the methodological deciphering of such images coincides with critical turning-points of history, the position of the *writer-interpreter* – writer of, on and with other forms of writing, decipherer of traces – is of no little importance. Benjamin writes in this unstable zone without assurances, where the work can unfold in networks of a heterogeneous element (in the sense used by Georges Bataille), through a concept which rises and goes beyond itself in figures that attempt to grasp this 'excess' of history, this return of the primal into the present. Such is the concept of *catastrophe*, as a way of thinking history and art, with its many variants: trauma, shock, Baudelairean spleen, surrealist and then Brechtian montage, melancholy, distancing, states of emergency and – the final representation of the non-representable – death. Such too is the Angel.

Benjamin's archaeology is situated half-way between Foucault's project in *Madness and Civilization* (making a silence speak so as to reconstruct the historical plinth of reason) and Freud's in *The Interpretation of Dreams* (rediscovering a primal scene that reconstructs a complete logic of the real/unreal unconscious). One might define it as an *archaeology of the imaginary of and in history*, which is at work in the decisive junctures of modernity. Or one might even characterize it with the formulation that Benjamin applied to photography as the art of modernity: 'It introduces us to unconscious optics as does psychoanalysis to unconscious impulses.'[26] Without this updating of *unconscious optics* there could be no conception of history which proves 'equal to death' (Bataille), nor of violence and 'positive barbarism'. As in the work of Ernst Bloch, but in a diametrically opposite sense, the unplumbed depths of modernity – its *irratio* which has to be deciphered and made dialectical – really lie in the archaic, the mythological, the buried hosts of a past which is not yet past. It is an eminently political task, because this *irratio* is always open to conscription 'from the right', as in Nazism.

But is it not the case that such a Saturnian perspective on history, such a primacy of the 'logic of dislocation' over the logic of transcendence, brings on stage a radical uncanniness which needs to be inserted into Freud's text, in a way liable to explode the Marxisms of progress and replace them with a rent Marxism, a Marxism of rending? Bicephalous, historical and sexual, the work involved in such a project might be said to rest upon a 'female', non-paternal principle with no filiation, a utopian-violent principle affecting the status of the 'nameless'. The young Benjamin, subject to all the labyrinthine emotions of sexuality, expressed this same principle in astonishing 'metaphorical' terms:

> But I prefer to avoid speaking concretely here and to talk rather of *male and female*: for how closely the two are intertwined in human beings! . . . Europe is composed of individuals (in whom male and female are present), not of men and women. Who knows how far the mind of woman extends? What do we know of woman? As little as we do of youth. As yet we have no experience of a *woman's culture*.[27]

Woman's culture, bisexuality: we recognize the echoes of a veritable *feminization of culture* in the second half of the nineteenth century and the early years of the twentieth, both in the French language (Saint-Simonism, then Baudelaire, Mallarmé, Lautréamont) and in German (Simmel, Weininger, Groddeck, Schnitzler, Kraus or Musil). The very notion of 'female culture' – *weibliche Kultur* – circulated more or less everywhere at the beginning of the century. We find it in Groddeck's 1903 piece on *A Woman Problem*, as well as the essay on 'Female Culture' that Simmel published in 1911 in his *Philosophische Kultur* collection.[28] It is as if, in crisis periods when the problem of modernity reappeared, it was impossible to approach the 'woman question' without considering the 'question of civilization' through a whole series of oppositions and myths.[29] In such periods – of which the nineteenth century is one – a major effort takes place to deconstruct the frontier between male and female identities, thereby calling into question the pre-urban, natural differences ravaged by the development of big cities, industrialization and the mass dimension of social phenomena. In the labour of writing, the metaphor of the feminine then rises up as an element in the break with a certain discredited rationality based upon the idea of a historical and symbolic continuum. It does this by designating a new heterogeneity, a new otherness.

From Baudelaire's allegory of the prostitute-mother to Musil's 'man without qualities' given over to mystical, near-androgynous incest with the sister, from the dehiscent gap of womanhood in Mallarmé to Rilke's vision of the Open: a whole network of negativity escaping the dominance of the Concept, a whole 'culture' of the feminine if not of woman, now comes into play. We might call it a culture of *Spaltung*, of splitting, where the position of writing is subject to a highly ambiguous feminine whose Angel could be the trace, allegory, theoretical interpretation. The ambiguity is lodged in the unconceptualized side of 'the modern'. On the one hand, it is necessary to utter – to write – the end of the classical Cartesian subject with its 'control' of itself and the world, and to express the dizzying abysses of bodily *jouissance* and new values. But on the other hand, this labour of feminization arouses fear, anxiety and combative misogyny, common to a Baudelaire, Nietzsche or Weininger. This ambiguity works upon the very text of Benjamin's writings: he is ever attempting a 'critical', profane reading of the great Baudelairean myths of prostitution and the lesbian, that 'heroine of modernism'.[30] We shall return to this in Part Two below.

But if the archaeology of modernity seems haunted by the feminine, how far can the power of images go? From the origin (*Ursprung*) to primal, archaeological history (*Urgeschichte*)? And perhaps to the edge of that 'primeval forest' (*Urwald*) which surrounds Benjamin, rather like the 'primordial landscape' (*Urlandschaft*) of allegory?

Notes

1. Sigmund Freud, 'The "Uncanny"', in *Complete Psychological Works*, vol. 17, London: Hogarth Press 1955.
2. Jacques Lacan, *Encore: Séminaire XX, 1972–73*, Paris: Seuil 1975, p. 14. [The English expression used here, 'sexual pleasure', gives only a very approximate idea of Lacan's use of the term *jouissance*. For a discussion of this concept, including a translation of that section of *Encore* which explicitly deals with the 'other side', 'the *jouissance* of woman', see Juliet Mitchell and Jacqueline Rose, eds, *Feminine Sexuality: Jacques Lacan and the École Freudienne*, London: Macmillan 1982. *Trans. note*.]
3. Walter Benjamin, 'Central Park', *New German Critique*, 34, Winter 1985, p. 36 [Rolf Tiedemann and Hermann Schweppenhäuser, eds, *Gesammelte Schriften* (hereafter *GS*) 6 vols., Frankfurt/Main: Suhrkamp Verlag 1972–, II, 2, p. 663. Translation modified].
4. This text, 'Agesilaus Santander', is reproduced and interpreted by Gershom Scholem in 'Walter Benjamin and His Angel', in Gary Smith, ed., *On Walter Benjamin: Critical Essays and Recollections*, Cambridge, Mass: MIT Press 1991, p. 59. Some of the material here has been borrowed from Scholem's article.
5. 'Theses on the Philosophy of History', in Walter Benjamin, *Illuminations*, New York: Schocken 1968, pp. 253–64.
6. Gershom Scholem, ed., *Briefe*, 2 vols., Frankfurt/Main: Suhrkamp Verlag 1978, 2, p. 629.
7. Ibid., p. 748.
8. Ibid., p. 762. English translation in 'Some Reflections on Kafka', in *Illuminations*, p. 143.
9. In *GS* II, 1, pp. 213–19.
10. 'Theses on the Philosophy of History', p. 257.
11. Ibid., p. 257.
12. Benjamin, 'Surrealism: The Last Snapshot of the European Intelligentsia', in *One-Way Street and Other Writings*, London: New Left Books 1979, p. 237.

13. *GS* I, 2, p. 678. English translation in 'Central Park', p. 47.
14. Benjamin appealed to a 'materialist attitude' and not a materialist philosophy. See *Briefe* 2, p. 524.
15. Theodor Adorno, 'A Portrait of Walter Benjamin', in idem, *Prisms*, Cambridge, Mass: MIT Press 1981, p. 20.
16. *Briefe* 2, p. 685.
17. *GS* V, p. 580.
18. Walter Benjamin, *The Origin of German Tragic Drama*, London: New Left Books 1977, p. 166. [It should be borne in mind throughout the argument that the author's French title for this work, 'the origin of German *baroque* drama', is more evocative of the *Trauerspiel* which forms its object. *Trans. note.*]
19. *GS* I, 2, p. 681.
20. Ibid., p. 666.
21. *The Origin of German Tragic Drama*, p. 176.
22. Fabrizio Desideri, *Walter Benjamin, il tempo e le forme*, Rome: Riuniti 1980, p. 262. Cf. Marc Sagnol's intervention at the Colloque: *Weimar and Modernity*, held at Saint-Cloud in 1982.
23. *GS* V, p. 579.
24. 'Paris – the Capital of the Nineteenth Century', in Walter Benjamin, *Charles Baudelaire: A Lyric Poet in the Era of High Capitalism*, London: Verso 1983, p. 159.
25. Ibid., p. 171.
26. 'The Work of Art in the Age of Mechanical Reproduction', in *Illuminations*, p. 237.
27. *Briefe* 1, p. 65.
28. For an English translation see 'Female Culture', in *Georg Simmel: On Women, Sexuality, and Love*, New Haven: Yale University 1984.
29. In using the term 'feminization of culture', I presuppose a number of correlations between crisis culture (on the model of Vienna or Weimar), deconstruction of the classical male, conscious subject, and a challenging of the male/female division: hence the resurgence of the great myths concerning women, and the 'feminization' of the written body. In France these correlations first appear with romanticism, are to be found at work in Baudelaire, and haunt all the poetry of the second half of the nineteenth century. See the pertinent remarks in Julia Kristeva, *Revolution in Poetic Language*, New York: Columbia University 1984.
30. *GS* I, 2, p. 594; 'The Paris of the Second Empire in Baudelaire', in *Charles Baudelaire*, p. 90.

1

ANGELIC SPACE

Angelus Novus, an Overwhelming Picture

The starting-point is an encounter like any other: impact, brain-storm, post-shock. On 21 June Benjamin bought a picture by Klee called *Angelus Novus*. It was love at first sight for this half-ironic, half-enigmatic 'new angel' with a floating, dreamy sexuality, its wide-open eyes staring into the distance and its hair curled in the form of (somewhat baroque) parchments. Klee was particularly fond of these intermediate creatures, and of the many paintings he devoted to them *Angelus Novus* is certainly not among the greatest. Yet, as we know from Scholem, who would himself later write a poem to the Angel, 'Benjamin always considered the picture his most important possession'.[1] On 23 July 1920, in connection with another painting by Klee, *Seduction by the Miracle*, he wrote to Scholem: 'Do you know Klee? I like him enormously.'[2]

Benjamin never lost this fascination with Klee, and with a picture that one would hardly hesitate to call a 'collage-object', juxtaposing as it does the most disparate aspects of the parental images.[3] He kept it hanging at home until his divorce, and remained unable to part with it except through death. It even followed him into exile at rue Dombasle in Paris, thanks to an acquaintance who got it across the border, and in the dark hours of the war it was finally hidden by Georges Bataille at the Bibliothèque Nationale before being forwarded to his friend Scholem. The *Kleeblatt* (which also means cloverleaf in German) was immediately caught in a web of signifiers, evoking the celestial clover as symbol of the Trinity. Soon it was Benjamin's 'little demonology', his new kabbalistic protector, 'his unique messenger from the *kabbalah*'.[4] Such then are the 'facts', if that is the right word – for the metaphor of the Angel reappears in every scene of Benjamin's life. In 1921 he planned a journal of current affairs that would seek to understand the epoch through 'vertical penetration' and 'a rationality driven to the limits of the possible'. It was to be called . . . *Angelus Novus*. In later years, in his articles on Kraus and Baudelaire or his experiences with hashish in Marseilles, the new biblical angel would recover its more familiar satanic traits. Invading dreams and delirium, then history itself, its 'little demonology' really seemed to comply with that *logic of the complementary world* – of the Complement – which he detected in Kafka and Klee.[5] At the end of his life, in his 'Theses on the Philosophy of History', Benjamin would take up this logic in a chess metaphor he shared with Stefan Zweig, another future suicide who had experienced the culture of crisis and Nazism.

> The story is told of an automaton constructed in such a way that it could play a winning game of chess, answering each move of an opponent with a countermove. A puppet in Turkish attire and with a hookah in its mouth sat before a chessboard placed on a large table. A system of mirrors created the illusion that this table was transparent from all sides. Actually, a little hunchback who was an expert chess player sat inside and guided the puppet's hand by means of strings. One can imagine a philosophical counterpart to this device. The puppet called 'historical materialism' is to win all the time. It can easily be a match for anyone if it enlists the services of theology, which today, as we know, is wizened and has to keep out of sight.[6]

In this curious staging reminiscent of Kleist's puppet theatre, in this irresolvable duel between puppet and hunchback that dominated the whole of Benjamin's life, the decisive element was his encounter in 1917–20 both with Klee and with non-orthodox, messianic and mystical, Jewish culture as mediated by Scholem's friendship and his reading of Rosenzweig and the *kabbalah*.

1917: Benjamin, interested in the multiple forms of languages and signs, writes a series of very short texts on modern art in which he contrasts the longitudinal section of representative painting with the horizontal section of graphics and certain kinds of symbolic writing.[7] Modern painting, especially Cubism and Klee which so intrigue him, constitute a symbolic language irreducible to 'the order of essence' (philosophy) or 'the order of reproduction' (classical space). Through this annihilation of the humanist tradition of representation, 'the problem of Cubism lies in the possibility of painting which is not without colour but fundamentally alien to colour; linear constructions dominate the picture, but Cubism does not thereby cease to be painting and turn into design.'[8] The quest for such picture-writing, where the sign becomes visible, brings Cubism and Klee into proximity with each other: 'in this sense the only one of the modern painters to have touched me is Klee'.[9]

Nearly fifteen years later in 'Erfahrung und Armut', one of his finest pieces of writing, Benjamin was doubtless more aware of what 'touched' him so deeply. Moving beyond the revolution in painting and his own early reflections on picture-writing, he found in Klee a radically destructive principle, a creative catastrophic element, an ambivalent adherence to his age composed of passion and lack of illusions. 'Among the great creators, there are implacable ones who first of all make a clean break. They actually want a board on which to draw; they have been constructors.'[10] And he goes on to mention Descartes, Einstein and Klee.

Klee's figures, projected onto this clear drawing board, have a linearity which 'responds above all to their inside – to their inside rather than their interiority. *And this is what makes them barbarous.*'[11] The Angel is like all Klee's intermediate, disintegrated beings: maskers, demons, puppets, dazed madmen, beastmen, plant-faces; they no longer participate in a humanist logic of inner subject and representation. By an ironic excess, they mark the passage from the visible towards the invisible, where our floating frontiers of the human and the inhuman, culture and barbarism, that whole concoction of the unnameable plays itself out. Like Loos and so many others, Klee shunned 'the solemn and noble traditional image of man, bedecked with all the sacrificial offerings of the past, and turned towards the naked contemporary who cries like a newly born child'.[12] That invisible is thoroughly ensconced in the crisis of the epoch, concealed in the logic of the commodity and the reproducibility of the artwork. And in making it visible, it is necessary to appropriate the unreality of the human, its precariousness and contingency, a whole principle of indeterminacy of reality. The 'stranger relationship' (in Rosolato's sense[13]) to the non-human can only reject the everyday language of things, the falseness of actuality, and look beyond the world of the living to a complementary world: it must 'invent *a new, complementary language*'. Klee lives the same madness as that of Kafka, and Benjamin: rejection of human language, of 'likeness to man [*Menschenähnlichkeit*], that principle of humanism'.[14] In this infinite struggle of language, Benjamin intersects with the whole 'crisis culture' of Vienna at its height. It led the Wittgenstein of the *Tractatus*, or the Hofmannsthal of 'The Letter of Lord Chandos', to seek on the shores of silence 'a language none of whose words is known to me, a language in which inanimate things speak to me'.[15]

In this endless accumulation of transmuted forms given over to the rule of a new theatre – 'Angel and puppet, there at last is spectacle' (Rilke) – the representations of Freud's uncanny multiply *ad infinitum*. Between Klee's Angel and the metaphor-parable of Kafka's animals, Benjamin detects the same return of the forgotten: 'Kafka did not tire of picking up the forgotten from animals.'[16] It is a Nietzschean active forgetting which here turns back in a suspension of linear, chronological time and 'messes a situation up'.[17]

That forgetting, that non-human which is also non-representational, powerfully marks Benjamin's (and Freud's) ambivalence regarding the values of culture – those documents of barbarism of which naive rationalism has no knowledge. We find in both the same radical, lucid pessimism in the face of history, the same deracination in an impossible Jewishness that is at once denied and claimed. Benjamin, who received a liberal not a religious education, experienced the 'Jewish question' in the shape of anti-semitism and through his encounter with mystical and messianic culture. He wanted all his life to learn Hebrew, and he continually planned to make trips to Israel or even to settle there. But he never reached it: he was caught up in other frontiers and lands of exile, above all France.

Benjamin elucidated this anti-humanist connection between the New Angel and history in an article that he wrote on Karl Kraus, another major figure in Viennese culture.

> Neither purity nor sacrifice mastered the demon; but where origin and destruction come together, his rule is over. Like a creature sprung from the child and the cannibal his conqueror stands before him: not a new man; *a monster, a new angel*. Perhaps one of those who, according to the Talmud, are at each moment created anew in countless throngs, and who, once they have raised their voices before God, cease and pass into nothingness.[18]

This is evidence of a remarkable consistency, for it was in virtually the same terms that the Angel had served in 1921 as the symbol for the journal *Angelus Novus*. Ephemeral, living/dying, beginning and end, the Angel *sings* for a moment in praise of God, as the naked man of modernity *shouts*. The voice here represents that ancestral, infinitely maternal, imaginary which still eludes the articulations of · law and language. The 'language of angels' is a pre-linguistic, non-verbal language in which our most basic drives become metaphorical: the life and death instincts, Eros and Thanatos. Or, to use Benjamin's own terms, it is the moment within which the apocalyptic and the destructive principle are fused together. *War and Fire* is the title of one of Klee's last paintings.

That might well sum up this first account of the Angel, where the world of the living is, so to speak, parabolically duplicated by another world of violence and uncertainty. Expressed in this world is the infant's enormous visual curiosity, the *suffering* and jubilation of the eye.

> He who wishes to construct theatre must have lived and suffered through the eye. He must have sworn a thousand times that only the visible exists, and a thousand times shudderingly wondered whether the visible, before all other things, does *not* exist. . . . He must have undergone love, hate and fear and felt how love, hate and fear transform a familiar valley, a

customary house or a most intimate chamber, so that they resemble the cavernous depths of Hades whose walls contort themselves in a grin when the incestuous matricide enters therein.[19]

Valley, house, room – all containers of the feminine – evoke that seeing/non-seeing which lay behind Freud's discoveries, because it was also the mark of 'feminized' Viennese culture in crisis here illustrated by Hofmannsthal. This whole *heimlich* dimension, which suddenly becomes *unheimlich*, clearly represents part of what Freud opened up for thought: the incest-barred phantasm of the mother's inaccessible and ineffable womb/genitals. There is more to be said, however, about this violence which suffers because of the eye.

In the same article on Karl Kraus, Benjamin counterposes non-man (*Unmensch*) or the inhuman to the all-man (*Allmensch*) or 'cosmic man' of tradition. The angelic messenger of the Bible (*maleakin*: angels; *maleak*: a sovereign's envoy) moves in each of us as *angel-interpreter*. Witness the Book of Daniel, which for the first time gives names to the angels – previously 'nameless beings', like demons – and thus transforms them into symbolic protectors. These angel-interpreters know unfathomable secrets: they watch over men caught between the angel for the defence and the angel for the prosecution.[20]

Angelus Novus, interpreting angel – that is clear enough. But the interpretation in question only liberates what is inhuman in us: the inhuman 'stands among us as the messenger of a more real humanism'.[21] Beyond the animated puppets evoked in Freud's text, the angels, animals, new-born, not-yet-born or scarcely born call to mind the ritual of a barely disguised cannibalism in which humanity, like Saturn, devours its own children. Death instinct. Pain of the eye that does not want to see, of the subject that cannot hear what belongs to the realm of the cry, song, shock, non-birth or devourment. It is not far from that violence of cracks and cleavages which Artaud evokes in his letter to Peter Watson: 'From time to time, dear Mr Peter Watson, life makes a leap, but that is never written into history, and my only purpose in writing has been to fix and perpetuate the memory of these cracks, cleavages or breaks, these sudden and bottomless falls.'[22]

That memory is much more than affirmation of the law, of its transmission/filiation; it is the body's memory, the scansion of voice and song, visual recollection. For in the passage from sight to speech, the unsayable moves in and through a distance which is precisely that of writing. Concerning sight Benjamin says: 'I now have an idea of Dürer's violence, and *Melencolia* in particular is of an unspeakable profundity and expressiveness.'[23] But of writing he asserts: 'I keep returning to the idea that a crystal-pure elimination of what cannot be said in language is given to us as the most accessible form of acting within, and thus through, language.'[24] Paradoxically, only 'objective and therefore highly political writing' can lead to this vanishing-point, to 'that which is denied to words'. In this sense 'only the intensive directing of words to the core of innermost silence can truly have an effect.'[25] This secret of what is constantly beheld but cannot be expressed – which alone allows us to understand a 'humanity that affirms itself in destruction' – is the space of *Angelus Novus*. Such a distance between sight and speech refers us precisely to the 'complementary world', to *what is mystical* as Wittgenstein put it. 'There are, indeed, things that cannot be put into words. They make themselves manifest. They are what is mystical.'[26] We should understand by this that the 'mystical' element – ethics which, for Wittgenstein, can neither form the object of propositions nor be formulated in a problem – essentially coincides with aesthetics: 'Ethics and aesthetics are one and the same.'[27]

Now, artistic modernity could confront this complementary world of our historical barbarism only by measuring itself with the terminus of the cultural, with that invisible 'other' which is the theological. It is quite a different matter from religion: the one excavates a lack, feminizes it up to the point of non-capacity or non-being, whereas the other blocks it up through a labour of illusion and institutionalization.

Angel of the Odd, new angel, satanic and terrible angel: these, then, organize a most curious archaeological route, in a century marked by the secularization of politics (from Marx to Max Weber), by ideologies of progress and scientific rationality, and by revolutions without precedent in history.

For, ever since Baudelaire – where they are alternately 'delightful' or 'disagreeable', 'elated' or defenceless, 'brazen-faced' or 'wild-eyed' – angels have never ceased to exercise a kind of invisible guardianship of modernity within the poetic act. Angelic spaces are magical spheres of all the correspondences and metamorphoses, all the metaphorical displacements of desire. They are the spaces of Klee's 'intermediate world', of all 'those worlds which are not visible to everyone and can really only be seen by children, mad people and primitives', as in that 'inner space of the world' (*Weltinnerung*) to which Rilke refers.

It is a floating, imaginal space where every frontier wavers between subjective and objective, inside and outside, real and unreal, male and female, so that it opens onto the non-human point of view of the phantasmic, the matrical, the invisible. Thus Rilke could write: 'This, a world no longer seen from the standpoint of people, but *in* the angel, is perhaps my real task.'[28] Faced with a shrinking experiential world of pulverized fragments, the poetic task is 'to transfigure things into the invisible'. The angel, in the *Duino Elegies*, will be this terrible, confounding figure of super-mundane beauty who gives access to a higher world that upholds invisibility. As Rilke put it in a letter to Witold von Hulewicz: 'The angel of the *Elegies* is that Being in whom the transmutation of the Visible into the Invisible, which we seek to achieve, is con-summated.'[29] To those who do not feel sure in 'the interpreted world', angelic space – 'as intact as a rose' – is there to represent that 'baroque' current passing from life to death, that unending flow between the 'two realms' which is covered by poetic metaphor.

Of course, the host of angels that Klee drew and painted in the harshest years of personal illness and world disaster (1939–40) are not these terrible, higher creatures peculiar to Rilke's dimension of the Open (*das Offene*). *Poor Angel* (1939), *Guardian Angel* (1939), *Of Angelic Nature* (1939), *Oblivious Angel* (1939): these all depict ironically distanced angels who are in the process of becoming, caught in the play of cosmos and history. In short, they suggest that *fou rire* of angels which Klee, in his writings on modern art, linked to moral seriousness: 'Moral seriousness goes together with the *fou rire* of angels regarding scholars and pontificators.'[30]

Whatever the differences from Rilke's poetic act, Klee's repre-sentation of angels achieves something equivalent in painting: that is, it makes the invisible visible, testifies to the cosmic genesis of creation, and opens up an intermediate realm beyond appearances, irreducible to the human, precisely the 'complementary world' of which Benjamin speaks. One cannot fail to be struck, therefore, by the extraordinary affinity between Klee's act of painting and the horizon of Benjamin's thinking about '*Urgeschichte*'. Since painting is not the law but 'above the law', a world of differences and imponderables, it always seeks a vanishing point in the direction of 'primal chaos', 'an original foundation': it must go back 'from the model to the matrix', to the archetype (*vom Vorbildlichen zum Urbildlichen*). Klee's quest for what he theorizes as the 'original code' (*Ur-Codex*) of a 'primordial sign' (*Urzeichen*), or for 'primal forms' (*Urbilden*), consigns his work to a perpetual passage from chaos to 'the formal cosmos', from the visible to the invisible.[31] The similarity between Klee's terms (*Urbild, Ur-Codex*, etc.) and Benjamin's is quite remarkable. Klee's intermediate world, to which the angels belong, delimits a veritable 'prehistory of the visible', as he himself puts it.

Through the angels, from baroque putti to Klee's ironic and tragic creatures, it is actually 'the eye which looks at us': the eye of the painter, after that of God. It is as if, at the height of modernity and at the price of a mystical atheism, the Angel's labour still resumes the great angelic utopia of the baroque, which consisted in making something visible, in being a pure apparition that made appearance appear, from a position just on its edges. For in the world of the baroque, the Angel opens the play of illusion, the light vertigo of theatre on the theatrical stage, the theatre of a painted visible where the eye would at once be in the wings and on stage. As Richard Alewyn writes: 'The baroque illusion is always conscious and intentional: it refuses to seduce the soul or even to deceive reason; it wishes to seduce the senses.'[32] If life is a dream, the world is truly a theatre, and theatre is that 'intermediate world', the metaphor for an invisible visible and a visible invisible – for an *ingannar gli occhi*, to use the Italian expression.

Now, in our modern world, which no longer believes in angels nor, doubtless, in the transcendence that animated the baroque flight of appearances, the Angel's 'light' – that unmediated language prior to language – changes its nature and function. The angelic, by virtue of its very *être-ange-té* in any reality test,[33] summons up the precariousness of the human. Bisexual or androgynous, it almost makes real a hallucinatory phantasm: namely, to see the look which sees the visible, to scan the invisible, or, as Klee writes, 'to see with one eye and consciously perceive with the other'. Hence the Angel's capacity to prefigure the Other, the elsewhere, an inhuman or a 'third sex'. Interpellated by poetry from Poe to Baudelaire or Rilke, the Angel foils reality, 'romanticizes' or interrupts it, and sketches the mysterious unity of correspondences peculiar to metaphor or allegory.

From the 'angelic' fascination of his youth to the hunchbacked dwarf of theology playing with historical materialism, Benjamin continually found in messianic mysticism a number of excess figures and metaphors with which to explore the underlying abyss of history. We can already see this in his early fixation on *Angelus Novus*. And above all, we find it in the concepts of catastrophe, redemption and messiah which Benjamin borrowed from the mystical-messianic tradition of Judaism, and then used to 'interrupt the flow of time' and to practise what we might call *suspensive violence* – violence which cuts off breath, voice, representation.

Faced with an economistic Marxism in thrall to a social-democratic conception of linear progress, Benjamin always asserted the need for an auxiliary construction. In a series of controlled metaphors, the theological dwarf was to free the spaces where an expanded and truly critical rationality would have to operate. These spaces would be precisely those where madness once waxed; the task, finally, was to make them 'cultivable' by advancing 'with the sharpened axe of reason, looking neither to right nor to left so as not to fall prey to the anguish beckoning at the heart of the primeval forest [*Urwald*]'.

It is a long journey into the arcana of Western history, a journey of rediscovery of allegory and baroque drama.

Notes

1. Scholem, 'Walter Benjamin and His Angel', p. 62.
2. Benjamin, *Briefe* 1, p. 242.
3. In the sense used by Joyce Macdougall in *Plaidoyer pour une certaine anormalité*, Paris: Gallimard 1978.
4. *Briefe* 2, p. 543.
5. Ibid., p. 762.
6. 'Theses on the Philosophy of History', p. 253.
7. *GS* II, 2, pp. 602–3.
8. *Briefe* 1, p. 154.
9. Ibid., p. 154.
10. Ibid., p. 215.
11. Ibid., p. 216.
12. Ibid., p. 216.
13. See Guy Rosolato, *La Relation d'inconnu*, Paris: Gallimard 1978.
14. *GS* II, 1, p. 216.
15. Hugo von Hofmannsthal, 'The Letter of Lord Chandos', in *Selected Prose*, New York: Pantheon 1952, p. 141. On the relationship between language and representation in 'modernity', see Allan Janik and Stephen Toulmin, *Wittgenstein's Vienna*, New York: Simon & Schuster 1973.
16. 'Franz Kafka: On the Twentieth Anniversary of His Death', in *Illuminations*, p. 132.
17. Ibid.
18. 'Karl Kraus', in *One-Way Street and Other Writings*, p. 290.
19. Hofmannsthal, 'Die Bühne als Traumbild', in *Prosa* II, Frankfurt/Main: Fischer 1951, pp. 78–9.
20. On this 'history' of angels in the Jewish religion, see André Caquot, 'Anges et Démons en Israël', in *Génies, anges et démons*, Paris: Seuil 1971; and on the Angel's function in the structuring of the Jewish Oedipus, see the chapter entitled 'Trois générations' in Guy Rosolato, *Essais sur le symbolique*, Paris: Gallimard 1979.
21. 'Karl Kraus', p. 289.
22. Quoted and interpreted by Viviane Forester in *La Violence du calme*, Paris: Seuil 1980, p. 52. See also her analysis of the 'violence of nothing' as woman-violence.
23. *Briefe* 1, p. 76.
24. Ibid., p. 127.
25. Ibid., p. 127.
26. Ludwig Wittgenstein, *Tractatus Logico-Philosophicus*, London: Routledge & Kegan Paul 1972, p. 151.
27. Ibid., p. 147.

28. Letter to Ellen Delp, 27 October 1915, in Rainer Maria Rilke, *Selected Letters 1902–1926*, London: Quartet 1988, p. 263.

29. Letter postmarked 13 November 1925, in ibid., p. 395.

30. All quotations from Klee are here translated from the French text in *Écrits sur l'art*, vol. 1, Paris: Dessain et Topra 1973. *Trans. note.*

31. Ibid., pp. 69, 76. On Klee's intermediate world, see the analysis of Jean-François Lyotard in *Discours-Figure*, Paris: Klincksieck 1971, pp. 224ff: 'The problematic . . . is that of an intermediate world, of another possible nature which prolongs creation and makes visible that which is not.'

32. See Richard Alewyn, ed., *Deutsche Barockforschung. Dokumentation einer Epoche*, Cologne 1965.

33. See the discussion of Lacan's decomposition of '*étrange*' into '*être-ange*', on p. 43 above.

2
BAROQUE SPACE

Trauerspiel: Allegory as Origin

Unlike Christianity and the conservative Judaism of the Book, the mystical-messianic Jewish culture which circulated from 1900 to 1920 throughout Central Europe and the German-language area always referred to a history marked by radical insecurity, an element of instability and catastrophe, a consciousness of rupture and utopianism.[1] As opposed to Christianity, which inscribes redemption within a historical directionality, Jewish messianism invariably conceives of the emergence from the state of exile and oppression – redemption – as a tireless waiting for messianic fulfilment.[2] There is an infinite separation between present time (*olam hazeh*) and time to come (*olam haba*), which can come to pass only from a series of catastrophes (revolutions, wars, famines . . .). The 'totally new' is as unpredictable as it is sudden. As Scholem writes: 'Jewish Messianism is in its origins and by its nature – this cannot be sufficiently emphasized – a theory of *catastrophe*', of 'the cataclysmic element in the transition from every historical present to the Messianic future'.[3]

Jewish messianism, then, is characterized by the lack of any idea of historical progress. In its pessimistic-critical vision of reality, the coming of the Messiah, redemption or – in the terms of Lurianic kabbalism – 'restitution of the world' create an unbridgeable gulf between the history of the oppression of the Jewish people and the history of its messianic freedom. From the one to the other, there can only be a qualitative leap, a 'destructive principle' as Benjamin described it.

This central aspect of historical discontinuity, with its utopianism that served as a transition for numerous revolutionary intellectuals in the 1920s (including Ernst Bloch), was initially inserted within a cultural context common to the whole Jewish intelligentsia of Mitteleuropa, from Vienna to Prague, Budapest or Berlin. It was an explosive climate in which neo-romantic critique of 'the illusions of progress' fused with the work of Tolstoy, Nietzsche and Strindberg who influenced the young Benjamin.[4]

Such messianism mostly went together with an 'anarchist' or even nihilist politics which had reached its peak in certain heresies of the seventeenth century, particularly the Sabbatian movement, for which the arrival of messianic time was a question of the present. Not only did Sabbatai Zevi lift prohibitions, reject anti-female taboos and introduce free sexuality: 'Eve could have married several men'; he even proclaimed: 'Blessed art Thou O Lord our God, King of the Universe, who permittest the forbidden', and preached that 'violation of the Torah has become its fulfilment'.[5]

We find in Benjamin's articles of the twenties on violence the same continual passing between Jewish messianism, centred on the idea of catastrophic rupture, and a 'metaphysical', anti-state 'anarchism' close to Sorel, with an incipient train of thought which borrowed from Carl Schmitt's early analysis of the political as 'sovereignty that decides in states of emergency'. This vocabulary impregnated *The Origin of German Tragic Drama*, as it would much later the 'Theses on the Philosophy of History'. We should be clear, however, that for Benjamin 'the political' was always over-determined and never had an autonomous existence. It was deployed in a network of metaphors and myths, in a plurality of languages which held together its extreme moments of violence and the 'complementary world' of theology, real history and history in its image and its imaginary.

This ascent to the extreme limits first came into play in 'Critique of Violence' and 'Theologico-Political Fragment'. In opposition to the major debates of the time, which treated the political as a rational juridical form (Weber) or an ideal norm (Kelsen), Benjamin reinvested a terrain that was also Freud's – the terrain of 'classical' philosophy and its *primal*, inexorable, state-channelled violence. In such a space, there is room only for an infinitely repeated cycle of 'executive' violence which makes and preserves the law and periodically revives its own origin in the archaic violence of nature, mythical violence thrusting itself forward as 'fate'. Hence the never resolved antinomy of natural and positive law: 'Natural law attempts, by the justness of the ends, to "justify" the means, positive law to "guarantee" the justness of the ends through the justification of the means.'[6] The two meet up as they stumble over the same blind spot: 'For if positive law is blind to the absoluteness of ends, natural law is equally so to the contingency of means.'[7] In the end both refuse to see that they are in the thrall of executive violence, the permanent excess of the state principle over legality and norms. This excess is codified and displayed with the reality of a 'right to war' and the 'harder', organized forms of police and military violence. 'Militarism is the compulsory, universal use of violence as a means to the ends of the state.'[8]

In making visible this state unconscious of the law, Benjamin could open himself in some degree to Bolshevik and syndicalist anti-parliamentarism, even if his real sympathies lay rather with the SRs whom he considered more 'nihilist'. He was also able to take over Sorel's idea of the political 'general strike' as a symbol of messianic violence. Thus the complementary world of theology was seen as a way of breaking the cycles of violence, interrupting the flow of time and establishing justice (*Gerechtigkeit*) as a distinct form superior to law (*Recht*). Only this violence of justice could be said to be a 'purer and sovereign sphere'. 'All mythical, law-making violence, which we may call executive, is pernicious. Pernicious, too, is the law-preserving, administrative violence that serves it. Divine violence, which is the sign and seal but never the means of sacred execution, may be called sovereign violence.'[9]

The word sovereign is here used in the strong sense, for the theological 'metaphor' indicates a historical gap or discontinuity which breaks the cycle of catastrophes. We should not understand this literally in terms of religious belief. Even before he began to describe himself as a materialist, Benjamin's encounter with messianic Judaism was an encounter *in and of thought*. Thus in the 'Theologico-Political Fragment', written in harmony with Bloch's *Spirit of Utopia* and under the influence of Franz Rosenzweig's recently published *Star of Redemption* (1921),[10] Benjamin rejected any 'political theology', any nationalist possibility of establishing a direct link between state and religion.

> The Kingdom of God is not the *telos* of the historical dynamic; it cannot be set as a goal. From the standpoint of history it is not the goal, but the end. Therefore the order of the profane cannot be built up on the idea of the Divine Kingdom, and therefore theocracy has no political . . . meaning.[11]

The profane order thus has only one foundation, 'the idea of happiness', and messianic intensity can at most only indicate an impulse towards a free humanity. There is here an irreducible and sustained opposition between 'profane illumination' and 'religious illumination', an acute awareness which only real understanding of the theological can render atheist and profane. For the impulse to happiness which obsesses the religious sphere – that intensity as eternal and fleeting as the Angel – has a meaning only in relation to the excluded of history. The early Benjamin's 'individualist social-ism', as he himself described it, therefore involves an *ethical* choice in favour of the 'mass of excluded ones' and a union of minds with 'those who are asleep'. In that historical slumber of anonymity lies a potential for 'revolutionary nihilism'. Between *law* and *justice*, the theological metaphor embodies a critical-utopian distance, a different idea of politics which Benjamin, influenced by Nietzsche, calls 'nihilist'.

Nevertheless, the metaphysical suspensive violence of those years, expressed in the Sorelian idea of the 'political general strike', does not yet define a critical gesture that yields philosophical interpretation. It might be seen simply in terms of a miraculous 'decision', and not of catastrophe as a process of thought and representation revealing the archaeological foundations of modernity. It is really in *The Origin of German Tragic Drama*, first published in 1928, that Benjamin fully comes to terms, philosophically and historically, with the relationality of Power, as 'power of the King' which always tends towards a state of emergency, and with an allegorical imaginary of a time of ruin and dislocation.

If all allegory shies away from *Weltanschauung* and focuses micrologically on the detail or the fragment – the non-intentional elements of reality as opposed to a whole that is always problematic – the philosophical method of allegory can only be the indirect one of the *Umweg*. As the 'epistemo-critical prologue' to the book explains, 'method is the indirect way: representation as the indirect way'.[12] This *Umweg*, while absorbing Husserl's critique of all historicism or psychologism and the neo-Kantian rejection of philosophy as a closed system of truth, remains no less distinct from the major philosophical positions of the epoch. Insofar as the object exists only in a fragmentary state as a non-intentional but signifying element, interpretative truth can result neither from an intentional, historical phenomenology that recaptures sedimented primal levels, nor *a fortiori* from lived experience in the sense of Dilthey's *Erlebnis*.

Since interpretative truth is actually the 'death of intention', the philosophy of modern art which began with seventeenth-century baroque drama (*Trauerspiel*) immediately situates itself outside the space of the subject, consciousness and intention, outside a philosophy of language whose aim is to break its mimetism, its *magical* aspects, its symbolism resting upon a whole network of 'non-sensory correspondences'. Thus critical language, being confronted with the different levels of signification present in every detail (a feature also of kabbalistic philosophy), seeks to construct that 'excess' past with the present. 'Truth is not a process of exposure which destroys the secret, but a revelation which does justice to it.'[13] Interpretation grasps an enigmatic (familiar and alien) reality by building a concrete mass of constellations and significations, where 'meaning' is never more than the effect of a machinery which condenses time and reveals it by relating it to the present. This concretion defines what Benjamin calls *Jetztzeit* or 'now-time', in contrast to that simple present of presence, the instant as *term* or *passage*, which one finds in philosophies of empty chronology where events are 'lodged' in time.

> A historian who takes this as his point of departure stops telling the sequence of events like the beads of a rosary. Instead, he grasps the constellation which his own era has formed with a definite earlier one. Thus he establishes a *conception of the present* as 'now-time' which is shot through with chips of messianic time.[14]

Jetztzeit – a German term first introduced by Jean Paul[15] – coincides with genuine actuality, with the past as crux of the present, with that depth of the forgotten which Benjamin tracked down in Kafka's animals and Klee's intermediate creatures. It is an active forgetting, peculiar to memory and the infinite capacity of reopening a past which the 'science of history' claimed to be over and done with. 'History is not only a science but also a form of memory. What science has fixed, memory can modify; memory can work in such a way that the unconcluded is brought to a conclusion.'[16]

The approach which awakens the forgotten is therefore archae-ological and interpretative: its scanning of historical time bases itself upon an acute consciousness of crisis and catastrophe, making time capable of being seen and thought. This is precisely what theatre does by catalysing an essence of time which cannot be reduced to the physical, mechanistic, empty time of chronology, or to its expression in the event. 'No empirical event can entirely register the determining force of the historical form of time.' But theatre can do this: 'Historical grandeur can be represented in art only in the form of tragedy':[17] and, what is more, in the form of modern tragedy which is the 'drama' of Shakespeare, Calderón and seventeenth-century German baroque *Trauerspiel*. As its name suggests (*Spiel*: playing; *Trauer*: mourning or grief), *Trauerspiel* is really a represen-tation of grief, mourning work taken up in allegory. The generaliz-ation of the scopic drive in the Baroque carries to an extreme 'the tension between the world and transcendence'. In the meta-morphoses of the body moved by suffering and pleasure, it makes visible the mortal frailty of the human figure caught in the secularization of time. Here, as in *Hamlet*, the dead become ghosts, and that is why *Trauerspiel* exhibits the 'amphibious form' of a time which is neither individual nor purely historical-universal, which is never fulfilled though it is now finite. 'The generality of its time is not mythical but spectral. It is intimately bound up with the specific mirror-nature of the play.'[18] *Trauerspiel* is thus a play of representation upon representation, the generalized mirror stage, drama henceforth destined to be *spectacle*: it envelops death in a time of repetition where the mystical is nothing other than the allegory of a dream-life. 'Its events are allegorical schemas, *symbolic images* of another play.'[19] The performance is divine and absent: the hero no longer dies of immortality as in Greek tragedy; he dies. Whereas in Greek tragedy the sacrifice of the hero – his act of seeing fate – permits the reconstitution of order, *Trauerspiel* represents 'a history of the sufferings of the world', a decadent, Saturnian history of mourning and melancholia.

Where there is shock – historical trauma – interpretation can therefore appear. It arises from within a historical dislocation, a contradiction unrelieved by the Concept and with no messianic resolution, a catastrophic partner standing opposite. In other words, it comes about through the impact of image and thought where politics displays itself at its most naked: in the friend–enemy antithesis, the logic of restoration (philosophy of the Counter-Reformation), the defeat of the vanquished. Any dialectical philosophical study therefore demands that due account should be taken of the privileged baroque moment of modernity. 'The baroque apotheosis is a dialectical one. It is accomplished in the movement between extremes.'[20] This philosophy of extremes unfolds in a cultural space marked by the political philosophies of the Counter-Reformation, with their focus on power as 'sovereign power' represented by the King. But it is also a philosophy of modernity, in Heidegger's sense of the term.[21] As soon as the world becomes 'represented world' or image, the subject as *subjectum* affirms itself in the certainty of a centred Self, of a mastery which at bottom is *sovereign will* before it is proclaimed 'will to power'. In this Cartesian moment the *image* of history, now bereft of its mystical symbolism, makes itself visible insofar as a sovereign presides over representative playing and *decides*. The allegorical space of *Trauerspiel* thus has two sides:

The subjectum side. According to Benjamin, baroque theatre displays the political as sovereign power which decides in moments of crisis, 'states of emergency'. Taking over Carl Schmitt's conception of politics as *sovereign decision* of the state irreducible to any law or norm, Benjamin remarks that in baroque theatre 'the sovereign is the representative of history. He holds the course of history in his hand like a sceptre.'[22] In this sense the Prince is the Cartesian God transposed to the field of politics. But this politics, which is sovereignty and omnipotence, develops only on the ground of *catastrophe*, of 'a discussion of the state of emergency, and makes it the most important function of the Prince to avert this'.[23] It is a vicious circle of the political, where absolute power rises up on the basis of catastrophes, in order to avert catastrophe.

Unlike all legalist philosophies, and unlike the system of modern reason which has seen the state as the site of human emancipation – of the move from 'savagery' to 'civil' nature, 'contract' or reason – the logic of power in baroque drama encompasses its despotic-worldly reality. Here the truth of history lies no longer on the side of law, norm or regulation, but, on the contrary, in the violence of a sovereignty that asserts itself to the extreme in states of emergency in which the political relation is laid bare as one of 'war'.

The side of the imaginary. In the face of such power, the total or totalizing world of 'beautiful syntheses' breaks into fragments. It is the endless fragmentation of allegory as frozen portrait of horror, as enactment of an ultimate difference which displays a world of ruins and materially represents the dead and suffering body. Thus if it is true, as Louis Marin has shown, that against the state sovereign of the seventeenth century Thomas More's utopia wrote a *picture* into discourse – a political image of desire and happiness alien to all ownership, to anything one's own and to any appropriation – then we could say that allegory shows in the black of destructive dispossession what utopianism paints in red, or pink. It follows that state power and state reason are twofold: life instinct (desire) and death instinct (allegorical ruin).

Benjamin sets out to theorize this imaginary. In the chapter on 'Allegory and *Trauerspiel*', he polemicizes against a whole philosophy of art, dominated by the Romantic tradition, which sees the primacy of the symbol in the 'manifestation of an idea', 'the unity of the material and the transcendental object', the language of the Infinite.[24] In fact, with the remarkable – and much remarked – exception of Schlegel, for whom allegory was 'the centre of the play and of poetic appearance', Romanticism was 'foreign to allegorical expression in its original' (baroque or even medieval) form. It went along with classical prejudices against the baroque, and above all with that opposition between allegory and symbol which, in Benjamin's view, formed the real starting-point for the negative appreciation of allegory. According to this opposition, which goes back to Goethe's article of 1797 'On the Objects of the Figurative Arts', allegory moves from the 'abstract' general to the particular by means of directly conscious signification: it is therefore utilitarian, conventional and impoverished, since it merely embodies well-known ideas such as Justice or Truth. The symbol, on the other hand, which moves from the particular to the general, is image

(*Bild*): inexhaustible, infinite, intuitive thought, caught in the opaqueness and irreducibility of a signifier in which the Infinite 'becomes finite'.[25]

With regard to the dual classical and Romantic tradition, Benjamin embarks upon a real aesthetic and gnoseological reversal by linking up with the whole baroque practice of allegory as *indirect* language. Far from being the mere embodiment of an abstract idea, allegory is 'emotional writing' which proceeds through *figuration* (*Bild*) and thereby suppresses all the mediations and correlations between the extremes, between figure and meaning. Allegory makes its appearance only where there are 'depths which separate visual being from meaning'.[26] As the language of a torn and broken world, the representation of the unrepresentable, allegory fixes dreams by laying bare reality. 'The function of baroque iconography is not so much to unveil material objects as to strip them naked.'[27] Through a veritable fragmentation of image, line, graphic art and even language, it breaks up reality and represents time by hieroglyphs and enigmas. It is like the angelic interpreter of the inhuman. As in Klee and Kafka, it brings on stage the reverse side of assertive humanism: 'the individual can appear here only in the form of enigma'. In contrast to medieval symbolism or the beautiful totality of future classicism, allegory anticipates the role of shock, montage and distancing in the twentieth-century avant-garde: it shatters its object and fixes reality by a kind of alienation effect similar to the logic of the unconscious. 'The deep perception of allegory transforms things and works into *writing that stirs the emotions* [*erregende Schrift*]. . . . In the field of allegorical intuition the image is a fragment, a rune.'[28] With the amorphous fragment petrified like a dream, allegory offers for interpretation its own inescapable ambivalence: 'The basic characteristic of allegory . . . is ambiguity, multiplicity of meaning.'[29]

Such writing 'that stirs the emotions' completely overflows the linguistic order, for it expresses *mourning as feeling*. But 'how can mourning as feeling find access to the linguistic order of art?'[30] – unless it is through the gap between the natural sound of the signifying voice and that other thing which, as we have seen, characterizes the 'cry' of modern man and the 'song' of the Angel: namely, music. In the endless *Trauerspiel* cycle of metamorphoses, natural sound tends towards music and 'the contrast between sound and signification remains something ghostly and terrible'.[31]

This fragmenting of language and representation gives rise to profane appreciation of the Now which is characteristic of allegory: that is, an unprecedented cultural shift in the relations between visible and invisible, tangible and non-tangible. The 'complementary world' of theology is certainly in evidence, but it is already subordinated to the power of the present, imprisoned by the *play* of images, confronted with a death that knows no immediate redemption: 'The mystical instant (*Nu*) becomes the 'now' (*Jetzt*).'[32] Indeed, the whole of nature may be personalized but it can never become internalized: it is there, devoid of a soul, condemned to be a 'dead object' for all eternity. Hence 'melancholy immersion' is a 'bottomless pit', even if it is saved at the last moment by a supernatural force.[33] Dead bodies, ageing body, female body, corpse-body, martyr-body or ghost-bodies: life is never produced except when 'seen from the point of view of death'; as if 'the allegorization of the physis can only be carried through in all its vigour in respect of the corpse'.[34]

Long before *modern* art, then, allegory testified to the preeminence of the fragment over the whole, of a destructive principle over a constructive principle, of feeling, as the excavation of an absence, over reason as domination. Only the fragment is capable of showing that the logic of bodies, feeling, life and death does not coincide with the logic of Power, nor with that of the Concept. What are represented in it are precisely the silent (hence music), the new (even if in death), the 'uncontrollable' and profoundly ungovernable catastrophes which, as it were, stage the very action of representation.

Allegory thus consigns reality to a permanent antinomy, a game of the illusion of reality as illusion, where the world is at once valued and devalued. Hence the peculiar seductiveness of the baroque: the primacy of the aesthetic – of appearances and play – joins up with metaphysical wretchedness on the ground of grief or melancholy. The metaphor of the world as theatre expresses this specific temporality of the baroque, an almost choreographic or 'panoramic' temporality, in Cysarz's expression that Benjamin makes his own. In this eternal reflecting of appearances one ubiquitous yet already distant spectator reigns supreme: God. But the gulf between reality and illusion cannot be bridged: theatre now *knows* itself to be theatre.

This explains the 'mule track' which, bypassing the 'sublime and fruitless mountains of classicism', leads directly from medieval and baroque drama to Brecht. In epic theatre, the interruption of the flow of things also becomes a kind of distancing, a refusal of identification: 'This discovery (alienation) of conditions takes place through the interruption of happenings.'[35]

In the seventeenth century, however, the analytic of representation was still caught up in the language of things. The perceptible world, however profaned and destroyed by the allegorical vision, continued to refer as appearance or dream to a theological 'elsewhere' which signified it. The imaginary objectified itself in exteriority. Only later, with the fragmentation of the world as an act of thought and imagination – in German Romanticism, Nietzsche and Baudelaire – did allegory come to speak of the forgotten, of the buried dead, of the female hidden in the ground. As Benjamin put it:

> Melancholy bears a different character, however, in the nineteenth century from that which it bore in the seventeenth. The key figure of the older allegory is the corpse. The key figure of the later allegory is the 'souvenir' [Andenken]. The souvenir is the schema of the transformation of the commodity into a collector's item.[36]

The Baudelairean break in modernity makes of the uncanny, which was already at work in German Romanticism, the generative figure of the archaeology of modernity. But meanwhile, between *The Origin of German Tragic Drama* (1928) and the materialist approach to Baudelaire, Benjamin's work underwent a philosophical recasting which led to a 'theory of historical knowledge'. Of course, already in 1924 Benjamin had espoused a communist praxis, under the influence of Lukács's *History and Class Consciousness* and of a Latvian revolutionary, Asja Lacis, who was a specialist in children's theatre, a colleague of Piscator and a friend of Brecht. But it was only after 1928 that the 'historical materialist' transformation took place in his methodology of the imaginary. From then on, the 'metaphysical images' of the *Trauerspiel* transmuted into 'dialectical images', and catastrophe into a fragmented *writing* of catastrophe.

Notes

1. For an analysis of this historical and intellectual context, see Michael Löwy, 'Messianisme juif et utopies libertaires en Europe centrale (1905–1923)', *Archives des Sciences sociales des religions*, 51, I, 1981. [See also, in English, Löwy's recently published book *Redemption and Utopia: Jewish Libertarian Thought in Central Europe*, London: Athlone Press 1992. *Trans. note.*] On the relationship between messianism and 'metapolitics', and on utopia as a way of 'overturning the classical issues of politics' by the force of its emotional intensity, see the article by Miguel Abensour, 'L'utopie socialiste: une nouvelle alliance', *Le Temps de la réfléxion*, 1981.
2. See Gershom Scholem, *The Messianic Idea in Judaism and Other Essays in Jewish Spirituality*, New York: Schocken 1971.
3. Ibid., p. 7.
4. On this background of the young Benjamin, see the chronology with which Giorgio Agamben opens the Einaudi edition of Benjamin's complete works in

Italian: *Metafisica della Gioventù*. Cf. Michael Löwy, 'Revolution against "Progress": Walter Benjamin's Romantic Anarchism', *New Left Review*, 152, July–August 1985; and the chapter on Benjamin in *Redemption and Utopia*.

5. Scholem, *The Messianic Idea in Judaism*, pp. 113ff.
6. Benjamin, 'Critique of Violence', in *One-Way Street and Other Writings*, p. 133.
7. Ibid., p. 134.
8. Ibid., p. 139.
9. Ibid., p. 154.
10. Ernst Bloch, *Geist der Utopie*, 1st edn, Munich: Duncker & Humblot 1918; and Franz Rosenzweig, *The Star of Redemption*, New York: Holt, Rinehart and Winston 1971.
11. 'Theologico-Political Fragment', in *One-Way Street*, p. 155.
12. *The Origin of German Tragic Drama*, p. 28. [Translation modified.]
13. Ibid., p. 31. On the status of such critique, see Jürgen Habermas, 'Walter Benjamin: Consciousness-Raising or Rescuing Critique', in Smith, ed., *On Walter Benjamin*.
14. 'Theses on the Philosophy of History', p. 263. [Translation slightly modified.]
15. See Franco Desideri, 'Ad vocem Jetztzeit', a paper presented to the Benjamin Colloque held in Modena in 1981.
16. Quoted by Desideri in ibid.
17. *GS* II, 1, p. 134.
18. Ibid., p. 136.
19. Ibid., p. 136.
20. *The Origin of German Tragic Drama*, p. 160.
21. See Martin Heidegger, 'The Age of the World Picture', in *The Question Concerning Technology and Other Essays*, New York: Harper Colophon 1977, pp. 115–36.
22. *The Origin of German Tragic Drama*, p. 65.
23. Ibid., p. 65.
24. Ibid., p. 160.
25. See Goethe, 'Über die Gegenstände der bildenden Kunst', in *Schriften zur Kunst*, Zurich: Artemis 1954, pp. 122–5.
26. *The Origin of German Tragic Drama*, p. 165.
27. Ibid., p. 185.
28. Ibid., p. 176. [Translation modified.]
29. Quotation from Hermann Cohen. Ibid., p. 177.
30. *GS* II, 1, p. 138.
31. Ibid., p. 139.
32. *The Origin of German Tragic Drama*, p. 183.
33. Ibid., pp. 231ff.
34. Ibid., pp. 217, 218.
35. Benjamin, 'What Is Epic Theatre?', in *Illuminations*, p. 151.
36. Central Park', p. 55. [The German word *Andenken*, like the French *souvenir*, may refer either to memory of something or to the object – 'memento' or 'souvenir' – through which something is remembered. *Trans. note.*]

3

BAUDELAIREAN SPACE

A Modern Baroque

Throughout his life Benjamin had a special relationship to Baudelaire, one of theoretical-historical understanding and personal fascination or projection. This is especially apparent in what was intended as his *magnum opus*, the *Passagen-Werk* or Arcades project. Begun in 1927, it was continually restarted and supplemented by other essays: 'Paris – the Capital of the Nineteenth Century' (1935), 'The Paris of the Second Empire' (1938), 'On Some Motifs in Baudelaire' (1939), a collection of fragments entitled 'Central Park', and a philosophical section sketched out in 'Theses on the Philosophy of History' (1940). The project as a whole points to an archaeological *summa* of the modernity which opened in the middle of the nineteenth century. As Benjamin conceived it, a critical–social interpretation of Baudelaire, using the circuitous approach of *Umwege* to decipher the experiences deposited in his *oeuvre*, would throw light on the forms of modernity at work in Haussmann's Paris, in the architecture of the 'Paris arcades', the spread of fashion and photography, and the new modes of seeing and living – myths and realities – characteristic of the big city. The ancient and the modern were constantly intertwined in Benjamin's 'only constructive conception of history': 'The modern: the masses; the ancient: the city Paris.'[1]

Such dialectical images are, as it were, immobilized in 'dream-images' (*Traumbildern*) which pass beyond unresolved contradictions and already indicate points of rupture with a newly installed system. The materialist aesthetic of modernity can therefore coincide only with a turning-point where the imaginary – the unconscious modes of seeing – is thrown into confusion by technological developments and the 'mass' dimension of all reality. Hence the return in force of allegory and its great female myths: Angel, prostitute, lesbian. Benjamin, who was perfectly aware of this intransigence imposed on him by the theme of Baudelaire, wrote to Adorno: 'I have my Christian Baudelaire carried to Heaven by *purely Jewish angels*.'[2]

It is in fact with Baudelaire, after Poe, that the very notion of modernity appears in all the richness of its aesthetic and philosophical articulations. With him begins that 'long suffering of the eye' of which Hofmannsthal spoke: a new definition of 'modern beauty' bound up with the uncanny and horrifying; a new consciousness of temporality and memory; a new status for the desanctified poet, bereft of any cultural aura and delivered to the fetishism of the market. This revolution opened a dangerous gulf between literature and life, provoking the 'impoverishment anxiety' of melancholia (Freud) and the alternating process of 'centralization and vaporization of the ego' (Baudelaire).[3]

Thus, in *Le Peintre de la vie moderne* Baudelaire unhesitatingly asserted that 'the pleasure we derive from the representation of the present is due not only to the beauty in which it may be dressed but also to its quality of being present.'[4] This *Jetztzeit* of the present requires 'a rational and historical theory'[5] of the beautiful that will welcome the relative, the transitory and the circumstantial, all the strangeness peculiar to the 'new passions' that Baudelaire analysed in Poe: in other words, the 'death instinct', that 'primitive, irresistible force', is 'natural Perversity'.

This humanity, caught between 'childhood regained' and the 'professional passion of embracing the crowd', now finds its pleasure in the stamp of the time, in the new, in modernity. 'Modernity is the fleeting and transitory, that half of art whose other half is the eternal and immutable.' Like all beauty, this present which emerges in the constant novelty of fashion, world exhibitions or painting salons carries 'its share of inevitable, synthetic, infantile barbarism'.

At the height of the nineteenth century, then, Baudelaire's caesural critique of the idea of progress inaugurates a veritable duel between a *will to see everything* and a *will to see something different in a different way*, to interrupt through spleen the flow of time and to operate what Agamben calls an 'appropriation of unreality'.[6] Henceforth the creative experience of writing will be this 'duel in which every artist is engaged and in which he "screams with fright before he is vanquished"'.[7]

To wish to see *everything* with this securing eye of the city-dweller, of the *flâneur* who is prey to the heaped proliferation of images – that is to condemn oneself to see nothing. Baudelaire's eyes can no longer apprehend the aura of the work, its profound *hic et nunc*. 'What is involved here is that the expectation roused by the look of the human eye is not fulfilled. Baudelaire describes eyes of which one is inclined to say that they have lost their ability to look.'[8] Such eyes are too glued to what can be seen nearby, to fetishistic objects, to the phantasmagoria of big stores, world exhibitions and the crowd; they are *unlooking eyes*, ever on the look-out for something new which is also always-the-same and therefore a deception. This unlooking gaze marks a turning-point: the end of the heroisms of old and the appearance of a '*modern heroism*' in the face of the world. Commenting on Baudelaire, Benjamin adds: 'For the modern hero is no hero; he acts heroes. Modern heroism turns out to be a *Trauerspiel* in which the hero's part is available.'[9]

Modernism is thus not only an aesthetic position towards life in which the poet avoids spleen by acting out all the roles: *flâneur*, apache or dandy. For this loss of reality, which makes experience ever emptier and reality itself ever more impenetrable, has a social substratum in the commodity and the ambiguity of big cities.

Benjamin redeploys Marx's notion of 'commodity fetishism' – generalized subordination of an evanescent use-value to a reified yet visible exchange-value – as a kind of matrix-image of the imaginary with which to grasp more clearly a *historical structure of the mode of seeing*. The modern is 'a store of dialectical images' bearing contradictions which are capable of development but which are now frozen in 'dream images'. Neither 'reflections', nor Jungian archetypes, nor the mimetic representation of an already present reality, these images call for a 'Freudianization' of the commodity hieroglyph that will stretch into the most remote, the most infraconscious and micrological regions of existence.

Thus *in order to see properly* – to rediscover a 'stranger relationship' which can no longer be based on religion or tradition – it is necessary to interrupt through a *shock* the temporal alienation of seriality, of the ever-different and ever-the-same. Benjamin would find this shock again in surrealist or Brechtian montage, as the practice of any 'modern' avant-garde. But it is already 'poetic principle in Baudelaire: the *fantasque escrime* [fantastic fencing] of the city of the *tableaux parisiens* which is no longer home. It is theatre and quite foreign.'[10] By introducing a theatrical distance, the forcible entry of shock suddenly shatters what Benjamin calls 'the empathy [*Einfühlung*] of the soul with the commodity', which is common to the new historical characters of the big city: *flâneur*, collector, forger, gambler, prostitute.[11]

This interruption that shock produces in the flow of time is nothing other than *spleen*. 'Spleen is that feeling which corresponds to catastrophe in permanence.'[12] In this sombre tête-à-tête of the subject with himself, the time of seriality, 'progress' and the early culture industry is interrupted or immobilized. It becomes memory, quintessence of history: spleen inaugurates a time that is 'outside history, as is that of the *mémoire involontaire*'.[13] This is why, unlike in the baroque where death and the abyss were objectified, death is internalized in Baudelairean spleen. 'Baroque allegory sees the corpse only from the outside. Baudelaire sees it also from the inside.'[14] The baroque becomes modern.

To have the corpse inside oneself – a radically disturbing novelty which demolishes the acquired certainties of the 'subject' – is also to do violence to oneself, to become victim and executioner, seer and seen.

> To interrupt the course of the world – this is Baudelaire's deepest wish. The wish of Joshua. Not so much a prophetic wish; for he did not think much of change. From this wish sprang his violence, his impatience and his anger. . . . Out of this wish came the encouragement with which he accompanied Death in his works.[15]

This desire marks an epoch and a break. Baudelaire, like Nietzsche and the late Blanqui of *L'Éternité par les astres*,[16] takes his stand against the philosophies of progress of his time, saturated with triumphant positivism and industrialism – the great 'heresy of decrepitude'. Against them he asserts quite a different conception of time: eternal recurrence, which 'makes novelty appear in the perpetual cycle of the same, and the perpetual cycle of the same within the new'.[17] This strange theoretical troika (Baudelaire, Nietzsche, Blanqui) is for Benjamin constitutive of a new modernity born out of the contradictions of progress. Thus 'it is to be demonstrated with every possible emphasis that the idea of eternal recurrence intrudes into the world of Baudelaire, Blanqui and Nietzsche at approximately the same moment.'[18]

Eternal recurrence is simply the mad 'attempt to link the two antinomic principles of happiness with each other: namely, that of eternity and that of the once again',[19] in a new heroism adequate to a world 'without God' and to the devaluation of values. Baudelaire opens this epoch by displaying the productive and destructive force of one alienated man. Shot through with this contradiction, he is truly the 'lord of antitheses', the one who can become 'only the secret agent of his own class', through a kind of rebellion that is less 'ideological' than lodged in the depths of the unconscious. He is a secret agent because he is a double agent. Socially and politically he speaks not only for those at the bottom but also for those at the top: he wishes, as he himself said, 'to feel the revolution from both sides'.[20] It is a historical, and also psychic, duplicity in which Eros and Thanatos are placed side by side. Baudelaire like Satan has a 'dual aspect' (*ein Doppelgesicht*).[21]

Two sides, two aspects, two political positions: the double of ambiguity haunts the infinite play of correspondences, transmuting all the figures of allegory into memory. 'The *souvenir* [*Andenken*] is the relic secularized. The *souvenir* is the complement of lived

experience [*Erlebnis*]. In it the increasing self-alienation of the
person who inventories his past as dead possession is distilled.'[22]
Thus allegory finally discovers all its depths of forgetting and being
forgotten, its true destructive principle, its 'most precious booty':
woman.[23] It is precisely she, the woman-prostitute, who is embodied in the poem 'Allégorie' in *Les Fleurs du mal*:

> Elle ignore l'Enfer et le Purgatoire
> Et quand l'heure viendra d'entrer dans la Nuit noire,
> Elle *regardera la face de la Mort*,
> Ainsi qu'un nouveau-né, – sans haine et sans remords.[24]

Only woman and the (crying) new-born child are capable of such
knowledge of the black night. The feminine in Baudelaire's imagination is all dark abyss, primal womb:

> Tout est abîme
> Action, désire, rêve.[25]

But this feminine bearing the uncanny is precisely an Angel,
dispenser alternately of perfume and poison, seraphic and hell-
black by turns. At any event it is enigma and otherness:

> Et dans cette nature étrange et symbolique
> Où l'*ange inviolé* se mêle au sphinx antique.[26]

This Baudelairean ambivalence seems to criss-cross all the great
Christian myths, whether woman is – as in Wagner – Angel or
Beast, Madonna or Salome, sterile Virgin or Whore, indestructible
Venus or Redemptress, Damned or Saved. But we should not be
led astray by this into a religious interpretation of Baudelaire, or
into simple denunciation of an ideological misogyny which is
certainly always there. For this male feminine – which the nineteenth century put on show, and photographed, in the shape of the
bodies of hysterics and other women at the Salpêtrière clinic[27] – was
actually vaunted by Baudelaire: 'I am cultivating my hysteria with
pleasure.' Besides, it loaded him with peculiar sufferings and
constraints, as he wrote of himself in a letter to his mother: 'The
doctor says hysteria! Hysteria! You must master yourself, force
yourself to walk.'

In overcoming this hystericization of the male body of the written
work, Baudelaire ends in something very close to panic anxiety
about the sexed body of women, alternately felt to be sublime and
profane. The cultural and existential anxiety is so radical that, in a
break with a whole philosophical tradition since Plato, he places the
feminine in a relationship not to nature but to culture, or, more
precisely, to the distance introduced by culture: make-up, artifice,

fashion, apologia for a modern urban beauty. Everything is called upon to re-mark and re-present a difference between the sexes that has been brutally changed by industrialization, female labour and the emergence of feminism (Flora Tristan, George Sand).

It is so radical, in fact, that the allegorical image of prostitution invades everything:

Angels: 'And so, the wandering *déclassé* women, those who have had some lovers and are called *angels*, in recognition and gratitude for the glittering inadvertence, light of chance in their existence.'

Art: 'What is art: prostitution?'

God: 'The most prostituted being is the being *par excellence*: God.'

Everywhere Baudelaire's obsession with prostitution inscribes an ambivalent male imaginary (angel or beast). Benjamin sees in this the anguish of male impotence, 'the calvary of the melancholic'. But above all, in analysing Baudelaire's sexual and satanic language, he deciphers a different, 'critical and non-metaphysical' language, the conversion of women's bodies into mass-produced objects to be placed on show.

> One of the *arcana* which has fallen to prostitution only with the development of the metropolis, is the masses. Prostitution opens up the possibility of a mythical communion with the masses. . . . In the prostitution of the metropolis the woman herself becomes *an article that is mass-produced*. It is this wholly new imprint of life in the metropolis which gives Baudelaire's reception of the dogma of original sin its real meaning.[28]

There is thus an analogy between the status of art without aura and that of woman as 'commercialized' sex-object, so that the destructive principle driving all allegory finds its truth only in confronting the female body and reactivating the 'great myths' through their destruction. 'The motif of the androgyne, the lesbian or the barren woman is to be dealt with in relation to the destructive violence of the allegorical intention.'[29] Once again, unlike other literary depictions of the lesbian, Baudelaire's image breaks new ground by portraying her as 'the heroine of modernity', the 'protest of "the modern" against the technological'.[30] In 'The Paris of the Second Empire in Baudelaire', Benjamin discusses this 'heroine' in connection with the Saint-Simonian cult of the androgyne, even adopting certain analyses of Claire Démar on the 'feminine' content of utopias.[31] Nevertheless, Baudelaire never understood the social or personal question of female homosexuality. He was always divided between praise and criticism, trapped within a 'contradictory orientation': 'He had room for her within the framework of modernism, but he did not recognize her in reality.'[32] The lesbian was a victim of bourgeois pressure, but Baudelaire was also uneasy about the shifting frontiers between male and female – as if the 'masculinization' of woman was connected to his own hysterical 'feminization'. On the horizon were that 'extraordinary androgyne' Madame Bovary, and the great myths of modernism: Salome or Lulu.

At the heart of this archaeology of modernity, in the unconscious depths of seeing, the feminine is therefore throwing established identities into confusion. Perhaps we could see the Angel as the symptom, buried in a 'scene of writing'[33] in which Benjamin, after Baudelaire, was himself an actor.

Notes

1. 'Central Park', pp. 47, 49.
2. *Briefe* 2, p. 825.
3. Charles Baudelaire, 'Mon coeur mis à nu', in *Oeuvres complètes*, ed. Claude Pichois, vol. 1, Paris: Gallimard 1975, p. 676.
4. Charles Baudelaire, 'Le Peintre de la vie moderne', in *Oeuvres complètes*, ed. Claude Pichois, vol. 2, Paris: Gallimard 1976, p. 684.
5. Ibid., p. 685.
6. Giorgio Agamben, *Stanze: La parola e il fantasma nella cultura occidentale*, Turin: Einaudi 1977, chapter 5. The same author's *Infanzia e storia* revives and develops some of Benjamin's motifs, especially his conception of time and of the expropriation of experience as a correlate of modernity.
7. 'The Paris of the Second Empire in Baudelaire', p. 69. Benjamin is here using a quotation from Ernest Raynaud, *Charles Baudelaire*, Paris 1922, pp. 317ff.
8. Benjamin, 'Some Motifs in Baudelaire', in *Charles Baudelaire*, p. 149.
9. 'The Paris of the Second Empire in Baudelaire', p. 97. [Translation modified.]
10. 'Central Park', p. 42. [Translation modified.]
11. See 'The Paris of the Second Empire in Baudelaire', pp. 55ff.
12. Ibid., p. 34.
13. 'Some Motifs in Baudelaire', p. 143.
14. 'Central Park', p. 51.
15. Ibid., p. 39. [Translation modified.]
16. Auguste Blanqui, *L'Éternité par les astres*, Paris 1872.
17. 'Central Park', p. 43. [Translation modified to accord with the French.] On Benjamin's relationship to Blanqui, see Franco Rella, ed., *Critica e storia: materiali su Benjamin*, Venice: Cluva 1980.
18. 'Central Park', p. 43.
19. Ibid., p. 50. [Translation modified.]
20. 'The Paris of the Second Empire in Baudelaire', p. 14, quoting from Baudelaire, *Oeuvres complètes* vol. 2, p. 728.
21. Ibid., p. 24.
22. 'Central Park', pp. 48–9.
23. Ibid., p. 39. [Translation modified.]
24. 'Careless of hell and purgatory alike, when her hour comes to step into the blackness of the night, she *will look upon death's face* without hatred or remorse, like a newborn child.' Baudelaire, *The Complete Verse*, bilingual

edition, trans. Francis Scarfe, London: Anvil 1986, p. 220. Except where otherwise indicated, translations are from the 1857 edition.

25. 'All is abyss, action, desire, dream.' Added in 1868 edition: 'Le Gouffre', *Oeuvres complètes*, vol. 1, p. 142.
26. 'And in her strange symbolic nature in which *inviolate angel* and ancient sphinx unite.' Poem XXVII, *The Complete Verse*, p. 88.
27. See Georges Didi-Huberman, *Invention de l'hystérie*, Paris: Macula 1982, p. 83.
28. 'Central Park', p. 40.
29. Ibid., p. 35. Benjamin's interpretation of Baudelaire will be discussed further in Parts Two and Three below.
30. Ibid., p. 39.
31. 'The Paris of the Second Empire in Baudelaire', pp. 91–3.
32. Ibid., p. 93.
33. In the sense used by Jacques Derrida in *Writing and Difference*, chapter 7, 'Freud and the Scene of Writing', London: Routledge & Kegan Paul 1978.

4

THE SPACE OF WRITING

The Angel and the 'Scene' of Writing: In the 'Primeval Forest' (*Urwald*)

1939–1940

It is October 1939. Interned as a German émigré in a camp at Nevers, Benjamin is already smitten by the 'horrible catastrophe' that will lead him to suicide. On the night of the 11th–12th he has 'a dream of such beauty' that he immediately writes it down in a letter to Gretel Adorno.[1] For 'after this dream I could not sleep for hours, out of happiness'. It is a strange dream of intense, elegiac happiness, in which the figures of a true 'scene of writing' take shape through the 'primeval forest' – 'emotional writing' characteristic of allegory and close to Freud's figurative writing (*Bildschrift*).

Benjamin narrates that he was in the company of Doctor Dausse (who had cured him of malaria) and that, having left some other people, they found themselves at an *excavation site*. Almost at the level of the ground: '*Couches* of a strange kind, the length of the *sarcophagi*'. But in fact, 'in half kneeling down, I realized that we were softly sinking into it as in *a bed*'. It was all 'covered with moss or ivy', so that 'the whole thing resembled *a forest*'. Suddenly the view changes: the forest becomes like a 'nautical construction' and 'on the deck . . . were three women with whom Dausse was living'. This sight does not disturb him any more than

> the discovery that I made *at the very moment* when I was leaving my hat on a grand piano. It was a real *straw hat*, a panama that I had *inherited from my father*. As I was *ridding myself of it*, I was struck by a *wide fissure* that had appeared in the upper part . . . with *traces of red* on the edges.

Then follow a number of events linked with women. The first of these women, a graphology expert, is particularly unsettling for the dreamer. 'I feared that some of *my intimate traits* might thereby be *disclosed*. I drew closer. What I *saw* was a *fabric covered with images*.' The only writing he can distinguish on it is the upper part of the letter D, the more 'spiritual' part. Some conversations then take place about this writing, and Benjamin retains a clear textual and oral memory. At a certain moment he said the words: 'The point was *to change some poetry into a scarf*.' But

> scarcely had I said these words than *something very intriguing happened*. I noticed that among the women was a very beautiful one lying in bed. When she heard my explication she had a brief movement like a *flash of lightning* . . . and drew aside a tiny piece of the blanket. . . . But what she wanted to *show* me was not *her body* but *the pattern of the sheet*, which displayed imagery similar to that which I had had to write many years ago when giving a present to Dausse. I *knew* very well that the lady was making that movement. But what told me this was a kind of *supplementary vision*. For *the eyes of my body were elsewhere* and I could not at all make out what the sheet had *fleetingly* thrown open to me.

End of dream, insomnia, intense happiness.

On the one side, then, is the paternal legacy of the old, discarded panama hat, covered with red traces and feminized at its 'wide fissure'. But on the other side there are the forest (*Urwald*) of bottomless anxiety, the water, the fissure itself and the red traces, the bed so reminiscent of death and sarcophagi, the fear of revealing his 'most intimate' traits to a female handwriting expert, the body of a 'very beautiful' woman revealed in a flash but not actually seen. On this other side, two women show twice in a flash – in a *shock* – what the dreamer does not wish to see but already knows because of 'supplementary vision'. His bodily eyes are *elsewhere*. Where an image-covered fabric and then a blanket-sheet present themselves, he in his wildly intense happiness can read only the 'spiritual' part of the letter D, and then the memory of an old piece of writing. Above all, like the Angel who sings for a moment, he has this to say about it all: 'Change some poetry into a scarf.'

He therefore prefers the red traces to the traces of writing, as if the writing-body of elsewhere could exist only through this bloody profanation, this male-constrained denial of the perceived body of the mother or woman. These 'arche-traces', as Derrida calls them, here represent a primal scene of incest, an act of violence committed where web and text cross over. As Benjamin writes in an article on Proust: 'The Latin word *textum* means 'web'. No one's text is more tightly woven than Marcel Proust's.'[2] It is a web of memories in which oblivion and the intermittency of recollection are 'the reverse of the continuum of memory, the pattern on the back side of the *tapestry*'.[3] In the same article he defines Proust's writing position: 'the sickbed on which Marcel Proust consecrates the countless pages which he covered with his handwriting, holding them up in the air'.[4] Foliage of trees – forest leaves.

But the red traces remain indelible on the father's hat, and the yawning depths of the primeval 'forest', which the castrating axe of reason must avoid looking at, return as a source of anxiety. It is the immemorial which is being repeated – the extremity, the catastrophe which has always happened before. Such is that 'suffering of the eye' which determines the writing, that site of non-power where the imaginary originates. Indeed, Benjamin could write to Adorno: 'I find the root of my "theory of experience" in a memory from childhood.'[5] Thus, with the loss of lived experience in modernity and the removal of the subject's control and sovereignty, only the 'redemption of the past' (*die Rettung der Vergangenheit*) can provide the basis for genuine experience (*Erfahrung*). Benjamin remarks elsewhere that 'Proust's distinction between involuntary and voluntary recollection' is not unlike Freud's differentiation in *Beyond the Pleasure Principle* between memory traces and consciousness.[6] *Mémoire involontaire*, in which 'the past is reflected in the baptismal mirror of the present', offers by itself an eternity of intoxication or happiness – by chance, in an instant, a flash, a shock. It is power over the imagination, *image*, for its imaginary belongs precisely to the order of 'non-mastery' (chance). What constantly reappears in Proust is 'the image, which alone is able to satisfy his curiosity, or rather to assuage his nostalgia'.[7]

Benjamin's dream brings us back to a primal scene where the oneiric structure supports the play of text/web, sex/writing, 'seeing/ not-seeing' the naked female body. Do we not find here the uncanniness of writing, the *modern* beyond all humanisms, the 'study of the *frontier area* defined by Kraus and, in another way, by Kafka' which 'preoccupies me [Benjamin] a great deal'?[8] Is this not the site where what Maurice Blanchot calls 'subjectivity without a subject', the 'non-human side of man', is revealed? However, this frontier area always includes its limits in memory, and its risk of straying into the madness of thought. Between the Baudelaire of metropolitan Paris and the Benjamin of the 'Berlin Chronicle' there is much more than a methodological affinity: there is the same bewilderment, the same disarrangement of the subject, the same labyrinth.

> Not to find one's way in a city may well be uninteresting and banal. . . . But to lose oneself in a city – as one *loses oneself in a forest* – that calls for quite a different schooling. . . . Paris taught me this art of straying; it fulfilled *a dream that had shown its first traces in the labyrinths on the blotting pages* of my school exercise books.'[9]

After the web, the blotting paper; after the forest, the city. But always a dream, the first, eternally repeated dream: a set of traces, a labyrinth, the triple cipher of the writing of sexuality and those without a name. For the labyrinth 'is the home of the hesitant. The path of someone shy of arrival at a goal easily takes the form of a labyrinth.'[10] It is the home of the sexual drive 'in those episodes which precede its satisfaction', the home too of 'humanity (the social class) which does not wish to know what will become of it'.[11]

The traces of blood, writing and social architecture deposited in the city re-enact this famous 'frontier area'. Is the key perhaps the Angel's stage, that Jewish Ariadne's thread? Is it not up to the Angel to rediscover that space of Klee, where very early Benjamin sought the juncture of (traditionally separated) figures and signs, the equivalent of a lost Adamic language?

May 1933

In a semi-delirious state, doubtless brought on by malaria, Benjamin writes two versions of a particularly enigmatic text, 'Agesilaus Santander', which Scholem has deciphered as an anagram of *Angelus Satanas*.[12] This time, there is no question of the boundless intensity of rediscovered happiness, but rather of a Saturnian angel and a thoroughly Baudelairean melancholy. The New Angel returns as a 'picture on the wall' – in terms identical to those we find in earlier texts – sings for a moment the praises of God and then dissolves into nothingness. As with Klee's Angel, its features 'had nothing about them resembling the human'. This actor of the non-human appeals to a future which already exists at the beginning, one from which it 'hopes for nothing new'. But above all, the picture on the wall reveals its true nature as *androgynous angel*.

> For in taking advantage of the circumstance that I came into the world under the sign of Saturn – the planet of slow rotation, the star of hesitation and delay – the Angel *sent its feminine form, after the masculine reproduced in the picture*, by way of the longest, most fatal detour, even though both were so very much adjacent to each other.[13]

Scholem deciphered here Benjamin's unhappy love for the 'angels' Jula Cohn and Asja Lacis, while Benjamin himself saw in it the figure of separation from all the persons and things that he loved. But these readings do not exhaust the allegory of the angelic, androgynous and bisexual, actor. The felicity it promises is now joined to 'that bliss of the "once more", the having again, the lived'.[14] Separation – death – appears as the sum of all Benjamin's extra-territorialities: exile from things, persons and a problematic national identity; the accumulated impossibles of Jew, German, Marxist, anti-fascist, caught up in the writing of modernity. In short, 'the end is in the beginning'.

But this lightning shock, in which the two figures and aspects of the Angel recombine, also says something else: that there can be femaleness in the divine and the angelic/satanic; that, in keeping with a long kabbalistic tradition quite unlike that of Christianity, God is feminized and almost bisexualized. In contrast to the traditional Jewish Oedipus saturated with law and symbolism – which Benjamin found unappealing in Kafka – the God of the *kabbalah is not*. This non-existence or *aïn*, this 'no thing', this divine nothingness has a reason for existence only in its own scopic desire: 'God wanted to *see* God.' And what is this fabulous pleasure of a self-seeing nothing, if not the female side of God – of a godhead marked by the disappearance of his Name – which is peculiar to negative theology and various forms of heterodoxy? As Lacan puts it: 'Why not interpret a side of the other, the side of God, as supported by female *jouissance*?'[15] Indeed, why should the other *jouissance* not be the great metaphor of the Other?

Now, in judaicizing the gnosticism of southern France, the kabbalah went so far as to bisexualize God. If God has no existence except in his emanations or powers – the ten *sefiroth* – in the *Zohar* the ninth and tenth *sefiroth* are identified with the feminine. The ninth, Yesod, consists in the union of male and female forms, in the secrecy (*sod*) which is essence and ground; while the tenth, the famous Shekhinah or 'presence of God' to which Benjamin refers on several occasions, is at once 'wife, mother and daughter of God'. This curious diffraction of the godhead, which was not without its influence on Fliess or even Freud, is given special emphasis by Scholem. 'The discovery of a feminine element in God, which the Kabbalists tried to justify by gnostic exegesis, is of course one of the most significant steps they took.'[16]

In this feminization and bisexualization of God, the historical cycle of the divine is interpreted as God's exile from himself, the *trace of a separation* where feminine and masculine have diverged as a result of human sinfulness. The split establishes an upper and a lower, a female and a male, which the final redemption will reunite by putting together the two aspects of divine androgyny, 'for the love of God and his Shekhinah'. The end is also in the beginning. . . .

But the beginning, like the repetition and the return, cannot avoid the threads of language and symbolism, of a relationship to the Name as primordial sign and writing. 'Every word – and language as a whole – is onomatopoeic.' The concept of non-sensory resemblance holds the key which enables us fully to elucidate this thesis. Non-sensory representation condemns language to allegorical representation. And an allegory is precisely what we find in

'Agesilaus Santander'. For the New Angel's appearance on the wall is due to a family scene which concerns the Name in a disturbed heredity/filiation. Benjamin relates that when he was born, the thought came to his parents that he might perhaps become a writer. Because of the prevalence of anti-semitism, they gave him two secret names which might one day serve as pseudonyms to disguise his Jewish identity. Walter Benjamin was actually called: Walter Benedix-Schönflies-Benjamin. The family scenario of desire had inscribed the Mother's name, Schönflies, alongside that of the Father. Benjamin further mentions a Jewish custom according to which male offspring always had a secret name entered on the religious register – a name that was only communicated to them when they reached puberty.

The change of name remained a possibility but it proved to be quite illusory. 'The precautions by which they meant to counter fate were set aside by the one most concerned.' Of course, Benjamin did go on to become a writer. But although he used various pseudonyms (including Ardor, 'flame', in his youth), he became known as 'Benjamin'. The other names remained secret, magical, rather as the title of this fragment 'Agesilaus Santander' (the name of a king of Santander) concealed a secret rebel: *Satanas*. Furthermore, Benjamin had a real passion for anagrams, and he often broke his own name down into *Anni M. B.* In *The Origin of German Tragic Drama*, after quoting Giehlow to the effect that the very word *rebus* 'originated on the basis of the enigmatic hieroglyphs' of Renaissance artists, he establishes a close connection between hieroglyphs, anagrams and allegory.[17] For if allegory fragments reality through interruptive violence and so destabilizes it as to represent the figure of the corpse, the words, sounds and letters which are reduced to signifiers in the anagram are 'emancipated from any context of traditional meaning and are flaunted as objects which can be exploited for allegorical purposes'.[18]

The bisexual Angel, the secret name of the mother at the core of the signifier of writing, may perhaps be thought of as the trace of all traces, as the indicator of a background Name that is heretical vis-à-vis the dominant paternal filiations – a name as bisexual as the Angel. Here are the roots of that scene of writing in which Benjamin takes his place together with the subjugated and de-classed, the working class, those who are precisely 'nameless'. Here too the Angel of the 'family novel' links up again with those of writing and history. This is doubtless where the fate of Benjamin himself plays itself out – Benjamin the writer who carried 'catas-trophe' as a cipher, the image and thought of that other catastrophe which is progress. The end was still in the beginning.

Now-Time

In this journey through the imaginary – picture, allegory, dialectical image, phantasm – the Angel has shown us the non-visible or unconscious of modernity, something referring to an uncontrollable violence which lies beyond and beneath political mediation. In his attempt to make unreason dialectical and visible, to penetrate into frontier areas with the 'sharpened axe of reason', Benjamin was compelled to bring into play *two languages* and *two worlds*. The one, political and Marxist, belongs to the dialectic as the site where the vision and praxis of the vanquished ceaselessly clash with the oppressive sovereignty of the rulers, if only in the silent anonymity of a history that is still to be rewritten.

The other is the complementary world of Kafka or Klee, that of the 'theological dwarf' and the Angel. It is non-dialectical: it points to the interruption of history, to catastrophe and the non-human dehiscence or loss of the subject. It induces us to think the archaic, barbaric side of our civilized societies, the 'thing-like tenor' of big cities, mass politics, anthill-states and modern bureaucracies. It is the prehistory of a history that Marx announced, but for which the 'weakened power' of Benjamin's messianism went in search.

The two languages and worlds define a practice of ruptured writing consisting of fragments, montage, quotation. As Maurice Blanchot puts it in *L'Écriture du désastre*, which is not always far from Benjamin's writing of catastrophe, 'the fragmentary, more than instability (non-fixity), permits disarray, disarrangement'.[19] That Benjamin's work is relevant to the problems of modernity, and that it is shot through with the metaphor-reality of a by no means nameless feminine, says a great deal about the reverse side of existing masteries and the certitude of the self-willed humanist subject. Female culture is ultimately universal culture, which makes it possible to confront difference within the self and the other. In this respect we should bear in mind Benjamin's words:

> All rulers are the heirs of those who conquered before them. Hence, empathy with the victor invariably benefits the rulers. Historical materialists know what that means. Whoever has emerged victorious participates to this day in the triumphal procession in which the present rulers step over those who are lying prostrate.[20]

This flow of alienated time was what Benjamin sought to interrupt by practising a fierce hostility towards anything that lay on the side of the established filiations, names and identities, of ruling violence and of history subordinated to a vulgar concept of linear, continuous, empty time. To that he opposed the project of a different history as the *construction of now-times*: an archaeology of modernity. Its plot would be an ever reopened split between the multiplication of visibles, knowledge and information, and the barbaric, anti-humanist loss of experience that was its hidden side.

This split involved a reason that one might call baroque: the reason of allegory and the Other, the reason of an unreconciled history. To that we are becoming deaf and blind. And Benjamin's Angel appears as a symptom of this crisis of perception, this rupturing of time. The 'storm blowing from Paradise' is progress which perpetually moves into catastrophe, ruin and mutilation. This storm has not finished blowing. Benjamin sees in it more than ever the alchemy of our contradictions: our now-time.

Notes

1. *Briefe* 2, p. 828. The account of the dream is here taken from this letter. Emphases added throughout.
2. 'The Image of Proust', in *Illuminations*, p. 202.
3. Ibid., p. 203.
4. Ibid., p. 215. On this 'writing position', see Jean-Louis Baudry, 'Écriture, mort et profanation', *L'Écrit du temps*, 1, 1982.
5. *Briefe* 2, p. 848.
6. 'On Some Motifs in Baudelaire', pp. 160–1.
7. 'The Image of Proust', p. 205. [Translation modified.]
8. Benjamin, 'Conversations with Brecht', in Bloch/Lukács/Brecht/Benjamin/ Adorno, *Aesthetics and Politics*, London: Verso 1980, p. 90.
9. 'A Berlin Chronicle', in *One-Way Street and Other Writings*, p. 298.
10. 'Central Park', p. 40.
11. Ibid. [Translation modified.]
12. Scholem, 'Walter Benjamin and His Angel'.
13. Ibid., pp. 57–8.
14. Ibid., p. 59.
15. *Encore*, p. 71.
16. Gershom Scholem, *On the Kabbalah and Its Symbolism*, London: Routledge & Kegan Paul 1965, p. 105. See also David Bakan, *Sigmund Freud and the Jewish Mystical Tradition*, Princeton: D. Van Nostrand 1958.
17. *The Origin of German Tragic Drama*, pp. 169ff.
18. Ibid., p. 207. On the pseudonyms and the status of the name, see Giulio Schiavoni, *Walter Benjamin – Sopravvivere alla cultura*, Palermo: Sellerio 1980.
19. Maurice Blanchot, *L'Écriture du désastre*, Paris: Gallimard 1980, p. 17.
20. 'Theses on the Philosophy of History', p. 256.

PART TWO

THE UTOPIA OF THE FEMININE

Benjamin's Trajectory. 2

Women in Baudelaire: the most precious booty in the 'Triumph of Allegory' – Life, which means Death.

'Central Park', p. 39

The motif of the androgyne, the lesbian or the sterile woman should be considered in relation to the destructive violence of the allegorical intention. .

'Central Park', p. 35

The lesbian is the heroine of modernism.

'The Paris of the Second Empire', p. 90

Baudelaire's heroic ideal is androgynous.

Passagen-Werk, p. 980

Love directed towards prostitutes is the apotheosis of empathy for the commodity.

Passagen-Werk, p. 637

Our second set of quotations all place the feminine in the midst of Benjamin's central concepts of allegory, modernity, experience, and empathy with the commodity. It illuminates a nodal point in his interpretation of Baudelaire, and is itself one of the arcana of modernity explored in the *Passagen-Werk*. This radical focus, continually enriched, is a constant feature of Benjamin's writings: from the early critique in 1913 of the cultural emptiness of modern erotic civilization, in which he notes the lack of any *experience* of women's culture, to the recognition of woman as the *allegory of modernity* deployed in Baudelaire's grand imaginaries (prostitute, sterile woman, lesbian, androgyne). To be sure, the theme is never taken up head on but is addressed in an indirect, fragmentary manner, in the space between concept and metaphor. But more than any other it lies hidden beneath the earth, joining the fiction and materialist formulation of reconstructed history with our own now-times – as in a labyrinth that has to be passed through again.

In 'Berlin Chronicle', Benjamin writes that in his Proustian Berlin of rediscovered childhood and remembrance – this forest-town, labyrinth-town – he encountered 'the haunts of that Ariadne in whose proximity [he] learned for the first time (and was never entirely to forget)' what he would only experience later: love.[1] And when the labyrinth metaphor invades 'Central Park' and the *Passagen-Werk*, this early engraved memory comes back together with the arcana of modernity in the Paris of the Second Empire: 'With the rise of the great cities prostitution came into possession of new secrets. One of these is the labyrinthine character of the city itself. The labyrinth, whose image has passed into flesh and blood in the *flâneur*, appears in new colours with prostitution.'[2]

The image moves from the labyrinth of big cities to the labyrinth of the commodity, and by no means least is the ultimate labyrinth of history – 'the home of the hesitant' – where the sexual drive 'in those episodes which precede its satisfaction' curiously meets up with 'humanity (the social class) which does not wish to know what will become of it'.[3] This 'not knowing' of the labyrinth defines a whole grid of thought in which the feminine, with its symbolic and imaginative divisions, finds itself caught up. Should we accept in turn that the feminine may today be an Ariadne's thread with which to rework those tangled routes?

For the question of woman really does seem the precise point at which the two scenes of Benjamin's work as a historian intersect: the 'sociological' determinations of history (urbanization, industrialization, dominance of commodity fetishism) and the idea of modernity as phantasmagoria and progressive aesthetic. The new imaginaries which burst forth with Baudelaire, originating in nineteenth-century French utopian currents (Saint-Simonism, Claire Démar's feminism, various religious sects) and continuing in Berg's *Lulu* or the pubescent flower-women of *Jugendstil*, are the material with which Benjamin reconstructs a whole modernist regime of the imaginary of women. To use one of his own expressions, we might call this a visual unconscious which parallels Freud's unconscious of drives.

There can be no mistake here. The image which has been engraved in the *flâneur's*, body, Baudelaire's 'passing woman' who is merely glimpsed in the haze of big-city intoxication,[4] are just particular cases of what characterizes modernity as such: the cult of images, the secularization/sublimation of fleeting and reproducible bodies. The feminine might well be one of these 'primal historical forms' (*urgeschichtlichen Formen*) of the nineteenth century, an origin (*Ursprung*) in which a 'pre-history' and a 'post-history' (*Vorund Nachgeschichte*), the archaic and the modern, are dialectically articulated. This would unavoidably point to a new historical regime of seeing and 'non-seeing', of what can and cannot be represented.

The aim of this section will therefore be to examine again the scenographies of this 'primal historical form', to draw something like a *Trauerspiel of the woman-body of modernity*. Certain determinations of Benjamin's notion of 'utopia' or 'a-topia' will be discussed in relation to what Maurice Blanchot, in a text on Marguerite Duras's *La Maladie de la mort*, calls the 'excess which comes with the feminine', or the 'indefinable power of the feminine over what seeks to be, or sees itself as, alien to it'.[5]

Rather as in multi-entry baroque spaces with doubled, ambiguous perspectives, the 'feminine' might be said to delineate certain scenographies of modernity and some of its negative or positive utopias:

1 *'Catastrophist' utopia*, in its tendency to destroy appearances or false totalities – or the female body as allegory of modernity.

2 *Anthropological utopia*: exploration of the subterranean (androgynous) history of the nineteenth century, from Saint-Simonism to Claire Démar, Ganeau, various sects and Baudelaire. Bisexuality is here the matrix of 'anthropological materialism',[6] which breaks with the anaemic humanisms of universal man (*Allmensch*).

3 *Transgressive utopia*: the appearance in writing and historical praxis of a purely imaginal space (*hundertprozentigen Bildraums*) which convulses established frontiers and forces people to think together a number of apparent opposites – catastrophe and progress, messianism and Marxism, feminine and masculine, novelty and repetition of the same. Here the scene of writing and

history might be linked to a reinterpretation of Klee's Angel as it appears in the 'Theses on the Philosophy of History', a 'Jewish' angel who is a metaphor for the 'divine androgyny' characteristic of messianic currents.

Notes

1. 'Berlin Chronicle', p. 294.
2. 'Central Park', p. 53. [Translation modified to accord with the French.]
3. Ibid., p. 40. [Translation modified.]
4. A reference to Baudelaire's poem 'À une passante' [*Trans. note.*]
5. Maurice Blanchot, *La Communauté inavouable*, Paris: Minuit 1983, p. 87.
6. Benjamin, *Gesammelte Schriften [GS] V: Passagen-Werk*, p. 971.

5

CATASTROPHIST UTOPIA

The Feminine as Allegory of Modernity

Modernity and the redistribution of feminine and masculine

Baudelaire's work expresses in all its dimensions the symbolic redistribution of relations between the feminine and the masculine which is characteristic of modernism and of the twofold (socio-historical and aesthetic) archaeological scene of Benjamin's work as historian of nineteenth-century France. On the sociological side stands the new status of women in large towns, subject to a certain uniformity of the sexes as a result of wage-labour and urbanization. This violent insertion of women into the process of commodity production destroys traditional differences, whether material (differential location) or symbolic. As labour and society assume a mass character, women themselves become 'mass articles' and lose both their 'natural' qualities (female essence defined by the repro-duction of life) and their poetic aura, the sublimated idealization of Beauty which surrounded Dante's Beatrice. This societal dynamic therefore made it essential to redefine the symbolic features distinguishing the feminine from the masculine, especially as the first part of the nineteenth century witnessed the development of early forms of feminism.

On the aesthetic side, new imaginaries of the female body – imagined bodies – were already beginning to take shape in the *lyrical experience* of Baudelaire, a 'feminized' poet reeling under his own androgyny who had to obey the market like a prostitute.[1] The integrity of Baudelaire's poetic Ego is exploded by the allegorical impulse to destroy the appearances of nature and the social order, and by the Saturnian gaze on a history where alienation develops together with the typically modern *atrophy of experience* (spleen, melancholy, *ennui*, emptiness). From now on, it will be subject to the same 'loosening of the self' (*Lockerung des Ich*[2]) that is experienced in the state of intoxication.

In his destructive rage at the impotence or 'calvary' of his solitude, Baudelaire becomes caught up in all the ambivalences (historical, psychic, poetic) analysed by Benjamin. Discovering his own androgyneity, he identifies now with the prostitute as image of modernity, now with the lesbian as heroic protester against it.

The connection between the historical and aesthetic dimensions is so close that Benjamin is left in no doubt: 'Baudelaire produces in lyricism the figure of the sexual perversion that seeks its object in the streets.'[3] Like the poet, woman becomes one of the privileged sites of the 'mythic correspondence' within which 'the modern technological world and the archaic world of the symbol' now operate.[4] This intertwining precisely defines a form of modernism radically different from the 'ideologies of progress', one which nearly always emerges out of the depths of a crisis: seventeenth-century Baroque, Baudelaire, *Jugendstil*, the Viennese and German crisis cultures of the twentieth century. The positions to be adopted towards progress and towards 'catastrophe' therefore sharply distinguish two types of modernism.

On the one hand, the modernity of progress, derived from the grand Hegelian synthesis and lodged in evolutionist and historicist interpretations of Marxism, postulates a linear continuum of time, a development of culture and productive forces 'without barbarism', an aesthetic of beautiful classical and Romanesque totalities, a vision of history in which a subject, however 'alienated', gives it meaning. On the other hand, for the modernity which Benjamin draws out of the Baudelaire–Nietzsche–Blanqui constellation, the overcoming of the illusion of totality, system and unicity in history makes it necessary to recognize an inescapable truth of catastrophist utopianism: namely, the eternal recurrence of barbarism, fragmentation and destruction as a critical force.

This latter conception of modernity, which I would call 'untimely' in Nietzsche's sense of the word *unzeitgemäss*, sets itself against the stream of modernist and historicist approaches. It bases itself not upon a plenitude of meaning, a unified and perfectly intelligible history, but upon a loss, an emptiness, a lack – a power of absence (as opposed to the immediately 'actual') which links together signification and death. Deepening of the experience of spleen, loss of aura or nihilist devaluation of values: these non-Hegelian negatives inscribe in writing a *vacant site* which Benjamin associated with Baudelaire when he spoke of his construction of '*blank spaces* which he filled in with his poems'.[5]

The fact that this 'loss of love' in melancholy can express itself in the new status of the 'feminine' and its *modern allegories*, and that it is even embodied with all its violence and ambivalence in the figure of the prostitute (from Büchner to Berg, with Baudelaire as an important milestone), tells us a great deal about the phantasms which haunt it.

For the prostitute is one of those monads who open themselves to the archaeological labour of the reconstruction of history. We have already stressed Benjamin's interest in the 'nameless ones' (*Namenlosen*) and the lower depths of history and literature. And this constant resolve to '*fix the image* of history in the humblest crystallizations' will produce a kind of constellation of thoughts and images, a chaos of metaphors revolving around that figure of the feminine which is the form of the *Trauerspiel* of modernity.

The *Trauerspiel* of the 'prostitute-body'

The development of big-city prostitution as a widespread phenomenon giving rise to legislation, which involved the conversion of female bodies into articles of mass consumption, expressed a more general historical shift that took place in the middle of the nineteenth century. This took the form of a crisis of looking: new relations between the visible and the invisible, representation of the non-representable, and a series of practices and discourses engendered by it. More than anything else, the female body is the support of this 'archaeology of the look' to which Foucault referred. A new stage-setting of bodies now makes them irreducible to their geometric visibility and endows them with a coefficient of obscurity or mystery.

This 'deeper' visibility of the female body forms the core of many of Benjamin's analyses of make-up, artifice, fashion and the new 'female fauna'.[6] In the most immediate terms, prostitution makes of woman a 'mass-produced article' which is displayed as such for purchase and consumption in the city streets and then in brothels. This 'article' expresses the new correlations between sex and labour: the prostitute can demand a price for her labour at the very moment when 'labour becomes prostitution'.[7] There is thus much more than a superficial historical analogy between a market society where everything has a price and the prostitute who charges for love-time that becomes ever more an object of accounting, exploitation and profit maximization. Wage-labour and the generalization of the commodity mark the 'decline' of the qualitative side of use-value and difference and their subordination to the abstract universality of exchange. In the same way, prostitution demonstrates the end of aura and the decline (*Verfall*) of love.[8]

In his sketch of a 'political economy' of the prostitute-body,

Benjamin traverses the realm of appearances in a way that carries him well beyond socio-economic analysis. Prostitution exhibits 'the revolutionary character of technology', so that the serial and serialized body is interchangeable like the body set to work in the factory. But it is not just a question of disciplines. In the very mechanism of prostitution there is 'an unconscious knowledge of man', practised through 'all the nuances of payment', the 'very nuances of loveplay, now familiar, now brutal'.[9] Strictly speaking, what is bought is not so much pleasure as 'the expression of shame' that commands it, 'the fanatical wish for pleasure' in its most cynical form. In mass prostitution, which is not limited to prostitutes, new and peculiarly modern figures of passion and human existence take shape: Eros is linked to Thanatos, love of pleasure to perversion, and an apparently Christian language (including in Baudelaire) to the language of commodities.

Here then is one of the Ariadne threads of our labyrinth: male desire seeks to immobilize, to *petrify* the female body. Or, as Benjamin writes: 'In the lifeless body which nevertheless offers itself for pleasure, allegory is united to the commodity.'

This union should be understood in terms of the imaginative and symbolic equivalences which Benjamin establishes around the 'prostitute-body': for example, between love for prostitutes, the mythic communion specific to big cities, and empathy with commodities; or, more crucially, between the new markings of the female body, its *traces*, and the destructive violence of allegory which makes of the prostitute a second-degree allegory of 'the commodity allegory'.

Hence the *Trauerspiel* of the prostituted body organizes itself within the dual movement of allegorical violence: *disfigurement* and devaluation of everything real, then its phantasmagoric *humanization*. Woman has now lost her aura, her religious and cultural *hic et nunc*, her absolute uniqueness, her female body betokening a celestial beauty peculiar to love. Beauty no longer sees, no longer speaks. Her eyes, like clear, inexpressive mirrors, are closed to any sublimated, ideal belief. *Beauty has been petrified.*[10] As Baudelaire writes in his poem 'La Beauté':

Je suis belle, ô mortels! comme un rêve de pierre,
Et mon sein, où chacun s'est meurtri tour à tour,
Est fait pour inspirer au poète un amour
Éternel et muet ainsi que la matière.[11]

This dream of stone, this silent, petrified, materialized love, recalls Benjamin's haunting description of allegory as 'image of petrified unrest',[12] as 'petrified, primordial landscape'.[13] It refers us to the dual movement affecting the love-object in modernity.

Whereas the culture of the Middle Ages knows only an unreal love-object reflected in fantasy, in what Auerbach calls the *figurative* precisely in connection with Dante, the loss of aura cannot but be a dual loss, legible and visible in the scenographies of the feminine.

On the one hand, it is a loss of that sublimated love linking Beauty and Truth which made the figure of woman – Beatrice in the *Divine Comedy*, for example – the mediator of another, more 'celestial' love. The Beauty of the 'immortals' has thus turned into the 'dream of stone' of *mortals*. On the female body the poet reads precariousness, mortality, his own 'castration'. As Benjamin puts it in a striking formula, Baudelaire's poetry is 'a mimesis of death'. Hence the radical separation between *eros* and *sexus*, represented by the prostitute, is an ever present possibility.

But on the other hand, the 'dream of stone' also introduces a desire for the death of desire into the lyrical experience – a perverted paralysis whose end-point is precisely venal love or male impotence. In Baudelaire, then, desire is for the first time polarized between perverse pleasure and mystical pleasure. As Benjamin notes, male impotence fosters 'his attachment to the seraphic image of woman'.[14] Here Benjamin's analysis partially overlaps with that of Lacan: 'The body as final signified is the corpse or the *stone phallus*.'[15]

Once it is petrified, Beauty can only disguise itself. As we have seen, Benjamin was especially interested in fashion, artifice and the painted body, and he saw in the ritual make-up of prostitutes an anticipation of the girl shows of the twentieth century. But such travesties do not succeed in concealing the protracted workings of death which invade Eros. The ontological ageing of the body which appears in the erotics of the skeleton (see Baudelaire's fascination for 'little old women'[16]) is a distant precursor of Freud's images of *the uncanny*. '*Ô charme d'un néant follement attifé!*'[17] Or again: '*Ô beauté, monstre énorme, effrayant, ingénu.*'[18]

In this de-idealized beauty stripped bare by the appearance-destroying gaze of the allegorist, in this curious 'ontology' of woman's nothingness '*follement attifé*', the female body is robbed of its maternal body and becomes desirable only by going to the limits as dead-body, fragmented-body, petrified-body. It is as if the death of the organic body can be represented only in the feminine, at the moment when Baudelaire internalizes or subjectivizes death and makes it a visual focus of all reality. As John E. Jackson remarks, since Büchner the finitude or ontological corruptibility of the body, as well as the aesthetic of the fragment that it induces, have crystallized in prostitution. Danton's love of prostitutes is well known. As he tried to assemble the Venus Medici piece by piece among all the bright young things of the Palais Royal, he called this 'doing a mosaic'. God knows at which limb he left it. It is painful to see how nature *breaks Beauty into fragments*, as Medea her brother, and scatters it in bodies.'[19]

Prostituted, scattered, fragmented bodies themselves express the destructive impulse of allegory: the loss of aura, veils and immortality. But this utopia is critical as well as destructive; it has not only a regressive but also a progressive aspect. 'The dissipation [*Austreibung*] of appearances', the demystification of any reality that presents itself as an 'order', 'totality' or 'system',[20] makes modernity a *task* and a *conquest*.[21]

Paradoxically, therefore, the prostituted body is not only fragment, ruin of nature, disfigurement of the 'sublime body'. It is also a staging in and through new imaginaries created by a thousand excitations: fashion, gambling, succession of images, the whole phantasmagoria of modernity. It is thereby re-idealized and humanized, for the prostitute is the way in which 'the commodity attempts to look itself in the face. It celebrates its becoming human in the whore.'[22] There is humanization and something more: the plenitude of allegory itself. Thus, in Baudelaire's work 'the prostitute is the commodity achieving the plenitude of allegorical vision'.

In this baroque of female bodies, allegory therefore appears in its *modern* interpretation. The full significance of this needs to be understood. *Only the status of the feminine, of the female body as at once real and fictitious, makes it possible to distinguish modern from baroque allegory.*

The woman-body as interpretative principle of modern allegory

In Benjamin's analysis, which cuts across the tradition of Romantic criticism, modern allegory has a number of traits in common with baroque allegory, the origin (*Ursprung*) of modernity. We may summarize these as follows.

- As rhetorical figure and interpretation, allegory both destroys and demystifies reality in its finely ordered totality. By its destructive intention, allegory *lays bare* reality and gives it the form of ruins or fragments. In the course of this process, history itself emerges in its own representation and in its most Saturnian aspects.

- This process engenders the *emotionally charged writing* characteristic of allegory – self-figurative writing which ties itself down in theatrical scenes. One of the key elements in Benjamin's interpretation is precisely the optical character of allegory: it has to do with images, sight, scenes linking the visible and the invisible, life and dream. History here presents itself to vision, in ambivalences fixed as a *series of scenes*. It practises a quasi-mystical language of bodies, and that is why 'the observer is confronted with the *facies hippocratica* of history as a petrified, primordial landscape'.[23]

• Because history here appears in its 'catastrophist', imaginative side (hence the theatrical model of Calderón, Shakespeare and Gryphius), the now-secularized perception of time differs from the tragic vision in that it takes place in and through feeling: *Trauer* (mourning or sorrow) and *Spiel*. It therefore refers us to typologies of passion and a complete anthropology.

• In this passionate yet self-distanced writing on passion, the dominant rhetorical figure for the stage-setting of extremes and contradictions is the oxymoron. 'Nothingness' is 'dressed up' – like burning cold, and dark brightness.

This is another way of saying that allegory is anti-dialectical or, to use Benjamin's terms, that it is *dialectic at a standstill*, frozen, fixed in images.

While allegory is defined by these principal characteristics, Benjamin locates its *modernity* at the precise point of its relationship to death. 'Baroque allegory sees the corpse only from the outside. Baudelaire sees it also from the inside.'[24] In leaving the external world for the inner world, in making of death what Freud calls an endopsychic image, *modern* allegory shakes off some of the limitations of the baroque and establishes itself against the background of a dual disappearance. Salvation, the absent/present redemption of the baroque, disappears with the radical secularization of time without transcendence and without a future, periodized by the ever-new and ever-the-same. Cosmos/nature, as a totality of opposites or an 'objective' metaphorical reserve, similarly disappears – as was already apparent in Romantic irony, particularly that of Jean Paul.

And so, what 'body' can now give 'flesh and blood' to the destructive impulse of an ever more 'feminized' poet, one who has been expelled from the great models of paternal filiation and mimicked by his own 'abyss'? The answer is precisely the bodies of the feminine, which polarize the sadistic and perverse impulse of the allegorical gaze. For allegory, 'to touch things means to violate them, to know things means to unmask them'. This should be taken literally. Thus:

• In connection with Baudelaire's poem 'Le Beau Navire', Benjamin writes that the baroque specification (*barocke Detaillierung*) operates on the body of woman.[25]

- It is again the woman's body, and especially that of the prostitute, which provides the metaphor for the extremes of desire and death, vitality and lifelessness, life and corruption – the skeleton. . . . It serves as a material conversion for the 'petrified unrest' which is the very formula of 'Baudelaire's image of life' (*Lebensbild*), the image 'that knows no development'.[26]
- Finally, this real/fictional body gives to modern allegory its condition of existence: its visibility, everything that revolves around the *Bild*. This is why, as we have seen, the scenarios of the 'female body' act as metaphors for those of the 'commodity-body'.

We could go on listing these procedures, which doubtless refer back to the most secret and pregnant of them all: the procedure of the *abyss*. For the Baudelairean taste for the void and nothingness, as well as the figures of modern *Trauer*, spleen and melancholy, live on a *continual metaphor* of the female sexual organs. The bottomless abyss, in which the poet experiences pregnancy as 'disloyal competition', triggers anguish and impotence. As Benjamin argues in one of his finest fragments: 'The sense of the abyss is to be defined as signification. It is always allegorical.'[27] Whereas for Blanqui 'the abyss is a star', which defines itself in the space of the world and finds its historical index in the sciences of nature, for Baudelaire 'it is starless', not even 'the exoticism of theology'. Rather, it is the 'secularized abyss of knowledge and signification'.[28]

In this highly suggestive parallel, where Benjamin wonders about the historical index of the Baudelairean abyss, he relates it to its twin sister, fashion, and suggests that the index might be 'the arbitrariness of allegory itself'.[29] For our part, we would suggest that this historical index has something to do with the shift in relations between the feminine and the masculine which took place in Baudelaire's work in the middle of the nineteenth century. For woman is not only *allegory of modernity*. In the great anthropological utopias of bisexuality, and in the two figures of the lesbian and the androgyne, she is also a *heroic protest against this modernity*.

Notes

1. On the androgynism of Baudelaire see Michel Butor, *Histoire extraordinaire: Essai sur un rêve de Baudelaire*, Paris: Gallimard 1961, and Leo Bersani, *Baudelaire and Freud*, Berkeley: University of California 1977, which relates it to the lost virility and dislocation of the Baudelairean Subject.
2. Benjamin, 'Surrealism', p. 227.
3. *GS* V, p. 343.

4. Ibid., p. 617.
5. 'Some Motifs in Baudelaire', p. 116.
6. *GS* V, p. 617.
7. Ibid., p. 439.
8. Ibid., p. 617.
9. Ibid., p. 615.
10. Ibid., p. 411.
11. 'I am beautiful, O mortals, as a dream in stone, and my breast, on which every man has bruised himself in his turn, is designed to inspire in poets a love as eternal and silent as matter itself.' *The Complete Verse*, p. 76.
12. *GS* V, p. 414.
13. *The Origin of German Tragic Drama*, p. 166.
14. 'Central Park', p. 36.
15. Jacques Lacan, 'La Relation d'objet', unpublished seminar of 5 December 1956, quoted in Monique David-Ménard, *L'Hystérique entre Freud et Lacan*, Paris: Éditions universitaires 1983, p. 203.
16. See the poem 'Les Petites Vieilles' in *The Complete Verse*, p. 180. [*Trans. note*]
17. 'What charm there is in Nothingness dressed to kill!' 'Danse macabre', in ibid., p. 192.
18. 'O Beauty, enormous, terrifying and ingenuous monster.' 'Hymne à la beauté', in ibid., p. 80.
19. John E. Jackson, *La Mort Baudelaire: Essais sur Les Fleurs du mal*, Neuchâtel: La Baconnière 1982, p. 75. The whole of Jackson's book concerns this 'internalization' of death.
20. *GS* V, p. 411.
21. 'Central Park', p. 35.
22. Ibid., p. 42.
23. *The Origin of German Tragic Drama*, p. 166.
24. 'Central Park', p. 51.
25. *GS* V, p. 415.
26. Ibid., p. 414.
27. Ibid., p. 347.
28. Ibid., p. 347.
29. Ibid., p. 348.

6

ANTHROPOLOGICAL UTOPIA, OR THE 'HEROINES' OF MODERNITY

The lesbian is the sister of the prostitute, in that she protests against the dominant interiority of the family scene, the reduction of love to family and pregnancy. But she is also an exactly opposite figure: she embodies 'a protest against the technological revolution' and a *'heroic archetype* of modernity'. Hence this pure love, this 'sublimation carried to the heart of woman', will serve Baudelaire as an erotic ideal and even a 'heroic guiding image'.[1]

The reference to modernity should here be taken in the strong sense. It is true that this image of the lesbian revives Greek Sapphic love and intertwines ancient and modern in the manner of allegory. It is also true that the figure of the lesbian was already firmly established in nineteenth-century literature, from Balzac's *Girl with the Golden Eyes* to Gautier's *Mademoiselle Maupin* or Latouche's *Fragoletta*. Nor should we forget the painters that Benjamin mentions in this regard: Delacroix, for example, whose work Baudelaire saw at the World Exhibition of 1855, or later Courbet. Nevertheless, for Benjamin the real origin (*Ursprung*) of this figure lies elsewhere. It is to be found in the reinscription of the myth of the androgyne within the first great utopianisms that accompanied industrialization: Saint-Simonism, especially in Claire Démar's feminist variant, but also the mystical-Romantic sects – the Ganeau current, for example.[2] Like all origins in Benjamin's sense of the word, it combined a pre-history with a post-history, both being linked to *the place of the anthropological question* within modernity and the strategy of the enlargement of experience. In a passage on the history of the sects, where he also quotes some extracts from Claire Démar's book *Ma Loi d'avenir*, Benjamin himself speaks of 'anthropological materialism'.[3]

Let us now consider Benjamin's 'montage' of the different forms of nineteenth-century androgyny, as the starting-point for the anthropological archaeology which, as it were, 'anticipates' the

Freudian discovery of bisexuality and underpins the critique of historicism.

First there is the *divine androgyny* of Ganeau, the celebrated magus who used to receive the publicists of the time at his mean bedside, and whose romantic heresy saw the bisexual Christian God – the figure of future liberty – incarnated in Jesus and Mary. Criticizing the paternal and 'phallocentric' symbolism of Christianity, he went so far as to create an alternative symbolism of the *Mapah* ('ma' and 'pa'). In 1838, in his first public declaration, he announced the opening of the age of *Evadah*, the created androgyne who mediated with divine androgyny. Benjamin notes all these features, and is especially attentive to the feminization of the religious which is rather reminiscent of the *kabbalah* and currents within Jewish messianism.[4]

Ganeau's heretical-Romantic delirium expresses a new historical evaluation of the feminine. In the bisexuality of the Christian God, Mary comes to embody the Liberty of 1789 'in the feminine', as the veritable priestess of the future world and of a reconciled humanity freed from its shackles.

Next comes *utopian and feminist androgyny, with its anthropological content*. Ganeau and many others mentioned by Benjamin (abbé Constant, for example, or Swedenborg, who influenced Baudelaire so much) refer us back to the true site of *androgynous modernity*: Saint-Simonism and the feminism of Claire Démar.

In particular, the religious Saint-Simonism of Prosper Enfantin proposed 'a new form of fusion between men and God'.[5] The architectural utopia of the Temple as the androgyne made real, the need for the androgynous principle to become the very basis of the cult (role of the Father and Mother): these linked Saint-Simonism to its two great 'modern' correlates, industrialization and feminism. Of the greatest interest to Benjamin, however, was the Saint-Simonian feminist Claire Démar: 'As far as its anthropological content is concerned, the Saint-Simonian utopia is more comprehensible in the ideas of Claire Démar than in this architecture which was never built.'[6]

This anthropological content of women's emancipation can easily be grasped in the manifesto of Claire Démar, *Ma Loi d'avenir*, which Benjamin quotes on a number of occasions. Women must derive their existence and social position from themselves – which entails a rehabilitation of the body, the freeing of love from marital constraints, the liberation of women from 'blood maternity', a critique of social exploitation and patriarchy.[7] Not only does this content account for the emergence of the *modern* figure of the lesbian out of utopianism and feminism. It also brings sharply into focus that famous 'anthropological materialism' which, according to Benjamin, aroused the hatred of bourgeois reaction in the latter part of the nineteenth century – through its critique of patriarchy, and its demand for freer and richer, but also more mysterious, relations between the sexes. To read this chapter of the *Passagen-Werk* today is quite an extraordinary experience, so deep do Benjamin's historical and theoretical insights now seem. Here we can see that gigantic anthropological utopia of modernity, in which androgynous bisexuality is combined with a critique of the 'dictatorship' of religious and monotheistic symbolism, and of the mass institutions of capitalism such as marriage and prostitution.

Benjamin's account, which bases itself on Firmin Maillard's book *La Légende de la femme émancipée*, takes us from Claire Démar to Fourier, evokes the movement of the Vésuviennes, and ends with the new protest against technology to be found in the flower-women of *Jugendstil*. Throughout, Benjamin is constructing a network of historical constellations in which past and present are telescoped together. Why this 'passion' for androgyny, more than twenty-five years after his first great youthful intimations that every individual is made up of male and female, that we have no experience of what a *female culture* would be like?[8]

The first answer that might occur to us is evidently a historical one: androgyny and feminism, for all Baudelaire's misogyny, are the true origin of this modern Sappho figure with her protest against industrial modernity and the subjection of women to the reproduction of bodies and images. This feminine is the bearer of a *new heroism* à la Baudelaire or Nietzsche. But it is a real heroism for Benjamin, who clearly sees the duplicity or ambivalence of Baudelaire. Whereas Baudelaire inscribes the *image* of the lesbian into modernity, he denies it in social reality and reserves for it the same ostracism that he showed for all emancipated women, beginning with George Sand.[9]

Although this answer is not without relevance, it does not go to what seems to me the heart of the problem: namely, Benjamin's notion of 'anthropology' and therefore of experience. Already in *The Origin of German Tragic Drama*, he detected in the figures of Time, *Trauer* and the passions of Power a veritable *dramatic anthropology*. Or rather: recognition of such an anthropology grounds the critique of historicism and distinguishes the baroque from the tragic. 'A basic stock of dramaturgical realia, such as is embodied in the political anthropology and typology of the *Trauerspiel*, is what was required in order to escape from the problems of a historicism which deals with its subject as a necessary but inessential transitional manifestation.'[10]

In other words, the staging of images and imaginaries pre-supposes a *wager of passion* on time, desire and death (sorrow and mourning), which are now liberated from Greek fate and represented in historical terms. Is it not here, in these territories given over to passion or even madness, that the 'axe of reason' must penetrate – as in a forest or labyrinth, where the buried feminine also lies within experience?

It is as if the feminine, with its power of images and imagination, mainly affected the status of writing and experience – or even historical praxis – through its potential for otherness and transgression.

Notes

1. *GS* V, p. 400.
2. Ibid., pp. 970–7.
3. Ibid., p. 974.
4. Ibid., p. 971.
5. Ibid., p. 981.
6. 'The Paris of the Second Empire in Baudelaire', p. 91.
7. *GS* V, p. 974.
8. See p. 49 above.
9. *GS* V, p. 400; and 'The Paris of the Second Empire in Baudelaire', p. 93.
10. *The Origin of German Tragic Drama*, p. 100.

7

TRANSGRESSIVE UTOPIA

'Image Frontiers' of Writing and History

Modernity is characterized by a loss of experience and a phantasmagoria of commodities which, like their opposite – the return to lived experience (*Erlebnis*) in Dilthey or Bergson – remain caught up in the fluid continuity of time. The experience of *Erfahrung*, on the other hand, always starts out from a break in time, in the empty, homogeneous continuity of historicism. 'Interruption of time', 'sectioning of time': this inaugurates an intensive, qualitative time of the descent into self, towards 'a state of resemblances' (Proust) or 'correspondences' (Baudelaire) or the 'complementary world' of Kafka and Klee. Here all experience is 'essentially linguistic': the uniqueness and unity of the subject break apart under the impact of shock and the involuntariness of time and chance. And yet, paradoxically enough, the moment of greatest happiness – the 'profane illumination' in which the everyday and mystery combine their powers – belongs less to the order of the linguistic and symbolic than to that of the imaginary: it becomes one flesh with images, with the whole realm of the *Bild*. It is as if an image were always necessary for the immemoriality of the past and the presence of now-time (*Jetztzeit*) to be telescoped together, as if a quite different aura could be constructed in the face of the loss of aura and cultural remoteness of the disenchanted world of modernity. Such a new aura, then, cannot be reduced to the 'commodity-aura' characteristic of the 'phantasmagoria' of modernity, nor, however, does it accord with Benjamin's most 'Brechtian' formulations which suggest that the decline of aura can be positively converted into the 'politicization of art'.[1] In fact, both Baudelaire's *correspondances* and Proust's 'time recovered' usher in an *untimely* experience of modernity. That which is lived becomes non-historical and even pre-historical remembrance: 'The *correspondances* are the data of remembrance – not historical data, but data of prehistory.'[2] As if the 'souvenir' alone, the internalized relic, could constitute the allegory of the modern, the ultimate utopia of the melancholic.

Yet involuntary memory born of 'shock', like the 'flashing' historical constellation of past/present, presents itself only in images or *figures*: in the archaic figure, on the one hand, and the non-archaic, historical figure, on the other, according to the characteristics that Benjamin attributes to the dialectical image in the *Passagen-Werk*.

In an author as attentive as Benjamin to the powers of the symbolic and the 'legible', the ubiquitous metaphors of gaze, face and *facies*, the vast grid of the *Bild*, and his own passion for theatre in general and baroque drama in particular, throw considerable light on the most intimate relations between the feminine and modernity: the unconscious of seeing.

First, with regard to the look or gaze, 'the *face* of modernity withers us with its look, as Medusa's did for the Greeks'.[3] It withers and petrifies because it deploys those ambiguous powers of the sexualized, maternal feminine which Freud analysed in his article on *'the uncanny'*. And yet, if 'the object become allegorical *under the gaze* of melancholy', there is another look which truly sees and calls up the aura. Thus in his *Trauerspiel* work, Benjamin notes that we are 'compelled to lift our eyes' by the 'schema' or diagram of baroque painting, which de-idealizes and deforms bodies and hollows out a space where no light (God or angels) appears. Benjamin defines the aura by the same movement of sight towards a representation of the unrepresentable: 'To perceive the aura of an object we look at means to invest it with the ability *to look at us in return*.'[4] It is the converse of that other, far from insignificant, look of Klee's Angel, the Angel of history, who, with 'staring eyes' and his *face* turned to the past, contemplates the storm of progress. In that angel's gaze, quite unprecedented relations take shape between the human and the inhuman, the ephemeral and the eternal, history and messianism, male and female. Acting out that which is non-human in man and history, the Angel passes across frontiers. For as we have seen in Part One, it really is an androgynous angel, stemming from the Jewish kabbalist tradition in which God is feminized, bisexualized and, as it were, theatricized.[5] In contrast to orthodox interpretations of Judaism, this God who is not (*aïn*), this divine nothingness, exists only through his own scopic desire: 'God wished to *see* God.' Conceived on the model of emanations and powers, this divine 'seeing' refers in the case of the tenth power to its feminized presence in the Shekhinah (wife, mother and daughter of God). And it is that Angel which 'appeared' to Benjamin in the overwhelming experience of 1933 which he described in his letter to Scholem from Ibiza. He the melancholic, who 'came into the world under the sign of Saturn', has been sent 'his *feminine form*, after the *masculine* reproduced in the picture, by way of ' the longest, most fatal detour'.[6]

This desexualized feminine – from the Medusa to the androgynous Angel – bursts forth as an excess, as a movement deconstructing frontiers, as an effacer of limits between representation and the unrepresentable. A figure of otherness, it provokes separation as fascination, inserting itself at the very heart of allegorical writing. For Benjamin such writing, with its power to stir the emotions, is shot through with two contradictory elements: tradition and expression (*Ausdruck*). While tradition refers to codes, rhetoric and a cold technique of dissociation from the object, the 'expressive form' (*Ausdrucksform*) manifests itself in 'showers of images', in metaphorical excess and transgression of the frontiers of reality. In this form, 'what is written tends to become image'. There is thus a permanent abyss between *figured Being* (*bildlichen Sein*) and signification (*Bedeutung*) – an abyss which breaks dialectical movement and fixes it in ambiguous, polysemic imagery detached like a fragment from the whole: 'In the field of allegorical intuition the image is fragment, a rune.'[7] Allegorical writing, then, is *figural writing* and destruction of the figurative in the strict sense of the term. For, as Gilles Deleuze shows in connection with the broken line of Michelangelo, 'the realism of deformation destroys all idealism of transfiguration'.[8] Things and forms are dehypostatized, deformalized, in a broken, theatrical movement of lines.

In more Freudian terms, we might say that baroque allegorical drama combines the cold, dissociative theatre of perversion, which idealizes the drive in scenarios and fetishes (the part for the whole), with the burning, excessive theatre of hysteria which summons up sexual pleasure [*jouissance*] in the proximity of seeing and spectacle. Burning cold or icy burning: such might be the formula of Baudelairean desire which pays the price of the decline of aura by separating Eros from love. But this structure which theatricizes reality and figures desire is so imposing that Benjamin, in a suggestive if debatable sociological parallel, goes so far as to discover baroque 'procedures' in the very movement of capital: for example, in the 'monumentalization of detail' typical of fragmented, disintegrated, unmitigated wage-labour.[9] Just as Baudelairean spleen expresses 'the entombment of the transcendental subject of historical consciousness',[10] the great baroque metaphor of the death's head is 'the product of a historical process'. This is why the loss of aura – its feminine symptom – chiefly refers to a loss of historical illusions: 'Lack of illusions and decline of the aura are identical phenomena.'

Thus, in his article on surrealism, Benjamin draws out the links between theoretical pessimism in the face of history and the need to refound 'materialist' political thinking that engages with the imaginary. 'To organize pessimism means nothing other than to expel moral metaphor from politics and to discover in political action a sphere reserved one hundred percent for images [*hundertprozentigen Bildraums*].'[11] This space of images is the one attained in intoxication, writing, and the space between the sensible and the conceptual which unsettles established frontiers. But how are we to explain this transgressive power of imagery in *Erfahrung*?

In fact, this transgressive inscription of a pure image-space into politics refers us to Benjamin's diagnosis of modernity and its political effects. In a fragment of the *Passagen-Werk*, he relates the decline of aura to the *petrification* of the imagination: 'The decline of aura and the petrification of imaginative representation [*Verkümmerung der Phantasievorstellung*] of a better nature are one and the same thing.'[12] Such petrification, as much sexual as political, evokes the parallel between working class and sexuality which is outlined in the magnificent image of the labyrinth: 'This petrification is due to the defensive position of the working class in the class struggle. For this reason the decline of aura and the decline of sexual potency are ultimately one and the same thing.'[13]

As a strategy for awakening from this petrification of all social and unconscious imagination, Benjamin lays stress on the powers to transgress and 'revolutionize' this image world. Such powers, he argues, could make it possible to transform political practices by giving them a potential energy or messianic intensity, within an auraless world condemned to 'profane illumination'. The imagination, as a visualization of the unconscious, is fundamentally ambivalent: destructive and constructive. On the destructive side, petrification – the petrified unrest of allegory – is 'a historical matter' involving the traces of all the 'violences of antiquity and Christianity that have been blocked in their conflict'.[14] As to anticipation of the future, Benjamin relates it to art but also to a certain logic of images present, for example, in fashion. 'It is well known that art *anticipates in images* the reality of perception . . . . Fashion has a more constant, more precise contact with things that are going to happen, thanks to *the incomparable flair of women for what is already at work in the future*.'[15] Thus fashion is 'a secret signal of things that are imminent'. Who knows how to decipher it?

Women's power over images, the staging of female bodies in the imaginaries of allegory or the protest against modernity, re-discovery of a bisexuality of writing, radical anthropological experience in the various utopianisms and modes of transgressing the normative division between feminine and masculine: all these new territories foreign to the 'historicist' reason of progress, all these 'primal historical forms' recaptured by 'dialectical images' which bridge the past and now-time, define the 'Ariadne's thread' of the labyrinth. And this 'pure space of images' proves to be an anthropological space which opens up experience to a time outside the space of historians or the linearity of meaning.

The 'utopia' of the feminine, in all its interpretative excess, might represent this intertwining of time, images and bodies in profane illumination. Benjamin 'knew' this with an unconscious knowledge – the knowledge of the labyrinth which guides his archaeological reconstruction of certain imaginaries of the modern and of its feminine allegories. There is an echo here of another voice, another heroic and irrational untimeliness of which Benjamin was fond. It is the voice of Nietzsche in the mouth of Dionysus:

Be wise, Ariadne! . . .
You have little ears, you have ears like mine:
let some wisdom into them! –
Must we not first hate ourself if we are to love ourself?
I am thy labyrinth.[16]

But Ariadne now knows that she is not wise, and she no longer welcomes wise words. At the heart of the labyrinth lies quite a different question. What does woman want?

Notes

1. See especially 'The Work of Art in the Age of Mechanical Reproduction'.
2. 'Some Motifs in Baudelaire', p. 141.
3. *GS* V, p. 72.
4. 'Some Motifs in Baudelaire', p. 148.
5. On this feminization of the divine, see Scholem, *The Kabbalah and Its Symbolism*, pp. 105ff.
6. Quoted in Scholem, 'Walter Benjamin and His Angel', p. 57.
7. *The Origin of German Tragic Drama*, p. 176.
8. On this notion of the figural, see Lyotard, *Discours-Figure*; and Gilles Deleuze, *Francis Bacon: Logic of Sensation*, Cambridge, Mass: MIT Press 1992.
9. *GS* V, p. 462.
10. This notion is taken up, in quite a different perspective, in Ferruccio Masini, *Dialettica dell'ebbrezza: Walter Benjamin, Tempo, storia, linguaggio*, Rome: Riuniti.
11. 'Surrealism', p. 238.
12. *GS* V, p. 457.
13. Ibid.
14. Ibid., p. 483.
15. Ibid., p. 112.
16. Friedrich Nietzsche, *Dithyrambs of Dionysus*, bilingual edition, Redding Ridge: Black Swan 1984, p. 59.

8

APPENDIX: VIENNESE FIGURES OF OTHERNESS

Femininity and Jewishness

> The only fear is of non-being, Nothingness, Evil;
> of madness, oblivion, discontinuity;
> of *woman*, of the double.
>
> Otto Weininger, *Über die letzten Dinge*

Discontinuity here breaks out in the form of the most radical and dangerous otherness – woman – and arouses the limitless fear stemming from self-hatred in which madness, the double and nothingness combine their evil powers. The *feminine* is thus directly indicated as a space of projections and phantasms, a mythical and allegorical corpus where other disclaimed differences, including Jewishness, take their place. For Weininger 'the woman' and 'the Jew', in their similarities and differences, make up the very spirit of modernity. 'Judaism is the spirit of modern life. Sexuality is accepted, and contemporary ethics sing the praises of pairing. . . . Our age is not only the most Jewish but the most feminine.'[1] An age, one might say, of nameless people 'without qualities'. For Weininger believes that fundamentally 'women have no name': like Kundry in Wagner's *Parsifal* or Lulu in Wedekind's play, they simply pile up forenames shaped by male desire: Eva, Nelli, Mignon. As *Namenlose*, they are excluded from the symbolic and are therefore 'without an essence', 'without identity', 'without a soul', 'non-logical' – a non-subject possessed by the omnipotence of its sexuality, 'amoral' and 'anti-social', 'ignorant of the State', prisoners of a libido of evil.

Such too is the figure of Jewishness which Weininger constructs not in the terms of biological or sociological anti-semitism, nor of actually existing Jews, but on the basis of a philosophical, 'Platonic' Idea. It is a Jewishness entirely permeated by femininity: 'Judaism is saturated with femininity, with precisely those qualities the essence of which I have shown to be in the strongest opposition to the male nature.'[2] Jews are thus judged in the name of a veritable *ontology of masculinity* which seeks to restore idealist and neo-Kantian values, to oppose the Nietzschean will to power with the 'will to value'. Jewishness, like femininity, is the negative reverse side of the virility inscribed within Western philosophy.

Weininger goes on to draw a series of further parallels between Jews and women. They do not know the need for property in the strong sense: for the assimilation of the soil in the form of individual landed property. Nor do they have any understanding of the nature of the State – hence their propensity to anarchism and communism. They lack 'personality', 'dignity', 'a soul' (a very Christian entity), or even 'immortality'. They are not so much anti-moral as 'amoral', inhabiting the family space of the reproduction of the species rather than living the free individuality of the 'Ego'.

This whole logic of exclusion evokes the precise origin of Weininger's discourse in his 'self-hatred' as a converted Jew and his dread of feminized sexuality. There is more than a touch of delirium in his discussion of sexuality. Trapped in the fused undifferentiation of bodies, femininity is incapable of separation and individuation. 'Woman is *only* sexual.' Sexuality 'is diffused over her whole body, so that stimulation may take place almost from any part'.[3] Happy in her polymorphous, narcissistic perversity, woman remains at the body-to-body level of a precocious generalized sexuality, and yet she is also dominated by the idea of coupling and the identification of the male with the phallus! Such femininity, with its frenzy of the body, is constructed in the image of Jewishness, and vice versa. For Jews who do not know themselves are similarly dominated by the idea of coupling. 'Always more absorbed by sexual matters than the Aryan' (!), the Jew has an 'organic disposition towards match-making' rather than 'marriages for love'. The metaphors are meant to be taken literally. As all sexual pairing tends to efface the boundaries of bodies and individuals, '*the Jew, par excellence, is the breaker down of limits*', the very figure of wandering non-citizenship.[4]

In contrast to aristocratic difference with its pathos of distance, the Jew represents for Weininger a false otherness in which distancing does not take place. He effaces and transgresses the frontiers between states, sexes or religions, and between the categories of thought that a philosophy of values seeks to maintain and reaffirm. In this blurring of boundaries, Weininger therefore detects a whole *space of ambiguity or ambivalence*: 'The psychological contents of the Jewish mind are always double or multiple. There are always before him two or many possibilities . . . He can never make himself one with anything.'[5]

In this way the effect of Weininger's text might be reversed. For if theoretical anti-semitism feeds off blatant, anti-egalitarian difference, a quite different status appears in the 'positive', dangerous and transgressive, difference which goes beyond the boundaries of subjects and the divisions of knowledge. This arouses in Weininger a fear so primeval that he goes so far as to identify coitus with murder. The confrontation with Judaism and femininity thus traps him in extremes which need to be interpreted, in the Freudian sense of the term.

The parallelism of woman and Jew appeared in fin-de-siècle Vienna *simultaneously* with a philosophical anti-feminism derived from Schopenhauer and a diversified culture of anti-semitism.[6] These were all commonplaces in the late nineteenth century and the early part of the twentieth. With regard to the status of the body as an object of love/hate throughout Western history, we find the opposition noted by Adorno and Horkheimer between the 'well-known, written history' of progress and rationalization, and an 'underground history' consisting in 'the fate of the human instincts and passions which are displaced and distorted by civilization'.[7] There is nothing surprising in the fact that national socialism disclosed the 'relationship between written history and the dark side' by means of these two figures of a denied and persecuted otherness. Thus in *Mein Kampf* women's emancipation is 'a Jewish invention' and 'the Jew steals our women through the forces of sexual democracy'. Jews and women (as emancipated Other), representing by turns defilement, hybridity, 'impurity' and the myth of a dangerous sexual prepotency, are completely alien to the 'male order' (*der Männerbund*) of the state and its death-dealing logic. For his part the Nazi ideologue Alfred Rosenberg, in *The Myth of the Twentieth Century*, evoked the order of the Teutonic Knights, the Templars and the Jesuits: 'A state model, a racial, social or ecclesiastical model, rests almost exclusively upon the discipline of a male order.'[8]

In reality, however, the parallel between femininity and Judaism did not operate only on the right. A positive variant, drawn in quite different terms, can also be found on the left: in Minna Cauer, for example, who wrote in 1908 that '*women*, the working classes and *Jews* are the oppressed of our century'. This lucid idea, which opens up a critique of oppression and exclusion, can be found under many pens, from Simone de Beauvoir to Adorno: 'Women and Jews bear the mark of an age-old exclusion from power.' It is as if critical discourse here managed to gather together in a single existential minority/majority all the figures of denied and destroyed otherness. But why, in what way, are Jewish and female otherness related to each other?

If the *Sex and Character* which so fascinated Kraus or Musil is at once an 'anti-utopia' (Ernst Bloch), a 'laboratory of modernity' and even 'a reactionary modernism' (Jacques Le Rider), is it not precisely because the figures of femininity and Jewishness are caught in an *irreducible ambiguity* which Weininger's philosophical project and his 'subject position' offer for interpretation? This ambiguity, or even ambivalence, operates entirely around the law, the 'frontier' and the 'limit' – a fact which did not escape Freud's cutting observation. 'In him [Weininger],' he wrote, 'the castration complex forms the link between Jew and woman.'

The play which *Sex and Character* makes with a certain status of 'limits', 'differentiation' or 'boundaries' has to do with Weininger's philosophical project as such: namely, to answer the challenges of Viennese 'crisis culture', and particularly the Nietzschean critique of the nihilist devaluation of values. It is hard to imagine today what Nietzsche meant for a whole generation. Stefan Zweig tells us in his memoirs: 'Under our desks we read Nietzsche and Strindberg.'[9] And as to Robert Musil, who never ceased to see Nietzsche as the man of a thousand new possibilities, he writes in his journal: 'Fate: that Nietzsche first came into my hands when I was exactly eighteen years old.'[10] Weininger did not escape that fate and tried to come up with a response. He wrote of man, for example: 'The most profound thing in him which distinguishes him from the animal is, in my view, *not the will to power but the will to value*.'

Weininger saw himself as opposing both Nietzsche and the empirio-criticism of Mach, which emptied the Subject of all substance and qualities ('the ego cannot be saved') and reduced the Object to a bundle of facts, as well as the drama of *Peer Gynt*, which he took as the archetype of desubjectivization.[11] Against this, Weininger called for a 'return to Kant', via the neo-Kantianism of his times and various Platonist mediations – a return to the theoretically and existentially neuralgic point of the ego, of self-identity. Weininger, then, sought to reconstruct a logic and ethic of identity, a new variant of a metaphysics of the ego centred on a veritable ontology of the masculine. Between Being and Nothingness lay an ontologically grounded inequality of the sexes: 'Women have no existence and no essence; they are not, they are nothing. Mankind occurs as male or female, as something or nothing.' In other words, if women do exist then men *are no longer*.

The extreme contradictoriness of this project, due to the character of the Viennese 'crisis culture', explains a large part of Weininger's ambivalence. For that very same crisis of values, so apparent in the novels of Musil and Broch, manifested itself as the crisis of a whole philosophy and epistemology stemming from the

Aufklärung. Modelled on the idea of progress, it actually rested upon a series of dichotomies affecting the 'differences' between subject and object, between positivistically justified knowledge and the untruth of illusion, between the representable and an emergent sphere of non-representability, between the masculine and the feminine. The collapse of these divisions opened the door to a whole zone of ambiguity and ambivalence irreducible to traditional logic and ethics – a zone which would be the archaeological base of Freud's discoveries. And as always in Western culture – from the Dionysiac through the Baroque to nineteenth-century utopianism – ambiguity entered into an alloy with the feminine.

Sexual difference could thus no longer be contained within the universalist Enlightenment paradigm of the 'human race', which consistently denied a 'specifically feminine' element. But the insertion of such difference into biologically defined nature also constituted a problem. The result: *a feminization of culture*, of its values and imaginaries, which undermined from within established male identities and filiations and exploded their virile certainties. Hence Weininger's dread of the lack of a reference centre, without which affects multiply until the possibility of communication is lost. This entire culture, despite or because of its oppressive social morality, now found itself facing what Simmel called 'female culture' (*die weibliche Kultur*), as opposed to the culture of the object and objectification.

If Weininger, up to his suicide in 1903, occupied himself so intensely with this boundary work, this dizziness of anxiety and guilt within a problematic 'male' subject, was it not because the status of the boundary unified Jewishness and femininity at the same blind point? For Weininger was a true *effacer of limits*, like his own figures of the 'Jew' and 'woman', and a *producer of new limits*, in the most radical and contradictory manner imaginable.

Obsessed with the feminization of culture, Weininger never ceased to proclaim that femininity and masculinity were only ideal types and not empirical realities. Thus, in opposition to the biologistic discourse of a Moebius, he stressed the impossibility of a radical *break* between female and male. Indeed, he argued that every human being is bisexual: 'There is neither man nor woman, but male and female'; 'all actual organisms have both homosexuality and heterosexuality'.[12] This structural bisexuality related to a real *anthropological revolution* shaking the crisis culture, one which, in France as in Vienna, crystallized in the return of the myth of the androgyne. Whether desexualized or oversexualized, the androgyne served as the mythical matrix for the whole post-Baudelairean 'decadent imaginary' of fin-de-siècle France, from

Redon to Gustave Moreau and J.K. Huysmans. But it is also to be found in Musil's great 'modern myth' of the incestuous utopia that tied Agathe to Ulrich as Isis to Osiris.[13]

In the language of myth or concepts, the nineteenth-century obsession with bisexuality is inseparable from the feminization of culture which deconstructed traditional roles and identities and liberated forces of the unconscious. It is expressed in those 'sexually intermediate forms' of which Weininger spoke, and also of course in homosexuality. This explains why Weininger, that 'Jewish' effacer of limits, struck out with a ferocity that entranced Karl Kraus at civilized morality and the kind of orthopaedia which unified and shackled 'sexually intermediate forms' and induced the 'hysterical duplicity' of woman. Whatever may have been the relationship of Weininger to Fliess and Freud, and regardless of the ensuing accusations of plagiarism, it must be recognized that his thought contains a dimension of ambivalence and bisexuality which brings into play an active, or even transgressive, feminine principle. And yet, he continually affirms the difference between the sexes in a combative ontological fashion, carrying it right up to a deadly hatred of sexuality and the female otherness of desire. What holds fast, then, if not that minute difference, that slight asymmetry, which does not spare Freud and will make 'psychoanalysis ill with bisexuality', to use the expression of Wladimir Granoff?[14]

Weininger enunciates with perfect clarity this tiny qualitative difference. Admittedly all beings are bisexual, but although 'man can become woman', 'woman cannot become man', except by masculinizing herself in a repulsive psychic feminism based on egalitarian principles. Hence there is no real psychic androgyny, and bisexuality remains 'conceptually composite'. For at the very place where otherness makes itself strong, dangerous and transgressive, it provokes the greatest male resistance. Like many others, Weininger finds an escape route: woman will be sexually omnipotent but ontologically null, a Nothingness. It cannot be denied, however, that the Nothingness is itself quite formidable, permanently oscillating between non-being and a 'mystical' and always feminized erotics of *jouissance*.

Having caught sight of sexual difference, Weininger responds with that German dream of *Natur-Natur* which Granoff analyses in relation to Freud. In her continual body-to-body clinching, woman will ignore separation and frontiers because she is nothing other than mother – unless she is courtesan and whore!

The feminine is truly present as this blind task in which differences and contradictions abolish each other through a kind of fusion prior to any representation of castration. In Ibsen's *Peer Gynt*,

Weininger finds again his problem and his ideal: the so ardently desired identification of Aase and Solweig, woman in love and mother, in a single redemptive vision of woman. For 'the mother is the permanent root of the species, the never-ending *rhizome*, the foundation from which man detaches himself as an individual.' The rhizome – underground stem, bulb and tuber – is thus the permanent principle of connection and heterogeneity, an anti-genealogy; it is the proliferating multiplicity where any point can be placed in contact with any other.[15] The truth of Weininger's feminine is rhizomal: a foundation (*Grund*) which is an abyss (*Abgrund*), a nothingness of anguish and proximity. Man tries to detach himself from this vital rhizome in order to be *an* individual, but not woman. And man here includes 'the Jew', however feminized and haunted by coupling.

It is at this point of resistance and blindness that the parallelism of femininity and Jewishness finally breaks down, giving way to an unstable, almost invisible frontier. The Jew who has 'overcome' his Jewishness and 'become a Christian' (like Jesus) may indeed 'be regarded by the Aryan in his individual capacity'.[16] Despite everything, Judaism has thus not completely broken with a spiritual (if inferior) element, whereas woman is totally devoid of one. If femininity and Jewishness resemble each other in their masochism ('neither believe in themselves'), they nevertheless differ in terms of belief: woman 'believes in others . . . in her children', while the non-religious Jew 'believes in nothing', 'is frivolous and jests about anything'.[17]

A symbolic element finally separates femininity and Jewishness. Curiously enough, Weininger's reference here to Bachofen's concept of symbolic 'paternity' links him to the Freud of *Totem and Taboo* and *Moses and Monotheism*. After all, the passage from 'matriarchy' (dominated by the sensible world, nature and the action of a feminine, maternal principle) to patriarchy, law and a monotheism which 'dematerializes God' is seen as a conquest of spirituality.[18] But on this symbolic frontier – the frontier of castration – Weininger and Freud part company. Weininger hesitates for ever because he feels the frontier to be dangerous and destructive, an object of deadly hate and guilt. Freud, more 'Jewish' than 'Christian', finds in it the 'power of thinking' (Spinoza) and therefore the lifting of all prohibition on the knowledge of sex. And that remains true even though woman remains 'dangerous' in her desire by signifying for man his own castration – a signification which grounds all real otherness.

Frontiers, no frontiers: this subtle game seems to indicate a place, a law, where German-language thinkers of Jewish origin reflected on their relationship to femininity and women. The ones who actually cross the frontier are those who take the risk of 'becoming woman' and find a truth of fiction in the imaginaries of the feminine: for example, Arthur Schnitzler, in his 'flight into the shadows'. Others, such as Weininger or Hofmannsthal, catch sight of the frontier and deny it in the attraction of the maternal and the fear of castration. Or, in the case of Freud, the frontier is endlessly skirted, put to work, as the basis for a new knowledge and a dark continent.

In this frontier game, Vienna was truly the 'city of four psychologies' which, as Musil writes in his journal, had 'fallen from heaven with its opera'.[19] A modern myth in its raw state. And if all myth is inscribed somewhere in the real novel or phantasm of the subject, it should be added that a position of female desire may encounter another history of cruelty, albeit at the price of imaginary identifications: a history of 'Jewishness' in which the archaic and the modern, the document of culture and the barbarism of the age, have definitively marked the Saturnian face of our history. For our history has always been completely intolerant of ambiguity, of *any* genuine otherness, and for that reason it remains intolerable.

Notes

1. Otto Weininger, *Sex and Character*, authorized translation from the sixth German edition, London: Heinemann 1910, p. 329. [This 'authorized' translation has been used throughout this chapter, although where phrases in the French edition have no equivalent in the English, they have been directly translated without a reference. *Trans. note.*]

   The present chapter, which first appeared in *L'Écrit du temps*, 5, 1983, is part of a longer paper, 'Culture de la crise et mythes du féminin', delivered at a colloque organized by the WIF in Salzburg in December 1983 on *Women and Fascisms in Europe*. On Weininger, see Jacques Le Rider, *Le cas Otto Weininger: Racines de l'antiféminisme et de l'antisémitisme*, Paris: PUF 1982.
2. *Sex and Character*, pp. 146–7.
3. Ibid., p. 91.
4. See the whole of chapter XIII of *Sex and Character*: 'Judaism'. This question of the relationship between femininity and Jewishness, to which we have alluded in our discussion of Benjamin, requires investigation that goes far beyond the limits of this chapter. It is one of the main axes in Eugène Enriquez, *De la horde à l'État: Essai de psychanalyse du lieu social*, Paris: Gallimard 1983, particularly of chapter 4 on Nazi anti-semitism.
5. *Sex and Character*, pp. 323–4.
6. On the crisis of liberal hegemony in Vienna and the rise of anti-semitism, see Léon Poliakov, *The History of Anti-Semitism*, vol. 4, *Suicidal Europe, 1870–1933*, Oxford: OUP 1984; and especially Carl E. Schorske, *Fin-de-siècle Vienna*, New York: Alfred Knopf 1980. We should recall that during this period Vienna was the only European capital to have given power to an openly anti-semitic list in municipal elections.

7. See the section entitled 'Importance of the Body' in Theodor Adorno and Max Horkheimer, *Dialectic of Enlightenment*, London: Verso 1979, pp. 231–6.
8. On all these points, see Rita Thalmann, *Être femme sous le IIIᵉ Reich*, Paris: R. Laffont 1981.
9. Stefan Zweig, *The World of Yesterday: An Autobiography*, London: Cassell 1943, p. 40.
10. Robert Musil, *Tagebücher, Aphorismen, Essays und Reden*, ed. Adolf Frisé, Hamburg: Rowohlt 1955, p. 37.
11. See Otto Weininger, *Über die letzen Dinge*, Vienna 1904.
12. *Sex and Character*, p. 48.
13. See chapter 10 below.
14. See Wladimir Granoff, *La Pensée et le féminin*, Paris: Minuit 1976.
15. See Gilles Deleuze and Félix Guattari, *Rhizome*, Paris: Minuit 1976.
16. *Sex and Character*, p. 312.
17. Ibid., p. 321.
18. See Freud, 'Totem and Taboo', in the *Complete Psychological Works*, vol. 13, London: Hogarth 1955, p. 144; and 'Moses and Monotheism', in ibid., vol. 23, London 1964, p. 131.
19. Musil, *Tagebücher*, p. 351. The 'four psychologies' are doubtless those of Bühler, Adler, Weininger and Freud.

PART THREE
BAROQUE REASON

G. Moreau, L'Apparition, Musée Gustave Moreau. © *Photo R.M.N.*

9

AN AESTHETICS OF OTHERNESS

For the state, woman is night, or more precisely sleep: man is waking.
She seems to do nothing: she is always the same, a relapse into healing
nature. In her the future generation dreams. Why has civilization not
become feminine? Despite Helen, despite Dionysus.[1]

It was thus through Nietzsche, at a moment in history when the
great certainties of the modernist philosophies of Progress were
crumbling (Reason, Subject, linear Time, Science of a transparent
reality), that something suddenly burst back into labyrinthine
existence. An obsessive question already delineated the pain of an
absence, of something incommunicable. Why has civilization not
become female?

It was certainly a strange question, condemned to repetition
without memory. Today, after years of permissiveness and feminization of values, the normalized but ever floating and contested
division between 'masculine' and 'feminine' is again being ques-
tioned with the same radical intensity as in every crisis culture.
Whether the division is held to be biological, social or cultural, it is
visibly inscribed within customs and laws. But it is also an uncertain,
phantasmic division, more insidious and invisible, which is troubled
by the unconscious and woven out of all the imaginaries, all the
anthropological utopias of a 'third sex' or of constitutive androgyny.
There, as Nietzsche puts it, woman is 'night' or 'nothing'. A space of
projection and allegory mingles together the seduction of Helen,
the deadly powers of a dangerous otherness, and the proteiform
androgyny of Dionysus.

But this night is one of potential desire and pleasure [*jouissance*],
the night of an abyss which makes things visible. It is a baroque
night – mystical perhaps. For it concerns that non-representable
nothing which has perpetually haunted Western philosophy as its
'oriental' Other, its limit, its difference. To this stage femininity has
continually been summoned. Weininger, of course, is quite blunt
about it: 'fundamentally women have no name'. But others too,
from remote times, say the same thing in a more mythical way: in
Hesiod, for example, the first woman is already nameless. She is

excluded from the symbolic: with no name, no identity, no being; lacking both essence and existence.

In this missing being of the subject, of desire and its language, woman seems relegated to negative theology, where the nothing that cannot be figured or rationally conceived leaves her with neither language nor voice in the void of a *jouissance* of complete fusion. Is she that word-absence, that word-hole which, like Marguerite Duras's *Lol. V. Stein*, can by turns captivate us or condemn us to the 'sickness unto death', to the stray multiplication of names modelled on the desire of the Other?

Through being so closely linked to nothing – to the primal chaos of nature or desiring passivity – the feminine hangs in suspense in that ambiguous, neuralgic zone occupied by Nothing in the Western tradition. In this respect, the difference is very great with those currents of oriental philosophy (Taoism, for example) where Nothing and the void are dynamic, active elements. If it is accepted as a basic principle, with concrete representations such as the valley, the empty Nothing situates and condenses 'the nodal point woven from potentiality and becoming, where lack and plenitude, the Same and the Other, coincide'.[2] This vast shape of the void, so reminiscent of Lucretius, which Chinese painting constantly seeks to recreate as a body of colour ('the void is not nothing, the void is colour'), is accepted by the dominant traditions of Western thought only if it is transcended in a stable Being or Creator or, at a later date, in the reflexivity of the Concept as a contradictory otherness productive of a totalizing meaning.

This accounts for the strange reversal in the figures of Nothing. On the one hand, nothing is nothing. Nothingness has no property, quality or identity. Because it cannot be represented or made an object of thought, even if it conditions all thought, Nothing manifests itself only in the most intellectualized or mediated forms: as irony, doubt or negativity in the service of mastery. But on the other hand, Nothing is all. By a kind of heretical-mystical and then baroque conversion, this 'nothing of being' changes into an infinity of ecstatic delight [*jouissance*], a plethora of forms. Consider, for example, the rush of angels in the great baroque paintings of the seventeenth century. Here the angels' aura forces us to look, to lift our eyes, to desire the impossible spiral of an ascending desire foredoomed to the earthly representation of appearances – an *erotics of nothing*. Or take that marvellous text of Saint Denis the Areopagite, which defined for both East and West the matrix of all negative theologies, the point of departure for what Michel de Certeau calls the 'mystical fable'. Since God is absolute and

unknowable Superessence, beyond all properties, essence or difference, he *is not*, or he is Nothing. Love, the chimerical point of
fusion in the enjoyment [*jouissance*] of the divine, is attained
through Nothing, through the mysticism of otherness and the falling
away of everything in the most luminous shadow of silence.

But if the feminine is kept too long in the toils of Nothing, one
ends up with that long and persistent absence: 'civilization has not
become feminine'. Thus the feminine has never ceased to oscillate
between the nothing of nothingness and the nothing of *jouissance*,
between non-representable Nothing which eludes all form (shape-
lessness, chaos, lack, matter, matrix) and the nothing of the 'female
side of God' (Lacan) or the super-*jouissance* allotted to women ever
since Teiresias. At no time, however, has the feminine found a
place within the exclusive egalitarian paradigms of the Subject.
Without an identity or symbolism of its own, it appears from the
beginning as that madness of the body in which the powers of Helen
are combined with those of Dionysus; later, it attains the wild *corps
à corps* of sixteenth-century poetry, or enters the seventeenth-
century theatre of baroque derangement of appearances that was
rediscovered by Baudelaire and Benjamin.

In rousing the intellectual and moral resistance of more than two
millennia of nihilist metaphysics, Nietzsche placed this symbolic
elision of the feminine under the dual sign of Dionysus and Helen,
two traversers of frontiers and languages facing a *polis*-state that
affirmed itself in a community of values. Again as early as Hesiod,
the feminine shifts over to the side of that 'beautiful evil' which
knows not the State. Dionysus, that polymorphously perverse god
of wine, ecstasy and theatre, of suffering and play, represents
precisely an 'anti-system' in the history of the Greek *polis*;[3] or, we
might say, the condensation point of all the metamorphoses and
border-crossings – between animality and humanity, consciousness
and the unconscious, male and female, the *polis* and its margins of
the foreign and mysterious. A savage hunter and eater of raw flesh,
Dionysus summons women from the private space of their conjugal
home. In the forest that appeared so primitive in comparison with
the *polis*, he seems akin to the figure of the Amazon queen
Penthesileia, a virgin so filled with desire that she fell into madness
and the eating of flesh. Although he was often held to be an alien, or
at least an 'Easterner' from other climes, Dionysus was also the
woman-god who orgiastically changed sex and the child-god of
reemergent life who played in the mirror.

A single theatrical space stretches from Dionysus to Helen, the
first mythical figure of all the eternal feminines. Carried off by Paris,
Helen is the symbol of Beauty and appearance, of ornament and

falsehood: she is the 'artistic power' or 'differend' on account of whom the space of war pits men and cities against one another. For she truly embodies that 'tyranny of the Logos' which Gorgias vaunts in his *Encomium of Helen*. If speech clings to passion and turns itself into a magical elixir of love, it is diverted from its real function of establishing communication and ethical consensus in the *polis* and within the realm of philosophy. It is then no more than formidable persuasion (*peithô*), not that fusion of rationality and power, that logic of identity propositions (X is A) which philosophically regulates the political community. Helen is defeated. But she is also innocent, since love binds itself to the look and body of the Other: 'So if Helen's eye, pleased by Alexander's body, transmitted an eagerness and striving of love to her mind, what is surprising?'[4]

Thus if civilization has not become female, despite Helen and Dionysus, theatre and sophistics, this is because language as dialogic consensus begins with a double murder, an elision of othernesses: murder of the multiform body of Dionysus, none of whose shapes can be fixed, identified or comprehended; and murder of the body-sex of Helen as the site of *polemos* or war. In the protean nature of Dionysus, or in the desire-filled, non-veracious plenitude of a body-form which cleaves to itself even in its act of appearing, we therefore see something quite different from the traditional dualist opposition between form and formless matter through which the male–female division operated in Plato and Aristotle.

This proliferation of unfixable forms generating non-identity logics constitutes a permanent deformation of the reality hollowed out by the void. It returns as a kind of repressed content in Western philosophical conceptions of form, haunting the very aracana of modernity in its allegories of the feminine. In Joachim du Bellay's *Olive* of 1550, for example, the parallel between man-god and deified woman already suggests an imperceptible slippage from the Godhead to the profane Deity. And what should we say of the Uranus figure in the scientific poems of Jacques Pelletier? A reincarnation of Dante's Beatrice, Uranus here holds all the secrets of the science of the heavens and atmospheric phenomena. In all this sixteenth-century poetry, the feminine is the site of knowledge where all the metamorphoses magically operate – witness the 'long and varied changes' that Ronsard attributes to Venus, or the rose-body of Mary that was sung of so much and so quickly lost. It is as if lovers' bodies acquired vegetable or mineral properties, linking up with the great cycle of Nature.

To be sure, the baroque poetry or theatre of the Counter-Reformation abandoned the pagan cosmology of the Renaissance.

But the endlessly martyrized or sublimated bodies are still there in excess, until the outer limits are reached in that hallucinatory aesthetic which Octavio Paz discovered in the work of Quevedo.[5] Such a theatricization of existence bespeaks a veritable 'hermeneutics of desire' (to use an expression of Michel Foucault), where the scenography of drives subjects bodies to energetic thought which does not allow itself to be enclosed merely within the model of representation. This *figural* power of the stagings of otherness (of the divine, the feminine, or death) makes the invisible visible, giving symbolic form to all the realms of nature and supernature in an infinite play of 'correspondences' in Baudelaire's sense of the term. This play offers itself for interpretation in the rhetorical and stylistic figure where opposites join together: in the oxymoron. Here the 'poetry of mystical paradox' analysed by Jean Rousset displays its infinite stream of 'inaccessible light', 'luminous fog', 'dark brightness', 'enrapturing horror'[6] – which meets up with what we might call a distinctively baroque *aesthetic of otherness and amorous paradox*. This marks a discontinuity vis-à-vis the cognitive, dialectical or even ethical otherness of Plato, Hegel and Kant/ Lévinas respectively; it thereby rejoins the Kantian notion of the sublime as informal form exhibiting the incommensurability of the heterogeneous Other.[7]

For if all knowledge proceeds through identification (Adorno) or assimilation (Lévinas), it can only effect a neutralization of the Other to the advantage of the Same of traditional ontology. And if all genuine otherness appears only on the ground of a non-synthetic, non-assignable element which destabilizes ego-identity, if it is truly 'forcible entry' or 'wonder', then perhaps it unfolds on a stage other than that of mere ethics and the salvation of the Law. The erotic relation, as paralogical logic or amorous 'paradox', would then be that backless backdrop characteristic of the 'modern' aesthetics of the baroque. Hence its special reception for the otherness of otherness, for the 'quality of difference' which, according to Lévinas, is the hallmark of the feminine.[8] It should be stressed, however, that this is not the feminine of modesty, mystery and motherhood, but one which is caught up in the surplus materiality of bodies, in an excitation which cracks appearances and consigns them to that deformation and transfiguration of which Deleuze speaks in connection with Francis Bacon.[9] In this 'germ of tranquil atheism' which marks the seventeenth-century Baroque, the figure is already subject to the order of accident, changeability, precariousness and mortality.

The idea of 'progress' in modernity is governed by the plenitude of reality: the plenitude of the 'great classical form', of a fulfilled meaning of history corresponding to reality, of Truth as a system and of the Subject as identity and centre. In opposition to this, the baroque presents from the beginning quite a different, 'postmodern' conception of reality in which the instability of forms in movement opens onto the reduplicated and reduplicable structure of all reality: enchanted illusion and disenchanted world, *engaño* and *desengaño*, to repeat Quevedo's great metaphor of the woman-city which opened this book.

Rousset sees the essence of the baroque in this 'interpenetration of forms within dynamically unified ensembles animated by dialectical movement'.[10] This evokes a *startling* interlacement – startling in the strong sense of surprise or chance à la Gracian – of Eros and thought, allegory and an 'untimely' understanding of history. If, in the baroque, history becomes a representation (see Benjamin), representation is itself subject to dramatization or theatricization of the sensible world in a backward movement towards a missing centre, towards that decentred centre which Pascal, the baroque thinker *par excellence*, placed at the heart of his scientific and religious paradigm. In this world with no centre, no site, no fixed point of reference, 'the centre is everywhere and the circumference nowhere': 'the fixed point has become a point of view'.[11]

As it becomes impossible to determine finitude and appearances in relation to any identity reference, any essence or substance, we are left with an infinite regress towards a point that is always slipping away, a pure otherness of figure. The regress carries us towards Eros: the seductive, beguiling theatre of bodies induces an active and dynamic image of Eros, through captivation or rapture, ecstasy divine or human. It is also a regress towards or of history: since it cannot be totalized and mastered, history is acted and frustrated against a background of wars and absolute power. It presents itself as a catastrophe which the great disorder of the world, or the cosmic disaster of the end of the world so dear to baroque poets, is alone capable of expressing in metaphor.

In this dual, 'postmodern' regress of reality, the great founding figures of modernity – the Subject, stability of representation, the Centre, Totality – are undermined from within by a logic of extremes, paradox and non-dialectical neutralization of opposites, such as they appear in oxymoronic writing. At the very moment when 'classical science' was establishing itself – a science which, from Galileo to Descartes and even Pascal, was highly critical of the powers of metaphor – poetry and theatre were asserting the claims of universal metaphor. For a time, the world as representation organized by *ratio* coexisted with the world as hieroglyph, when the famous 'metaphor dispute' broke out at the height of the century of classicism. The relations between image and *ratio* were then fixed in terms that are highly revealing for the archaeology of the modern.

On the one side were those like du Perron, Descartes and Mersenne who attacked metaphor in the name of the new science: 'Metaphor is a petty similitude, an abridged similitude; it has to *pass quickly*; one must not linger on it when it is *too constant*; *it is imperfect* and *degenerates into enigma*.'[12] On the other side was Mlle de Gournay, Montaigne's adopted daughter, who defended the poetic and even epistemological powers of metaphor against the moralists of language, and affirmed discordance or excess in the beautiful; for her, metaphor was 'the art of discerning a conformity in opposites'.[13]

As we know, the debate was eventually settled through the withering of metaphor and, above all, the splitting of scientific from poetic language in a process bound up with the collapse of the old cosmos of resemblances and its ontological foundations. However, the classical *episteme* was not thereby definitively unified. The same century which produced the orderly representative paradigm also yielded a theory of allegories or emblems, of generalized theatre bringing into play that which has been 'made metaphorical'. This is certainly a weighty paradox, and some light is indirectly thrown upon it by those who interpret modernity as a 'world image' linked to the appearance of a representative Subject bearing 'science as a project' (Heidegger), or by those who define modernity in terms of *episteme*. As Michel Foucault has written: 'At the beginning of the seventeenth century, during the period that has been termed, rightly or wrongly, the Baroque, thought ceases to move in the element of resemblance.'[14] The baroque itself is inscribed within the structure of representation that we find in Velázquez's *Las Meninas*: the visible refers us to a reverse side, to an invisible that is at once present and absent. But if thought discards the analogic paradigm for the order of signs and representation, perhaps it should be added that one is talking of scientific thought, a certain philosophical *ratio*, the new forms of knowledge. In any case it is not *all* thought: poetry, and indeed the *topos* of the world as theatre, impose their analogical logic of ambivalence and reversal. At the limits of scientific-representative space, the poet even takes on the 'role of allegory'.[15] Beyond the order of signs, he will rediscover the role of correspondences. In fact, Descartes himself inserted baroque disillusion ('*Life is a dream*') at the heart of the classical *ratio*, even if his methodical doubt used it to undo the old relations between similitude and reality.

There is thus a kind of *metaphorical semantics* (in Hans Blumenberg's fine expression[16]) which haunts the representative context itself, reduplicating the archaeology of scientific concepts in one of *figural*, theological or already secular constellations or configurations. If all representation now plays upon a relation of identity and difference, there is also 'another' difference: the difference of the Other. In this respect, we might say of the baroque what Louis Marin wrote of Pascal: 'Pascal keeps intact the representative model which he *makes metaphorical* outside its own domain. Pascal draws representation into the infinite play of difference.'[17]

In opposition to all substantialist ontology (that of Descartes, for instance), Pascal could welcome a thought of *nothing* (scientific vacuum or metaphysical-theological nothingness) and a thought of radical difference. The two come together in the status of the figural, of *figuratives*: 'Figure includes absence and presence, pleasant and unpleasant. Cipher with a double meaning, of which one is clear and says that the meaning is hidden.'[18] Pascal's concept of the figurative is here very close to that 'baroque apotheosis' which, according to Benjamin, takes the form of the blocked dialectic of extremes, dialectic 'at a standstill', frozen in the 'dialectical image'. The logic of an ambivalence which no synthesis can move beyond is inscribed within the very language of difference, of the elsewhere. This language is evidently theological in Pascal, for whom the Name of God is that of the unnameable Other, the true 'degree zero of the proper name' (Louis Marin), the infinite gap and maximum difference which deconstructs the metaphysics of presence, specificity and identitarian appropriation, or even of the subject. For the Pascalian 'subject' is already 'sundered' and consigned to the Other of all its impenetrable simulacra and abysses. It cannot represent itself by reflecting itself in a fixed point, a Centre: it is 'difference without a subject', in Derrida's sense.

But this figural bears *pleasure and displeasure* with regard to the otherness hidden within it. This explains why, in the overembodied universe of the baroque, the almost materialist passion of bodies always oscillates between a cruel, macabre theatre in which the death's head and the corpse prowl around, and an ecstatic and mystical theatre of love in which the sublime and sublimated Eros becomes pure lyricism. Eros and Thanatos, aesthetic of otherness and ontology of precariousness, unfold in a number of allegories, including the all-powerful one of the feminine and its uncertain, bisexual or asexual, double: the Angel. Gérard Genette has shown that 'modern thought perhaps invented the baroque as its mirror'; but it may be that it was a distorting or broken mirror. For if convulsive beauty is the hallmark of times of trouble and distress, the allegorization of the feminine may be said to recur in a kind of *modern baroque* peculiar to the arcana of the twentieth century.

We find confirmation of this in the reversal space where the Romantic Schlegel of *Lucinde* meets up with the 'melancholic' and very Baudelairean Proust of *À la recherche du temps perdu*, through an allegorization of the feminine more and more bereft of aura. For the one there is wonderful, vigorous, utopian, androgynous allegory: 'I see here a wonderful, deeply meaningful allegory of the development of man and woman to full and complete humanity. There is much in it – and what is in it certainly does not rise up as quickly as I do when I am overcome by you.'[19] For the other there is the post-Baudelairean allegory of a petrified feminine:

It was indeed a dead woman that I saw when, presently, I entered her room. She had fallen asleep as soon as she lay down; her sheets, wrapped around her body like a shroud, had assumed, with their elegant folds, *the rigidity of stone*. . . . Seeing that expressionless body lying there, I asked myself what logarithmic table it constituted, that all the actions in which it might have been involved, from the nudge of an elbow to the bruising of a skirt, should be capable of causing me . . . so intense an anguish. . . . And so I remained, in the fur-lined coat which I had not taken off since my return from the Verdurins', beside that twisted body, *that allegorical figure. Allegorizing what? My death? My love?*[20]

Here the fine anarchy of Romantic allegory – Schlegel's 'beautiful chaos of sublime harmonies and interesting pleasures' – has completely broken up. Allegory no longer makes it possible to run through all the degrees of a future humanity in which male and female become alike in a third, androgynous sex; now it figures the death of love and even a death wrapped around in shrouds. The allegory of dissipation and infinite intensity has given way to Quevedo's 'ashes of the sensible' (*serán ceniza mas tendrá sentido*) and 'amorous dust' (*polvo enamorado*).

And yet, the allegorical powers of the feminine hold together and make a comeback that perpetuates a very long history. Already in the first century AD Philo of Alexandria, introducing the Old Testament into philosophy through an allegorical method of symbolic interpretation and exegesis, saw in the biblical Eve the signifying figuration of sense perception. Was 'Adam's offence' not the confusion and division that gripped the mind under the sway of sensory images? It was for this reason that the feminine appeared within a twofold androgynous structure which broke with the feminine as biological genus. Eve is at once woman and female side of man: every human being, qua mind and sense perception, is at once Adam and Eve, within a constitutive androgyny.

The same allegorical power of the feminine as Other is present in the philosophical representation of woman, the *donna gentile* of Dante's verse: 'L'imaginava lei fatta come una donna gentile.' No doubt this is because she has the understanding of love, *l'intelletto d'amore*,[21] and because since Dotima in Plato's *Symposium*, via Boetius and Cicero, philosophy has been a female figure. Derrida once remarked apropos of Nietzsche's idea of truth as woman: 'Perhaps woman – a non-identity, a non-figure, a simulacrum – is distance's very chasm, the out-distancing of distance, the interval's cadence, distance itself, if we could still say such a thing.'[22]

Thus allegory brushes aside all essentiality, all identity or unique-ness, in accordance with its almost etymological nature: the Greek *allegoria* coming from *allos* ('other') and *agoreuein* ('to speak'). For allegory consists precisely in saying something other than what one means, or in saying one thing so that, by oblique procedures, *another* thing will be understood. But this *discourse through the other* is also *discourse of the Other*, a vocalization and staging of an otherness which eludes direct speech and presents itself as an elsewhere. Therefore, before allegory became feminine, it embarked on an indeterminate adventure and set its sights on what slipped away from it: on the Most High God. As Origen wrote: 'There are matters whose significance cannot be duly expounded by any human language.' To this failing of human communicative language – a failing vis-à-vis the Other – allegory lends its figural force, its lack of mediations and explicit correlations, its 'emotional writing'. As the Romans held, it is an *inversio* 'which designates one thing in words and another thing, if not an opposite thing, in meaning' (Quintilian).

That this *inversio*, from Baudelaire to Proust, crystallized the decline of aura says a great deal about the strange introduction of seventeenth-century baroque death into the height of modernity. For *petrification* (the stone body, marble body, fixed and frozen body) is a baroque metaphor *par excellence*: so that in the poems of Le Moyne, the dead Litie is already marble, with 'cold and heavy blood'. Death, as an accident breaking the beautiful continuities of time, strips the disguises of love: 'Such an accident makes of Litie a piece of marble. . . . Fear and pain freeze her spirits.'[23]

Benjamin is thus absolutely right to insist on the novel aspects of modern allegory bound up with the loss of aura, the internalization of death being a writing experience which reintroduces a figural – an *optisch* – into modernity.[24]

Although allegory does not give birth to a style in the nineteenth century, its very reappearance in Baudelaire and its later persist-ence require some fresh consideration – if only to understand the curious *baroque reason* which has been at work in the twentieth century in thinkers as diverse as Benjamin, Barthes and Lacan. One of these, Lacan, has written: 'As someone recently noticed, I am placing myself – who is placing me? . . . – on the side of the baroque.'[25]

'Baroque Reason': the term may appear provocative, so greatly has the explaining [*rendre raison*] of reason obliterated the *plurality* of classical reasons and obscured the baroque as a paradigm of thought and writing which overflows conventional models of identity, essence and substantiality. For those who identify reason with its 'long chains', Cartesian or other, it seems impossible that a *ratio* should be stylistic and rhetorical, that it should be permanently at grips with its theatricization and dramatization, that it should act itself out in 'bodies'. But in the baroque, the reason of the unconscious and the reason of utopia present themselves to be interpreted. The baroque signifier proliferates beyond everything signified, placing language in excess of corporality. At the risk of appearing still more paradoxical, we might say that baroque reason brings into play the *infinite materiality* of images and bodies. And this being so, it always has to do with otherness as desire.

Lacan has written that the Baroque is the 'lesser history of Christ', in which his importance is established 'through his body'. By this Lacan has in mind not only the precariousness of the body in the Christian doctrine of salvation, but also the very modalities of the enjoyment [*jouissance*] of the Other's body. For if the body of Christ assumes importance only through oral incorporation (the Catholic act of communion/devourment as a sublimated oral drive), it is because somewhere the display of the body evokes infinite *jouissance* and thus defines the Baroque: 'Everything is bodily exhibition evoking *jouissance*.'[26] To the exclusion even of the sexual act, obscenity shows itself here at the level of desire – the desire precisely of the All. The same madness presents itself in the *jouissance* of God and of woman: 'The other side of madness is total *jouissance*, imperative and continual; and that appears as woman.'[27] Concentrated here is precisely what Lacan calls 'the female side of God', the intersection of divine and female otherness.

It should be made clear, however, that the bodily *jouissance* of the Other remains trapped in a curious asymmetry. Whereas man aims at the 'phallic' *jouissance* of the sexual organ, woman, who 'is not whole', always has in view the additional *jouissance* of the body as such. In other words, 'regulation of the soul through corporeal scopics' – which defines the Baroque for Lacan – is precisely what woman is concerned with. For in the baroque affinity between thought and Eros, she recognizes herself – I recognize myself – as the work of a difference alien to the metaphysics of identity.

By inserting us into the logic of the phantasm, the baroque leads us into the utopian reason of writing while leaving space for the 'principle of sufficient reason'. In allegorical writing, opposites join up and cancel each other, with no unitary hierarchy of the whole. Reality proliferates in all its dissonant, exuberant details, without the form of the 'grand style' ever being able to contain or dominate it. The resistance of the baroque in the modern world is the resistance of a heterogeneous, alien and inassimilable element, ever incomplete, in which 'deformalized' forms achieve a space of purely qualitative movement: thought of the body, or rather, of the generation of space on the basis of movement, the presence/absence of the corporeal.

Only metaphor and figuration, by radicalizing the fluidity of phenomena, are able to accomplish the destruction of the ontologies of high 'modernity' in which the subject and reality are content or substance. The price for this is noted by Musil in his speech on Rilke: 'The spheres of the categories of being, separate from each other in ordinary thought, no longer seem to form more than a single one.'[28] This reason therefore 'founds languages', and we can understand why Roland Barthes, like Lacan but from a different point of view, saw in the baroque and the pansemic nature of the image, the site of excess meaning, *obtuse* meaning, a signifier without a signified, which governs aesthetic pleasure. The 'baroque region', from Loyola to Fourier, is the one where 'meaning is destroyed beneath symbol' and 'one and the same letter can signify two contraries'.[29] The fact that the 'symbolic' effect of the letter overflows and suspends any logic of meaning accounts for the links between the rhetoric of desire and what Barthes calls '*a baroque semantics*' or '*a topos of the impossible*',[30] always stylistically modelled on the oxymoron: the sun here becomes dark.

In Barthes's analyses of Loyola and Fourier, baroque semantics involves a rejection of the great classical dichotomies, descending from the seventeenth century and the Enlightenment, which counterpose subject and object, real and unreal, masculine and feminine. Baroque semantics presents for interpretation a whole 'hieroglyphics' which operates through the deciphering of series and correspondences between all the realms and forms of the universe. Thus Fourier's construction of '*marvellous reals*' follows the stylistic procedures of the seventeenth-century Baroque:

• Totality is made impossible by the writing of a manifold, multiple-entry text (or picture). 'Language, the field of the signifier, presents relations of insistence, not consistence: centre, weight, meaning are dismissed.'[31]

• The permanent excess which eroticizes 'the real' by staging phantasm 'founds meaning on matter and not on concept'. This materialization or 'corporealization' of the invisible in image issues in the 'imperialism of seeing'.[32]

• Detail, as part of the whole (metonymy), is promoted to become *adorable detail*, the promise of happiness: 'Perhaps the *imagination of detail* is what specifically defines Utopia (opposed to political science); this would be logical, since detail is phantasmatic and thereby achieves the very pleasure of Desire.'[33]

• There is systematic recourse to a problematic of difference and ambiguity. This *topos* of the impossible thus bears upon the difference between the sexes as such. As Fourier wrote: 'In order to confound the tyranny of men there must exist for a century *a third sex*, male and female, stronger than man.'[34] Only this third sex can 'denaturalize' the fixedness of instinct and delineate new epistemological categories of analysis: the space of the neuter, the ambiguous. Fourier's world rehabilitates the ambiguous, which 'is not allowed in our customs', and demands infinite variation of pleasures by asserting their differences. As he writes in *Le Nouveau Monde amoureux*: 'All omnigyny is necessarily sphneistic and every woman a pederast – otherwise these characteristics would lose their pivotal quality which is philanthropy or devotion to the other sex.'[35] One could go on forever listing the powers of this 'neuter' which governs all transitions (from childhood to old age) and brings extremes together. Love, that 'hyper-neuter', blossoms at its outer limits: sapphism, pederasty or even incest. The ambiguous, the ambivalent: there is the qualitative value of Fourier's world 'in harmony', the very possibility of all differences!

Benjamin, Baudelaire, Lacan, Barthes: something like a *baroque paradigm* asserts and establishes itself within 'modernity'. Against any idea of self-enclosed language, any logical metalanguage, this paradigm continually appeals to the same tropes and stylistic procedures: allegory, oxymoron, open totality and discordant detail, the real emptied of its superabundance of reality. This whole rhetoric of affects presents difference as excess and 'obtuse' meaning: an aesthetics, but also an underground site where the baroque paradigm touches the paradigm of desire. It is as if the great modern myths of the 'feminine' (Lulu, Penthesilea, Agathe) simply put that impossible difference on stage. One name sums them all up: Salome.

Notes

1. Friedrich Nietzsche, 'Nachgelassene Fragmente: Herbst 1869 bis Herbst 1872', in *Nietzsche Werke*, vol. III, Berlin: Walter de Gruyter 1978, p. 154.
2. François Cheng, *Vide et plein: Le langage pictoral chinois*, Paris: Seuil 1979,

pp. 21ff. The possibility of identifying man with the void 'is at the origin of the images and shapes' (p. 34), and 'the brushstroke art, *yin-hsien*, is the art of the visible–invisible' (p. 52). This should be considered in relation to Klee's problematic as outlined in Part One above.

3. See Marcel Détienne, *Dionysus Slain*, Baltimore: John Hopkins 1979.
4. Gorgias, *Encomium of Helen*, Bristol: Bristol Classical Press 1982.
5. See, for example, Octavio Paz, *On Poets and Others*, London: Paladin 1992, p. 159.
6. See Jean Rousset, *L'Intérieur et l'extérieur*, Paris: Corti 1976. On all these questions see also Rousset's classic study, *La Littérature de l'âge baroque en France*, Paris: Corti 1970.
7. On the Kantian problematic of the sublime as a display of the non-representable, as energy sign and anticipation of 'postmodernity', see Jean-François Lyotard, *La pittura del segreto nell'epoca postmoderna, Baruchello*, Milan: Feltrinelli 1982; and *The Differend: Phrases in Dispute*, Minneapolis: University of Minnesota 1988, pp. 165ff., where the 'sublime of nature' is seen as something which may be 'without form' (Kant).
8. Emmanuel Lévinas, *Time and the Other*, Pittsburgh: Duquesne University 1987, p. 36. Lévinas's conceptualization of the feminine as 'the very origin of otherness' has given it a central and quite exceptional position in 'the economy of Being'. See ibid., pp. 85–8, and *Ethics and Infinity*, Pittsburgh: Duquesne University 1985, pp. 65ff.
9. See Gilles Deleuze, *Francis Bacon: Logic of Sensation*, Cambridge, Mass: MIT 1992.
10. Rousset, p. 250.
11. See Michel Serres, *Le Système de Leibniz*, vol. 2, Paris: Gallimard 1968, pp. 675ff.
12. On the 'metaphor dispute', see Rousset, op. cit., p. 60.
13. Ibid., p. 63.
14. Michel Foucault, *The Order of Things*, London: Routledge 1991, p. 51.
15. Rousset, p. 63.
16. On the relations between modernity and 'metaphor' or 'world image', see Giacomo Marramao, *Potere e secolarizzazione*, Rome: Riuniti.
17. Louis Marin, *La Critique du discours*, Paris: Minuit 1975. Much more could be said about the links between 'Pascal's semiology' and the 'symptomatology' of the subject in which qualities have no substantive foundation (p. 131), nothingness is difference (p. 133) and everything is figure (pp. 139ff.)
18. Blaise Pascal, *Pensées*, Harmondsworth: Penguin 1966, p. 109.
19. Friedrich Schlegel, *Lucinde*, Minneapolis: University of Minnesota 1971, p. 49.
20. Marcel Proust, *Remembrance of Things Past*, vol. 3, London: Chatto & Windus 1981, pp. 366–7.
21. On allegory in general, and Dante's use of it in particular, see Jean Pépin, *Mythe et allégorie*, Paris: Études augustiniennes 1958; and *La Tradition de l'allégorie de Philon d'Alexandrie à Dante*, Paris: Études augustiniennes 1987. See also Jacqueline Risset, *Dante ou l'Intelletto d'amore*, Paris: Seuil 1982.
22. Jacques Derrida, *Spurs: Éperons*, bilingual edition, Chicago: University of Chicago Press 1979, p. 49.
23. *Anthologie de la poésie baroque française*, ed. Jean Rousset, Paris: Armand Colin 1968, p. 30.
24. Benjamin, 'Central Park', p. 52.

25. Lacan, *Encore*, p. 97.
26. Ibid., p. 102. [On Lacan and *jouissance* see also pp. 43, 50. above. *Trans. note.*]
27. Ibid.
28. Robert Musil, 'Rede zur Rilke-Feier', in *Tagebücher*, p. 893.
29. Roland Barthes, 'The Spirit of the Letter', in idem, *The Responsibility of Forms: Critical Essays on Music, Art, and Representation* [a translation of *L'Obvie et l'obtus*], New York: Hill & Wang 1985, p. 100.
30. Roland Barthes, *Sade, Fourier, Loyola*, London: Jonathan Cape 1977, pp. 99, 118.
31. Ibid., p. 6 [Translation slightly modified.]
32. Ibid., pp. 62–6.
33. Ibid., p. 105.
34. Quoted in ibid., p. 119.
35. Cf. ibid., pp. 106, 115.

10

SALOME, OR THE BAROQUE SCENOGRAPHY OF DESIRE

In a passage of his journal where he discusses his *Man without Qualities*, Musil defines modern myth as follows: 'The novel has been accused of perversity. Answer: the archaic and the schizophrenic are expressed in art in a concordant manner, even though they are totally different. Similarly, incestuous feeling may be perversity and it may be myth. Incidentally: *a modern myth* contains intellectual elements. It involves "a partial solution".'[1]

If it is true that modern myths have a theoretical dimension, if they offer an experience of utopian thought which disaggregates and destabilizes the given by introducing Nothing and the Other, if, that is, their logic is one of divergence or difference from any real of plenitude, then this would rather paradoxically establish their proximity to what Benjamin calls allegory, in both its antisubjective stylistic forms (decline of the subject and of social identities) and in its opposition to the forms of Greek tragedy. At the same time, these characteristics of allegory bear within them a *Trauerspiel*, a theatricization of the existent which always seeks to 'remove the limits of language', as Barthes said of baroque semantics.

To theatricize the existent here means to deploy it in multivocal scenographies with an unconscious circulation of figures and bodies, veritable metaphors for what is to be thought. And even at the height of 'modernity', does this not always write back into its languages the baroque paradigm of desire and thought? Is this not what is involved in *Les Fleurs du mal*, and in those great modern myths of otherness as non-reciprocity, as femininity, whose names are Lulu, Carmen and Salome? In all these scenes the Other appears in its most radical, 'excessive' form, as the fundamental reference of women, as a violent semantics of drives in which sexual non-reciprocity definitively links together Eros and Thanatos.

Salome is certainly among the most exemplary of these fin-de-siècle myths, the one in which the issues and forms of the baroque paradigm offer themselves for interpretation. Its unprecedented fascination is evident from the names of Flaubert, Mallarmé, Huysmans, Wilde, Moreau, Beardsley, Klimt, Strauss – just to mention a few of those who gave it representation in the literature, painting and music of the second half of the nineteenth century and the early part of the twentieth. Already a legendary history steeped in the Gospels had given rise to an exceptionally rich and charged iconography: in the sixteenth century alone, the figure of Salome bearing John the Baptist's severed head on a silver platter appears with matchless allegorical power in, among many others, the work of Jacob Cornelisz, Josef Heinz, Bartolommeo Veneto, Bernardino Luini and Titian. But her decisive importance comes with Oscar Wilde's play (1890), Gustave Moreau's paintings (*Salome Dancing before Herod, The Apparition*) and Richard Strauss's opera (1905) – which together 'invented' Salome.

They did so by giving her a name, with all its power of excitation and all its dense mystery. In Wilde and Strauss the girl who for centuries had been 'the daughter of Herodias' called herself: Salome. And this power of the proper name, this language of language, sealed her first impossible encounter with Jokanaan/John, who immediately consigned her to the anonymity of prostitution:[2]

'I am Salome, the daughter of Herodias, the Princess of Judaea.'
'Stand back, daughter of Babylon! To the chosen of God approach not.'[3]

But to give her a name, to inscribe her in the order of the signifier, is also to introduce her through this active signification into a world, a history, a destiny. Here nominal existence opens the language of her desire, the reappropriation of her mythical body. Whereas, before Wilde, the 'daughter of Herodias' was a young Jewish virgin who fulfilled her mother's wish for vengeance and not her own, it is now Salome who desires and decides. And what a desire!

It is born of hearing the voice of Jokanaan the prophet rise from the depths of the cistern/prison:

Thy voice is like sweet music to my ears.

Next the desire of his body:

Jokanaan! I am am'rous of thy body. Jokanaan! . . . Ah, let thy white body be touched by me.

And then the mad, 'peremptory' desire of decapitation:

I would that they presently bring me in a silver charger . . . the head of Jokanaan. . . . I do not heed the voice of my mother. 'Tis for my own pleasure that I ask the head of Jokanaan in a silver charger.

Finally, the more cannibalistic, necrophiliac desire to kiss the head of his corpse:

> Ah! Thou wouldst not suffer me to kiss thy mouth, thou wouldst not, Jokanaan. Well, well, it shall now be kissed. And with my teeth I'll bite it, I will bite it as one bites in a ripe fruit.

Seeing, touching, cutting, kissing, eating: these are Salome's gestures, the extremist baroque somatology, which Strauss's music carries to its paroxysm of dissonance and which Wilde's play scripts in the form of asymmetrical otherness:

> I was a princess, thou hast scorned me. I was a virgin, thou hast deflowered me. I was chaste, thou didst fill my veins with fire.[4]

The gestural – which includes dance – is so much the figurative element of Salome that in Moreau's paintings the whole pictorial space is organized by her outstretched hand, resolute, frightened, vengeful, clutching a lotus flower that is the metaphor of sexuality. It is the gesture of desire become plastic force, desire which designates its own 'part object': the auratic, radiant, bleeding head of the dead Jokanaan. The gesture is a kind of impossible pictorial hyphen between two bodies: Salome's body of seeming appearance and the mystical body, the *apparition*, of John. We can see why, although Moreau devoted a number of paintings to this theme, it was his *Salome Dancing before Herod* which drew more than five hundred thousand visitors at the *Salon* of 1876, and why both Wilde's play and Strauss's opera were banned by moralistic censors (in London in 1891 and Vienna in 1905). For this gesture of female desire threatens to be a founding gesture, in that it transgresses the 'Christian scene' of the sacrament which is also a (symbolic) incorporation of the body. In taking as the object of her desire the absolute Other of sainthood, Salome presents a highly Christian, and hardly Jewish, relationship to the body. For the Christian religion simultaneously requires that there should be a body (the body of Christ crucified, the body of the Church, the body of the sacramental host) and that there should not be a body – or that it should be cast off or doomed. On the one hand, the prohibition expressed in saintliness robs desire of any body; on the other hand, the flesh is guilty in itself. As Michel de Certeau writes: 'The "corpus mysticum" – the *Apparition* – always presents itself as the quest for a body.' Indeed, he defines mysticism as 'the production of a body', 'a cinematography of the body' which refers back to the origin of Christianity in 'the loss or disappearance of a body'.[5]

This exacerbated relationship to the present/absent body, which is a feature of all baroque, also characterizes Salome, with one additional nuance. Salome rejects Christian 'mourning work': instead, the affirmation of a woman's desire, as burning as it is virginal, supposes and 'devours' the body of the Other. It thus reverses the woman–death mimesis of Baudelaire's baroque allegory – the dead, frozen, stone-like Albertine, for example – in which the 'queen of the graces', the 'star of my eyes', the 'sun of my nature' is but vermin, carrion and decomposing love. Salome well embodies Baudelaire's 'bloody apparatus of destruction' by sanctifying the severed head of her desire, by pushing the destructive principle of modern allegory to its extreme in the fragment, the ruin, the wound as dead/living head of desire. But this auratic head is already sacred, holy, out of reach, twice forbidden. The religious figure serves to demonstrate the impossibility of this *jouissance*, this movement in which the embers of desire ice over in the *idée fixe* of kissing Jokanaan's mouth. It is a hallucinatory scenario, a kind of metaphysical orgasm in which the 'bitter taste' of love and the madness of death combine in the macabre theatre of the seventeenth century.

Allegorical violence leads Baudelaire to reinvent the female body, to produce a different, mutilated sexual body:

Et faire à ton flanc étonné
Une blessure large et creuse.[6]

But in the case of Salome, it results in a severed dislocation of the erotic, mystical body of man. It is no longer the breast/tomb of Baudelaire's *femmes damnées* but this severed head of desire which moves 'presentation' in the baroque imaginaries.

This named desire, then, upturns not only the Christian scene but equally Freud's future historical novel of the birth of humanity. For Freud, the founding act of the social is also a murder or an act of devourment, but it is murder or devourment of the Father by the Son. In short, it is a question of Saturn rather than Helen. By placing sex above all divine, social or human law, Salome rejoins a whole line of 'excessive', dangerous women who have proclaimed the necessity of a 'revolution' in the symbolic – the very women whom modern myths bring up to date or create.

In a poem he wrote in 1923, 'Isis und Osiris', Robert Musil himself traced the great incestuous myth of Ulrich and his sister Agathe back to his own pre-history. Here we find the same scenography of limits: androgynous devourment of brother and sister takes the Elizabethan form of a physical and symbolic interchange; I give you my sex for your heart.

Gently then the sister removed the sex
From the sleeper and ate it up.

And gave her sweet heart in return,
Hanging her crimson heart upon him.
In dream the wound did heal
And she ate the beloved sex.[7]

The mutual devouring of genitals and heart, the baroque apotheosis of love, functions here as the grand metaphor of otherness, of the *other state* (*der andere Zustand*). In his incestuous passion for Agathe, Ulrich lives that radical experience of erotic anarchy, where the male subject without ego, qualities or subjectivity discovers himself to be 'human' in the female double who gives him a body, a reality. The androgynous dimension has been noted by many critics and accepted by Musil himself within the framework of the novel. 'Can it be understood why, all over the world, the ideal of lovers is to become one being, even though these ungrateful creatures owe nearly all the charm of love to the fact that they are two beings of delightfully different sexes?'[8] And yet, what Ulrich and Agathe attain in the 'other state' is this 'dream of being one person in two separately moving bodies' or 'two goldfish in a bowl', a dream of absolute twinship, androgynous and mystical. The 'delightful difference' would appear to exist only to be negated in a utopia in Musil's sense of the term. 'Utopia means an experiment in which one observes the possible change of one element and the effects that it would produce in the complex phenomenon we call life.' Or again: 'Utopia – that is, the equivalent of a possibility.'

This experimental component of sexual difference therefore makes it possible to destabilize the established reality, to 'de-simplify' the elements at work in the very structure of the bisexual phantasm. 'Baroque reason' is very close to the Freudian knowledge drive: the knowledge of both sexes at the same time. We might say that this reproduces in modernity the position of Teiresias in Greek tragedy, the seer who became blind from having glimpsed the naked body of the goddess Athena and who himself experienced a change of sex and the infinite *jouissance* of the feminine.

This cannibal love recalls many another. Kleist's Penthesilea, for example, in the play of the same name, tears and eats the body of Achilles and proclaims the tragic irreducibility of her desire: 'Kisses, bites – the two rhyme together. And whoever loves with all their heart can take the one for the other.'[9] Agathe, Lulu, Penthesilea, Salome – all represent that everything/nothing erotics characteristic of baroque desire. The body is devoured and affirmed as an 'adorable detail', however bloody it may have become. The severed head, the devoured genitals stand as a 'perverse' metonymy of desire, in which the mutilated part fetishizes a primitive oral drive in place of the totality of love. Desire, by being desire of the Other, kills and raves as it hollows out an impossible otherness. And that otherness is the critical problem of the whole fin-de-siècle 'decadent imaginary' which the paintings of Salome condense in the form of myth.

It is the otherness of a girl, a Jewess who always appears highly pagan and oriental in relation to the Christian body. The whole imaginary of a libidinized East is here mobilized by a declining 'colonialist' West that is prey to archaeological trials and tribulations. Gustave Moreau, the great painter of myths such as those of Oedipus, Orpheus, Helen and Moses, even goes so far as to rehabilitate allegory. Of his *Messalina*, he writes that it concerns 'the unsatisfied desire of woman in general, but of a perverse woman acting in pursuit of her ideal'; and in this debauch of Eros and death, 'the scene is conceived in the form of allegory', as if once again the theatricization of the pictorial – 'the scene' – were joined with the power of allegory.[10]

The very body of Salome, which is the focus of seventy of Moreau's 120 sketches on the subject, bears the marks and traces of this mytho-logy. At first he wanted her to be a naked dancing figure, but Salome is gradually reclothed with all the 'tattoos' of a living archaeology. Her outstretched arm is decorated with a lotus flower (sign of sensual pleasure) and a bracelet bearing an eye (the Egyptian *oudjat*, as the sign of magical fluid). Salome's jewel-bedecked body is covered with various shapes, including heads of monsters with apotropaic eyes – a veritable sign-body made totally unreal. Salome thus operates in a universe of symbols: a black panther (lasciviousness), a sphinx, a statue of Diana of Ephesus and two of Ahriman (the Persian figure of evil), while the temple and altar settings place the whole scene at the border between the real and the unreal.

In this plethora of symbolic and theatrical detail, Salome epitomizes all the archaeological phantasms of a society which dreams its cold and alluring *femmes fatales* in the shape of an oriental Other. We can see why, in his famous *À Rebours*, Huysmans saw in her 'the symbolic incarnation of undying lust, the goddess of immortal hysteria, the accursed Beauty . . . the monstrous Beast, indifferent, irresponsible, insensible, poisoning, like the Helen of ancient myth, everything that approaches her, everything that sees her, everything that she touches'.[11]

We might also consider here that female bestiary which male humanity has continually produced and updated, in imagery by no means confined to the Christian zoo. Antiquity already had its devouring monster-seductresses, dangerously alluring female figures who usually bore phallic symbols and were often equipped with deadly, narcissistic mirrors to entrap the soul. Part-woman, part-scorpion, -viper, -serpent, -winged beast, -dragon – such are the great figures of devouring seduction: Lilith, Scylla, Sirens and Gorgons, the Mélusine fairies of French legend, and many others. To grasp the allegorical and decadent power of the ancient myths, one has only to look at the wild paintings of Mucha, where a 'perverse' girl with hair of vultures and skulls holds in her claw-hands thousands of torn and martyred bodies.

Actually, we might go further and see in Salome the last in the line of those nineteenth-century Medusa Beauties or 'Dames sans merci' that Mario Praz has so thoroughly analysed.[12] For the middle of the nineteenth century was a real watershed when the fated romantic 'hero' irreversibly shifted into the *femme fatale* and sublimated sexuality began to dream of a different, castrating sexuality. Hence the tradition of oriental Lady Macbeths, Messalinas and Cleopatras, praying mantises thirsty for the blood of their desire. The vampire woman (from Gautier to Swinburne) and the *femme fatale* (Cecily, Carmen, Messalina, Penthesilea, Mary Stuart, Venus) now had a brilliant future ahead of them.

It should be recognized that this involved a real shift in the relationship to the body, which was alternately rehabilitated and condemned. At the moment when labouring bodies were being ever more confiscated by machines, reshaped and destroyed in their appearances, subjected to industrialization and urbanization, woman became guilty of that inherence in the body which has been analysed by Jean Starobinski: 'Nineteenth-century man develops an inverted, complementary image of idealized femininity. According to this myth, woman is the great temptress because her nature makes her incapable of absenting herself from her body.'[13] Men do not have, or no longer have, this body-obsessed body which is allegorized or mythified as nature, excess, flower-body – so many formal correlates of an increasingly instrumental reason. Witness the ambivalent positions of Baudelaire: fascinated by make-up, female artifice and fashion, he nevertheless despises 'emancipated' women (George Sand) and 'horribly' natural women. And yet the female face, with its melancholic voluptuousness and its vacancy lending itself to conjecture, expresses the Baudelairean idea of Beauty.

It was thus on the basis of the female body that this industrious, at times puritanical, society drew the figures of boundary-crossing, the topologies of excess, the curious alternation of angelism and demonism which ruled an imaginary in the throes of secularization. In fact, woman moves any imaginary which seeks to liberate itself from the established polarities. The fin-de-siècle 'feminization of culture' stemmed both from the decline of the traditional aura and from the formal 'deconstruction' of the great philosophical and epistemological antinomies handed down by the Enlightenment: feminine/masculine, real/unreal, rational/irrational, and so on. In Baudelaire as in Nietzsche, the forms open into a yawning 'chasm' or 'abyss' of meaning. The real no longer presents itself as a fact, a meaning, a full form, a horizon of objects: it is now furrowed with absence, to be interpreted like a hieroglyph in the process of its withdrawal. Not only does beauty rise up from the abyss; there is no form except on the basis of a primal, chaotic, maternal formlessness, which explodes the classical Hegelian hierarchy of form and content. This accounts for the strange similarity and theoretical contemporaneity between Baudelaire, poet of the 'decline of aura', and Nietzsche, philosopher of the nihilist decline of values. The one writes in his 'Réflexions sur quelques-uns de mes contemporains': 'Everything is hieroglyph. . . . What is a poet . . . if not *a translator, a decipherer*?'[14] The other sees in morality and metaphysics a 'hieroglyphic text' and makes of interpretation the hermeneutics of the will to power.

This 'untimely' modernity therefore destroys the appearance of meaning and plenitude in the beautiful systems and totalities. The modern aesthetic of *fragment* and ambivalence naturally rejoins the aesthetic of seventeenth-century baroque. It brings forth a principle of dissonance and shock which dislocates, pluralizes and deformalizes forms. The digging of the void that we find in spleen, together with the structure of disillusion in nihilism, break apart the great manifest truths of a reality structured by perspectival space and unilinear time. The baroque region of modernity derives from the labour of a plural, heterogeneous negativity, post-Hegelian and non-Hegelian, which Adorno detected in the music of Schönberg: 'a chaotic anarchy, the precedence of disorder over order'.

Thus, beyond the particular historical referents, the labour of limits and differences which takes the feminine as its basis accomplishes 'the testimony of a passion come from elsewhere and aimed at elsewhere'.[15] In this anticipation of a nowhere, an ineffable place, an interstice, we find a baroque topology of the impossible peculiar to *modern myth* in Musil's sense of the term. It is something quite different from irrationality: the utopia of an anthropological and symbolic revolution affecting the distribution of values and sexes.

Modern myth, then, always includes its own anthropological critique, its own non-rational reason, through a whole series of correspondences between antiquity (Greek, Persian, Egyptian) and a modernity dominated by the look and by theatre. The otherness of the feminine is reinforced by the play of other aesthetic, cultural and even unconscious othernesses.

First of all, it is a strictly pictorial otherness of a colourist's world, somewhat 'Egyptian' and very visual or tactile, composed of luminous aggregates and disaggregations which irradiate bodies to the point of rendering them unreal or 'poetic'. In Moreau's paintings, beyond the murder and the violated taboos, Salome's pale-white body joins Jokanaan's brilliant radiance in a virginal, androgynous kinship. The otherness is reduplicated in the tragedy of the asymmetrical look which is dominant especially in Strauss's opera.

Salome, who sees and is barely seen, is the deadly intersection of looks which engenders unhappiness. As the Page who will die of love for her says directly to Narraboth: 'You always look at her. You look at her too much. It's dangerous to look at people in such fashion. Terrible things may happen [*Schreckliches kann geschehn*].'[16] *Schrecklich* – something dangerous and terrible – is the veritable leimotif in the libretto of *Salome*, and Richard Strauss made it correspond to the female 'dissonance' of the clarinet (Salome's musical motif) with its range of thirds.

If Salome sees too much, Jokanaan is precisely the one who will not, cannot, see with 'fleshly' eyes because he wants nothing to do with her:

Who is this woman who is looking at me? I'll not have her eyes resting upon me. Wherefore doth she look at me with her golden eyes under her gilded eyelids? I know not who she is. I do not wish to know who she is. Bid her go. To her I would not speak.

This 'I do not wish to know' (because I know), this I do not wish to see (because I have seen her 'golden eyes'), recurs in Salome's final contemplation of the dead man's head:

Ah! Wherefore didst thou never look at me, Jokanaan? Thou didst put upon thine eyes the cov'ring of him who seeketh God in all His glory. Well! Thou may'st have seen thy God, Jokanaan, *but me, me, me thou didst never see*. If thou hadst looked at me, thou wouldst have loved me.[17]

The visible and the invisible, eyes of the body against eyes of the spirit: this *imperialism of sight* theatricizes desire and leads to a kind of deictics of the female body. Salome's 'this is my body' – the dance of the seven veils in which she strips before the lustful gaze of Herod – is a challenge to the 'this is my body' of religion. More than immodesty or perversion, Salome expresses the body's metamorphoses carried into their representational alienation, where the feminine is consumed and consummated in the eternal 'hysterical' encounter of seduction and theatre.

She performs the *phantasm of love* in all its senses: first, as an unreality which since the Middle Ages has shifted from immediate seeing of the Other to its imaginary, to the figure as love of the image; but also in the more precise sense of those 'funereal strategies' that assert themselves in Baudelairean melancholy or Freudian perversion. The phantasm of love becomes partial, fragmentary object, bounded and set in perspective. Object of pleasure and suffering cut off from the body, but in fact a somatic extension of the self, the fetish object is strictly speaking metonymic. It is there to veil and unveil, to display and conceal the sexual object. The final scene in which Salome kisses the severed head of Jokanaan becomes clearer in light of what Rosolato writes of denial: 'What appears in the encounter between a look and a seen, what is unbearable in the spectacle, is the horror and apoplectic effect which arise in the flash when phantasm and reality are telescoped together.'[18] The telescoping is so strong and so sublimated that the destructive intent in the allegory and in Salome's sadistic love drive are all but transformed into tenderness, 'cannibalism of tenderness' or 'metonymic tenderness', to use the formulations of Masud Khan.[19]

All the othernesses therefore converge on that 'metonymic effect' of the severed head that we find in other paintings of Gustave Moreau (including *Orpheus*) and especially those of Odilon Redon. Is the *Apparition* not this wild telescoping of reality and phantasm?

As in the masterpieces of Caravaggio, where angels destabilize space by making the Other, the distant light, suddenly visible, so here the head of Jokanaan creates an infernal incandescence, a halo or aura. It refers us to the whole mystique of the severed head and the eye peculiar to the pictorial symbolism of the epoch, with Odilon Redon again the prime example (see his *Head of a Martyr*). Eyes delineate 'luminous bodies which open onto the infinite'; with their power of dream and mystery, they already see the limits of the representational scene. As Redon wrote in his journal for 1902: 'The meaning of mystery is to be always in ambiguity with double, triple aspects; in the hints of aspect (images in images), forms which will be, or which become according to the state of mind of the beholder. All things more than suggestive because they *appear*.'[20]

The equivocal, the double, the play on appearances, the nascent form: everything here evokes the baroque procedures of the language of the Other which infringes codes by overturning their limits. Redon himself relates this 'appearance' to Goethe's famous *Urphänomen* which Benjamin discussed in connection with baroque drama: 'There is perhaps a primary vision in the flower. Organ of totality (Goethe). Bisexual.'[21]

Through its 'uncanny' visual effects, the severed head constitutes a kind of figuration of desire, a trope in the precise sense that Condillac, following Du Marsais, systematized: 'The advantages of tropes are, first, to designate things which have no name, and second, to give body and colours to those which do not fall under meaning.' To disturb flat representational space, to unravel through *concordia discors* the harmonious relations originating in the Renaissance between form of the eye and form of theatre: such is the trope of desire in which the great obsessions of the fin-de-siècle imaginary are condensed – panic fear of sex and castration, obsession with virility smitten with impotence, the impossible *jouissance* of the feminine. Nor should we pass over the mystical metaphor of the act of slicing: 'Slicing is the process of union when it is the Absolute which delineates because it removes.'[22]

Behind this erotics of the fragment and its threefold scene – the baroque, 'modernity' and Freudianism – the basic theme of the post-Baudelairean Modern Style is already being acted out: namely, the transfiguration of sterility and virginity. Salome is on fire because she is still a virgin: she is at once Baudelaire's 'cold majesty of the sterile woman' and Mallarmé's 'horror at being a virgin'. Stripped of her traditional auras, woman revives the accents of the oxymoron and the baroque apotheosis: 'cruel snow', Salome 'burning with chastity' (Mallarmé). Twenty years later, in another crisis culture prone to the Modern Style, Gustav Klimt's *Judith* rediscovers the other Salome, that relationship between sexuality and death, that aesthetic of cutting and fragmentation. A gold and jewel necklace separates the head from Judith's body, reduplicating in a highly distanced ornamentation the severed head of Holofernes. There is the same orientalizing (here Byzantine) style, the same modernist and baroque overprinting, the same imperialism of the image and of the bodily section, the same theatricization and allegorization of the feminine, that metaphor of male castration. The rehabilitation of myth and allegory common to Moreau and Klimt seals these new relations between the ancient and the modern, nature and technology, which were already at work in the Baudelairean 'revolution'. On the one hand, the decorative, orientalist cutting of bodies is clearly modernist and close to all the aesthetics of shock and montage; but on the other hand, nature is here a primitive, archaeological *arche*, a femininity of life which, though all-powerful, is highly controlled in its proliferation of ambiguous, perverse, sometimes bisexual bodies.

In this metaphorization of the love and death drives, Salome/ Judith updates the exasperation of love in Baudelairean allegory, the experience of the 'terrible' and 'delightful' which originates in a radical transformation of the notion of reality. The experience of melancholy – now marked by the internalization of death, withdrawal, non-plenitude, the abyss – gives birth to an ontological perception of the 'dearth of reality' in the real. But Salome reincarnates it by inverting its psychic economy and inserting a desire that was absent from Baudelaire's work: female desire. Thus the baroque style of Baudelaire's poems, his cult of images and theatre, his procedures for staging and sectioning bodies (what Benjamin calls baroque *Detaillierung*), work themselves out again in Salome as a logic of realization and almost 'materialization' of the Other-being of allegory.

Baudelaire's 'modern baroque' certainly established itself within this awareness of the loss of reality, this spleen which covers the whole tradition of melancholy from the Middle Ages (acedia) to the Renaissance and Dürer's *Melencolia* (1514) or Robert Burton's *Anatomy of Melancholy*. But modern melancholy or *Trauer* arises from the new experience of decline of aura, subjective depreciation of the self, destruction of the appearances of both Subject and world. As Benjamin writes: 'The decisive ferment which, in entering the *taedium vitae*, transforms it into *spleen* is that of self-estrangement.'[23] Such estrangement establishes a void within a problematic subjectivity permanently trapped between 'centralization' and 'vaporization' of the self, to use Baudelaire's own terms. The poetic Ego is now marked by melancholic duplicity: to desire, while barring the road to desire, will maintain that self-relationship of play and theatre which is 'modern heroism'. To live in disillusion and permanent unreality is the condition of the poetic Ego and its dramaturgy:

Mais mon coeur, que jamais ne visite l'extase,
    Est un *théâtre* où l'on attend
Toujours, toujours en vain, l'Être aux ailes de gaze![24]

Not only is modern big-city life an endless theatre of 'dialectical images' without aura or 'gauze-winged being', but this *Trauerspiel* renews the characteristically baroque perception of the world. Permanent catastrophe and not straightforward progress, loss of any stable referent in history and not the subject as bearer of an already accomplished meaning: 'For *Spleen* the buried (corpse) is the "transcendental Subject" of historical consciousness.'[25] Henceforth melancholy feeds on a negative, catastrophist utopia: life knows neither future nor evolution; it is 'pure, *frozen* agitation', deployment of an organic vision and sadistic, machine-like imagination, which separate love from *modern, auraless erotics*.

The horizon of melancholic loss or withdrawal of the love-object explains why the poetic experience focuses on bodies, and especially on the female body which is confronted with its most destructive othernesses: death and the angelic aura of nostalgic, impossible love. Such an experience is profoundly ambivalent, for it takes shape in the infinite quest for the lost love-object – hence its archaic regression towards the correspondences of memory, the 'green paradise of childhood loves' and the powerfully desired body of the mother. And yet, as in all melancholy, desire is gripped by a kind of 'heroic fury' or 'lovesickness', a sublimity and bodily excess. For the melancholic gaze, as for the baroque gaze, the body always announces itself as lost and overly present. The ambivalence is so 'ontological' that it falls in with allegorical writing itself – an emotionally charged writing of opposites which lays reality bare and flattens its antinomies. Undermined by an insurpassable conflict, such writing is at once cold technique (which returns to the rhetoric of antiquity), convention and animated 'expression' which bursts forth in a shower of images. The creative antinomy makes of it a writing of excess. But the image ever present in Baudelaire's stage-settings is often there only as immobilized in pictures, as realized in part, fragment or fetish: 'In the field of allegorical intuition, the image is fragment.' Through its figural excess and constant fragmenting, allegorical writing might be said to be both 'perverse' and 'hysterical'. It is perverse because the rhetorical and poetic over-coding corresponds well to the 'mentalization' of drives in Freud's theory of perversion; words and the creation of language substitute for desire, and the poetic I is there only as spectator or witness in a theatre where all actions are *seen* and are performed by others. It is hysterical because the 'cult of images' has to endow the body with its own materiality, a thoroughly imaginary proximity, a non-renunciation of the primal, archaic maternal body.

Theatre, entertainment, play: these words indicate something quite different from a merely psychological state. The 'untimely' experience of modernity is rooted in an ontological toppling of the real, a movement in which signs meet the infinite chasm of meaning. Hence the formal correlates of the melancholic Eros: the female body so fragmented as to produce a pathos of detail; the body so phantasized as to yield mystical obscenity and an eroticization of the corpse, the skeleton and death in general. Love gives rise to all these 'funereal strategies' of which Salome holds the secret.

If we take Baudelaire's great poems which display this erotics of severance and fragmentation – 'Les Bijoux', 'Le Balcon', 'À une Madone' – we immediately see that the *Detaillierung* of bodies gives rise to a baroque 'scenography' of desire. Thus, in 'Le Balcon', beauty as 'mother of memories' breaks down into partial images caught in the movement of desire: the 'dear body' is only 'breast', then 'bouquet of your blood', then 'your knees' in which I 'live my past again'.[26] The dislocated unity of the woman's living and desiring body transforms it into what Bersani calls an 'image-producing machine'.[27] Hence the baroque paradigm of desire peculiar to allegory. 'The object grasped by allegorical intention is torn from the context of life. It is at once broken and preserved'[28] – that is, broken in reality, and preserved in memory and decomposed love. At the limit, the living body turns into its opposite. In 'Une Charogne' the 'queen of graces' becomes 'carcass' or 'carrion', while in 'À une Madone' 'the spellbound statue' is gradually covered with a 'gown of desire', 'dainty shoes of respect' and finally 'seven keen blades' plunged into 'your throbbing heart, your sobbing, gushing heart'.[29] The scene recalls *Penthesilea* and still more *Salome*, where destructive rage follows the movement of love in its cutting of the body.

In Strauss's opera, Salome's desire is subject to the same 'imperialism of sight', the same 'cult of images', from the first look that grips her heart and instantly triggers 'lovesickness'. This rendering of desire as event is characteristic of the whole figural realm, and the sudden perception of 'dissimilar likeness' telescopes reality and phantasms from the first scene where Salome meets Jokanaan. The telescoping is metaphorized under the sign of the moon, the female principle and symbolic measure of *Trauerspiel*. Even before Salome appears on stage, the moon is there in all its 'uncanniness':[30]

> *A Page of Herodias*: See the moon, oh look, how strange the moon seems. She's like a woman rising from a tomb. . .

> *Narraboth*: How pale is the Princess. Never have I known her to look so pale. She is like the shadow of a snow-white rose in a mirror of silver.

The same lunar metaphors are used by Salome:

> How good 'tis to see the moon. She is like *a little silver flower*, cold and chaste.

And it precisely this lunar flower, cold and chaste, which Salome finds in Jokanaan's body:

> I'm sure he is chaste like the moon. His flesh must be cool, cool like ivory.

White, chaste moon, black and deadly moon, red moon bloody with passion: this organic cycle is in the image of Salome's desire and the whole movement of the opera. As in Baudelaire's 'Le Balcon', Salome's desire refers us to an extremist, coloured somatology which brings into play two well-known baroque procedures: *Detail-lierung* moving from the whole body to its last part; and a constant reversal of images into their opposite, dialectical images with no synthesis.

1   First, there is the *lyricism of whiteness*, of the whole body in its virginal purity: 'Jokanaan! I am am'rous of thy body. Jokanaan! Thy body is white like the lilies of a wide field that the mower never has mowed. You look as white as the snows on the hills of Judaea. . . . Ah, let thy white body be touched by me.'[31]

2   Then, after Jokanaan's rejection, comes the reversal into its opposite and the appearance of a *lyricism of blackness*:

> Thy body is hideous. It's just like the body of a leper. It is like a plastered wall where vipers have crawled; like a plastered wall where the scorpions have made their nest. It is like a whited sepulchre, full of loathsome things. It is horrible, thy body is horrible. It's thy hair that I'm enamoured of, Jokanaan. Thy hair is like clusters of grapes, like the clusters of black grapes on the vine trees of Edom. Thy hair is like the cedars, the mighty cedars of Lebanon, that to lions and robbers give their shade. . . . Nothing in the world is so black as thy hair. Let me touch thy hair.[32]

3   Further rejection by Jokanaan leads to the appearance of a *lyricism of redness* and the 'partial object' of desire, the kissable mouth.

> Thy hair is horrible. With mire and dust it's covered. It is just like a crown of thorns which on thy head is placed. It is like serpents awrithing round thy neck. I love thy hair not. It is thy mouth that I desire, Jokanaan. Thy mouth . . . is like a sweet pomegranate cut with a knife of silver. . . . Thy mouth is redder than the feet of the men who tread the wine, stamping in the winepress. . . . Nothing in the world is so red as thy mouth. Ah, let me kiss thy mouth, kiss thy mouth.[33]

Six times Salome repeats this *idée fixe*, this meeting of reality and phantasm which issues in the final cannibalism of love when she kisses the dead man's mouth. Lily-white, grape-black, pomegranate-red: the coloured segmentation of Jokanaan's body symbolizes Salome herself as virgin, murderess and passionate would-be lover. The allegory of modern baroque thus seems to produce a kind of perverse scenario of the feminine. The part detached from the living body becomes a fetish object of lack, a surrogate which bursts into the visual field on a mirror-equivalent, a silver platter, or in the form of an 'apparition' in the painting by Gustave Moreau. Salome, then, feels the impalpable, crosses the last frontier of all law to obtain the wiping out of her narcissistic wound. A whole utopia, 'black' and destructive, liberates in the inorganic limit the partial and fragmentary, the pathos of detail. As Benjamin writes: 'Sadism and fetishism interpenetrate in the phantasms which seek to push back all organic life towards an inorganic foundation.'[34] The feminine is its grand metaphor, the site of its greatest legibility where ancient and modern intertwine.

But this possible reference to a scenario of perversity does not make of Salome the incarnation of the castrating *femme fatale* of nineteenth-century archetypes, even if Moreau saw in her the embodiment of 'evil'. The body of the Other is never, as in Sade, perverted and subjected to the cold logic of the libertine. At the most it is constituted and saturated as an amorous body by Salome's desire, which is never of a cerebral nature. Salome, unlike the pervert, does not organize 'tableaux vivants' involving a whole representational game, mechanical and icily erotic. She *is* this tableau vivant, this play of images and mirrors, where her own desire is caught in a murderous lack of reciprocity. The internal space of feeling rises up from the irreducible distance of desire towards an otherness which inscribes the phantasm in lyricism and vision.

The *Trauerspiel* of Salome is a *Spiel* (or play, in both senses) on the modern *Trauer* of suffering born of the ambivalence of Eros and Thanatos. In contrast to a whole classical tradition, passion is here never disorder or confusion of the body. As in Baudelaire, it is a logic of excess which petrifies or crystallizes in the *idée fixe*, in the 'mystical' meeting-place of all meanings and all opposites:

Ô métamorphose mystique
De tous les sens fondus en un!
Son haleine fait la musique,
Comme sa voix fait le parfum.[35]

Salome reproduces this Baudelairean cleavage between the excess of desire, its 'fury', and the moment of mystical meta-morphosis and sublimated fall. It is an 'upward fall', as Octavio Paz writes in connection with the spirit of the baroque, where 'falling may be a way of rising'.[36] But the characteristic of such upward falls is to feed on a curious 'empathy with the inorganic', a fascination for corporeal matter excluded from all commodity circulation, a final, dead matter:

Désormais tu n'es plus, ô matière vivante!
Qu'un granit entouré d'une vague épouvante.[37]

This is erotic matter, as it were, in which poetry, like Strauss's music, falls into catalepsy – a 'mimesis of death', as Benjamin puts it.

This is why, from Baudelaire to *Salome*, this whole baroque, allegorical region gives birth to a modern aesthetic that is at once nihilist and imbued with the idea of progress. It is nihilist in the sense that the 'cutting of bodies' – the distant origin of aesthetics of shock and montage, or photo-montage – exorcizes appearances and exacerbates the contradictions between nature and technology. This modern aesthetic destroys the beautiful naturalness of appearances, with their aura and ideal sublimity, by bringing into play a novel circulation of symbols between *the infra- and supra-human* – which Benjamin detected in Kafka or Klee – and the regime of the sensible. The nihilist instance of the destruction of values summons up the limits of representation, by allowing the non-representable to be seen on the side of the Other. The allegory of the feminine thus relates to a world caught on all sides by a 'corpse-like rigidity'.

For this reason, however, the nihilist aesthetic carries the idea of progress: it grounds desire on images, scenes, matter; it materializes difference and excess at the very site of a logic of ambivalence; it creates 'language', in the strong sense not of an 'irrational' other of reason as this is traditionally understood, but of a reason of the Other, with all its effects of 'estrangement' [*étrange* and *être-ange*].[38] In other words, whereas the reason most often invoked by modernism is that which has created the modern state and an ever more 'rationalized' civil society, perhaps there is a different reason, or even a different modernity, which appeals to the interstices of reason and feeling – to the 'senti-mental'. This is the reason to which Musil alludes: 'the type of reason which would forgo producing wholly verified knowledge – such as people use to roll iron, to fly in the air or to secure nourishment – but which would strive to discover and systematize other knowledge capable of offering bold new directions to human affectivity.'[39]

In this reason, baroque stylistics and semantics now require a different interpretation of the modern, for which Baudelaire and Benjamin have laid the foundation stones.

Notes

1. Musil, *Tagebücher*, p. 355. On myth and the question of the double, see the special number of *L'Arc* (Aix-en-Provence), 74, devoted to Musil, especially the article by Jean Molino: 'Doubles'.
2. For this analysis, I refer the reader to the excellent special issue on *Salome* of the journal *L'Avant-scène*.
3. Richard Strauss, *Salome*, Sony Classical libretto, p. 66, incorporating Lord Alfred Douglas's translation of Wilde's French text.
4. Oscar Wilde, *Salome*, translated by R.A. Walker, London: Heinemann 1957, p. 107.
5. Michel de Certeau, *La Fable mystique*, Paris: Gallimard 1982. See especially

chapter 3: 'La science nouvelle – le corpus mysticum ou le corps manquant' (pp. 158ff.) and 'l'art de parler' (p. 198), where the author analyses the function of oxymorons in mystical speech as being 'to produce in the language of effects that which does not exist in language'. This 'ontological figurability' of desires is common to both mystical and baroque speech.

6. 'And cleave into your astounded side a wide deep wound.' 'À celle qui est trop gaie', in *The Complete Verse*, p. 280.

7. 'Isis und Osiris', in Musil, *Gesammelte Werke* 6, Hamburg: Rowohlt, p. 465. A French translation of Musil's poem appears in the aforementioned special issue of *L'Arc*, 74.

8. Robert Musil, 'Das Sternbild der Geschwister, oder Die Ungetrennten und Nichtvereinten' [a posthumously published draft-chapter intended for a Part Four of *The Man without Qualities*. *Trans. note*], in *Gesammelte Werke* 4, p. 1348. See also the draft for chapter 55 of Part Three, 'Atemzüge eines Sommertages', which immediately precedes this in *GW* 4, pp. 1324–37.

9. *Kleists Werke*, vol. 2, Weimar: Volksverlag 1963, p. 299.

10. See Pierre-Louis Mathieu, *Gustave Moreau*, Oxford: Phaidon 1977, to which I am indebted for some of the details in this section.

11. J.K. Huysmans, *Against Nature*, Harmondsworth: Penguin 1966, p. 66.

12. See Mario Praz, *The Romantic Agony*, 2nd edn, Oxford: OUP 1970. Chapter 4, 'La Belle Dame sans Merci', and chapter 5, 'Byzantium', are largely devoted to the figure of Salome.

13. Jean Starobinski, *Portrait de l'artiste en saltimbanque*, Paris: Champs-Flammarion 1970, p. 67. Noting the hiatus between 'the glorious female body' and 'the mediocre male body', Starobinski analyses the function of the dancer (Salome, for example) in this process of metaphorization.

14. Baudelaire, *Oeuvres complètes*, vol. 2, p. 133.

15. Ibid., p. 132. The angelic/demonic polarity also connects Baudelaire to Rilke and Klee: the same 'reserve of non-meaning to pass to meaning' (pp. 131ff.).

16. Strauss's *Salome*, p. 42.

17. Ibid., p. 126.

18. Guy Rosolato, 'Études des perversions sexuelles à partir du fétichisme', in idem, *Le Désir et la perversion*, Paris: Seuil 1967. Rosolato speaks of 'metaphoric-metonymic oscillation' as abolition of meaning. Perversion as allegory manifests 'a duality without mediation between Good and Evil': p. 39.

19. See M. Masud Khan, *Alienation in Perversions*, New York: International Universities 1980.

20. Odilon Redon, *To Myself: Notes on Life, Art and Artists*, New York: George Braziller 1986, p. 84. Quoted in Robert L. Delevoy, *Le symbolisme*, Geneva: Skira 1977.

21. Quoted from Delevoy, *Le symbolisme*.

22. De Certeau, *La Fable mystique*, p. 184.

23. 'Central Park', p. 33.

24. 'But my heart, never visited by any ecstasy, is a theatre in which the gauze-winged being is for ever awaited in vain.' 'L'Irréparable', in *The Complete Verse*, p. 129.

25. 'Central Park', p. 35.

26. *The Complete Verse*, pp. 100–1.

27. Leo Bersani, *Baudelaire and Freud*, Berkeley: University of California 1977, pp. 64ff.

28. Benjamin, *GS* V, p. 415.

29. Ibid., pp. 91, 133–4.

30. Strauss's *Salome*, pp. 40, 44, 50, 64.

31. Ibid., p. 68.

32. Ibid., p. 70.

33. Ibid., pp. 71–2.

34. Ibid., p. 448.

35. 'O mystic transformation, whereby all my senses are fused into one: her breath becomes music, and her voice, perfume.' 'Tout entière', in *The Complete Verse*, p. 110.

36. Octavio Paz, 'Quevedo, Heraclitus and a Handful of Sonnets', in idem, *Convergences: Essays on Art and Literature*, London: Bloomsbury 1990, p. 228.

37. 'Henceforth, O living matter, you are but a granite form shrouded in vague horror.' 'Spleen' (LXXVI), in *The Complete Verse*, p. 156.

38. See p. 43 above.

39. 'Die Geistliche, der Modernismus und die Metaphysik', in *Gesammelte Werke* 8, Hamburg: Rowohlt 1981, p. 989.

11

THE STAGE OF THE MODERN AND THE LOOK OF MEDUSA

I am human and what am I? house of sorrows,
Plaything of false happiness, stray light,
Theatre whose actors are terrors and sufferings,
Burnt-down candle and springtime snow,
Life without life . . .

Abyss, o utter woe.

Andreas Gryphius

In 'Paris – the Capital of the Nineteenth Century', Benjamin considers the nature of the modern in Baudelaire and refers to the title 'Spleen et Idéal' which he gave to the first cycle in *Les Fleurs du mal*: the oldest foreign word in the French language being coupled with the most recent. For Baudelaire there was no contradiction between the two concepts. He saw in spleen the last of the transfigurations of the ideal, while the ideal itself seemed to him the first of the expressions of spleen. In this title, where the *supremely new* is presented to the reader as a *supremely old*, Baudelaire gave the most vigorous form to his concept of the modern. The whole axis of his theory of art is 'modern beauty', and the hallmark of modernity for him is that it is fated one day to be antiquity – as it already shows to those who witness its birth. Here is the quintessence of the unforeseen, which for Baudelaire is an inalienable quality of the beautiful. '*The face of modernity* withers us with an immemorial look, as the look of Medusa did for the Greeks.'[1]

The 'female' look of Medusa, petrifying and immemorial, is thus summoned up at the very heart of the modern. Modernity becomes a face or look which interpellates us with all its power of the *new* and unforeseen, as well as its capacity for repetition of the ancient as *ever-new*. It is thereby linked to the imaginary space of the great phantasmagoria in which historical and oneiric appearance meet and subjugate each other. It is this which characterizes the paradigmatically modern in Benjamin's work: the famous Parisian *passages*, closed shopping arcades which are half gallery-streets and half blocks of buildings. In them is already crystallized the primal structure of history peculiar to modernity, with its frozen dialectical images.

For the arcade, more than anything else, embodies the optical model of Baudelaire's *flâneur* and allegorist: the imperialism of seeing. Everything there is fundamentally ambiguous, ambivalent. This inescapable ambiguity is bound up with the real and derealizing functions of the arcade: street-gallery and block of buildings, passageway in which luxury goods are exposed to view, sanctified and sublimated in their commodity-aura. But the *passages* are also places where nothing happens: society dreams itself in them, frozen in utopian time and protected from any catastrophe. In this sense: 'The arcades are buildings and galleries which, like a dream, have no outside.'[2]

Town and world in miniature, the arcade is a monad of modernity which carves out a space floating between inside and outside, reality and unreality, commodity devaluation of every object and the new aura of the unforeseen, the new, 'modern beauty'. It reinvents modernity by embodying a pre-Freudian temporality of repetition, of a new that is always new. This is why 'modernity' is not only a dynamic social project based on rationalization and industrialization and oriented towards the future; it is also an ensemble of collective dreams – a historical dream (*Zeitraum*), as Benjamin says – which becomes material in objects, buildings and constructions. The modern therefore takes the form of a *baroque phenomenology* internal to the phantasmagoric display-form of the market, which can be seen in museums, salons, collections, world exhibitions, and arcades. Through all these buildings, 'the construction plays the role of the unconscious'.[3]

A single mirror-universe, a single 'world of images', deploys itself between the stylistic space of baroque ambivalence and the space of the modern, between allegory which lays bare reality and exposes the barbarism of any accelerated modernization and the awesome, enchanted world of phantasmagoria. In this mirror-universe, a look captivates, theatricizes, vivifies and petrifies its object of desire, which is ever new and undermined by death. And it is precisely this look of Medusa, this apotropaic zone of the Greeks from which one turns away in fascination mixed with horror, which forms the basis of Baudelaire's concept of 'modernity' and the poetic experience of allegory. The 'philosophy' of the imagination is one and the same.

In both cases, John E. Jackson remarks, the internalization of death as 'perceptual focus of the real' divests time of the future and 'transforms the full substance of the present into an allegory of loss'.[4] This allegory of shrunken reality and corporeality commits the poetic I to the ambivalent powers of the image: the pseudo-presence, pseudo-body takes the place of the real, intensifying and exacerbating it in all its polarities. For Baudelaire, as for Kant or Novalis, the imagination is thus the constitutive 'queen of faculties'. With its power of analysis and synthesis, its anticipation of possibility and infinity, the imagination creates something new and functions as a kind of coded language of figures, forms, sounds and perfumes:

> It is the imagination which has taught man the moral sense of colour, contour, sound and perfume. It created analogy and metaphor at the beginning of the world. It splits up all creation, and with the materials assembled and laid out according to rules whose origin can be found only in the depths of the soul, it creates a new world and produces the sensation of novelty.[5]

Between the 'moral sense' and the realm of 'sensibles', the imagination constructs an allegorical grid of correspondences which transposes the different spheres of existence: it spiritualizes the material and materializes the spiritual. As in Kant, the imagination progresses *ad infinitum*, makes present the non-representable, and secures the possibility of the image. It furnishes sight and the ontological horizon of any possible image. In this baroque compenetration of images, the imagination shatters the false antinomy of 'reasoning reason' and 'feeling feeling'. 'By its substitutive nature, the imagination contains the critical spirit.'[6] Using the terms of Novalis – so close in some respects to Baudelaire's – we might say that the imagination is 'an imagining intelligence' in which 'thought is felt'. By a kind of genetic imitation, imagining consists in 'awakening in oneself a foreign individuality'.[7]

To make of One Many, of the Same another and Others: such is the alchemy of imagination, that baroque reason of intersubjectivity in which everything is material for sensual pleasure, conversion and inversion, captivation by the phantasm and the Other. It is not at all surprising, therefore, that Baudelaire sees in imagination the very power of allegories and makes of allegory the substance of the poetic act:

> The intelligence of allegory assumes in you proportions unknown to yourself; we will note in passing that allegory – such a *spiritual* genre which awkward painters have accustomed us to treat with contempt but which is truly one of the most primal and natural forms of poetry – resumes its rightful sway in intelligence illuminated by intoxication.[8]

The poet, under the sway of allegory, is no more than a decipherer, a translator: 'He has the curiosity of an Oedipus obsessed by innumerable sphinxes', as Baudelaire said in relation to Victor Hugo.[9] But Beauty remains enigmatic and silent, like 'a misunderstood sphinx'. Its eyes are of marble: 'The implacable Venus gazes far into the distance, at the unknown, with her marble eyes.'[10] Hence the endless confrontation of the eye with 'the abyss', 'chasms', 'great night', 'vaults', all the non-representable reverses of the image. In this terrible look something appears which connects the baroque paradigm of desire – from Baudelaire to Salome – with the Freudian uncanny. For do not allegory and the uncanny bring into play the same procedures: ambivalence, the double, the organic and non-organic, living/artificial body, fixation on sight and the anxiety of losing it, and above all the dread of the fragmented body? 'Dismembered limbs, *a severed head*, a hand cut off at the wrist . . . all these have something peculiarly uncanny about them.'[11]

This 'something of desire' is haunted by the uncanny, by baroque contradiction, by a constant shifting between the familiar and the strange, the same and the other. An impregnable signifier is this Freudian act of seeing, this *Übersehen* which, as Jean-Michel Rey has shown, only occurs *post festum* and only sustains itself on a 'not-seeing', on a constitutive relation to bisexuality.[12] Now, the ubiquitous metaphors of the eye and the petrifying dual look (divine/ infernal), like all the formal correlates exhibited by the image, define the Baudelairean theatre of the modern and of the feminine. Or rather, modernity is this theatricality which *is constantly eroticizing the new*. For if the eye functions here as the organ of the passions and of their aggravation, the theatre for its part is unreal and lacking in affect – masquerade and artifice which Baudelaire's apology for appearances and fashion makes quite manifest.

In fact, unlike all the philosophemes of traditional aesthetics of the beautiful, Baudelaire's critical texts never fail to associate modernity with fashion, and more generally with an aesthetic of appearances, artifice and play which promotes the baroque values *par excellence* of spectacle, unexpectedness, ephemerality and mortality. In 'Le Peintre de la vie moderne', the solitary individual endowed with an active imagination is in permanent quest of 'modernity', which is precisely 'the transitory, fleeting and contingent, the half of art whose other half is the eternal and immutable'.[13] It exists entirely in the person's gait, look, gestures and mannerisms. Fashion, 'stamped by the age', expresses the essence of the present as such: novelty.[14] It is that 'special beauty which protects from death and eternity', that 'ritual by which the fetish Commodity wished to be worshipped'.[15] Like the continual speeding-up of information and commodity circulation, fashion 'seeks to do away with any interruption, any sudden end'.[16] More than anything else, it thereby expresses the baroque phenomenology of the modern – the ever-new, the 'eternal recurrence of the same'. It sets all the standards by which the commodity is identified, but its commodity-value disappears in the newness of 'modern beauty'. There is thus more than one analogy, however dissembled or denied, between Madame Death and Madame Fashion. In 'The Salon of 1846', Baudelaire saw the black dress fashionable during the July Monarchy as 'the rind of the modern hero'. For does its twilight colour not correspond to that beauty originating in the passions, that distinctive beauty of a modernity without illusions: suicide?

Fashion is truly the historical index of modernity: it expresses in the realm of the real the same arbitrariness and theatricality which allegory expresses in the poetic experience. As Benjamin writes in a formula which sums up his understanding of the modern: 'The hero who presents himself on the stage of modernity [*auf der Szene der modernité*] is actually first of all an actor.'[17] Similarly, in Baudelaire's 'Les Sept Vieillards', the poet finds himself in 'a background not unlike an actor's soul' and 'steels his nerves' like a hero, hunted and haunted by 'all the baroque spectres', by the 'satanical procession' of the seven old men who are the allegory of death.[18]

The idea of modernity as a stage where the commodity-aura of the 'ever-new' has replaced the theological paradigm of the seventeenth-century Baroque is not specific to Baudelaire or Benjamin. One finds the same theatrical metaphor in 'The Eighteenth Brumaire of Louis Bonaparte', where Marx seeks to think through a history which no longer simply obeys the laws of progress or a dualist model of classes in struggle – a dark, splintered history written under the impact of an actual defeat (the 'theatrical' coup d'état of Louis-Napoleon Bonaparte). At that moment history becomes Shakespearian: it is given over to a deadly, inhuman dimension and trapped in a labour of repetition where the past returns in the retro- or neo-masks of comedy:

> Men make their own history, but not of their own free will. . . . The tradition of the *dead generations* weighs like a nightmare on the minds of the living. . . . And precisely in such epochs of revolutionary crisis they timidly conjure up the spirits of the past to help them; they borrow their names, slogans and *costumes* so as to stage *the new world-historical scene* in this venerable disguise and borrowed language.[19]

As in Baudelaire, theatre rolls back the limits of representation: it displays a non-represented of history (the peasantry in Marx's text) and probably a non-representable where 'death holds its court' (Shakespeare).

The theatricality of desire or history therefore accomplishes the project of modernity as representation, while destabilizing it towards the vanishing-point of the non-representable Other. In 1855 Baudelaire wrote an essay on the World Exhibition of that year, a festival of industrialist and commodified modernity, in which he analysed at length the rise of a *cosmopolitan gaze* that appropriated the foreign variety of all cultures by placing them on display. The new which bursts forth here is at once bizarre ('the Beautiful is the bizarre') and astonishing ('the Beautiful is always astonishing').[20] But the break is never inscribed within a continuous history of progress, understood as an indefinite series capable of guaranteeing the future. No doubt this is because the historical time of modernity remains profoundly antinomic: time of progress and time of destruction, time of a dialectic in movement issuing from the Enlightenment and time of a frozen 'baroque' dialectic gripped by corpse-like rigidity. The coexistence was so explosive that it led Benjamin to conclude that 'belief in progress, in endless perfectibility . . . and the idea of eternal recurrence are complementary'.[21]

At any event, the appropriation of the Other which distinguishes Baudelairean modernity has nothing in common with a mere commodity-euphoria of 'the new'. For behind the cosmopolitan gaze lies hidden the different, terrorized gaze of the allegorist and the poet. True 'novelty' cannot be reduced to apotheosis of the commodity. Strangeness [*l'étrangeté*] as 'indispensable condition of beauty' really is uncanniness [*une inquiétante étrangeté*]. Thus in Baudelaire's writings on Edgar Allen Poe, 'natural perversity' – that primitive, irreducible force in every human being – dwells in the unexpected, the sudden, the 'new'. In opposition to all eighteenth-century philosophy, but in the line stretching from Sade to Freud, Baudelaire places evil, horror, abjectness within nature. Appearance, the artifice of culture, always establish themselves as a defensive bulwark or game keeping at a distance the constant physical dread and vertigo before 'the abyss'. The true 'morality' of appearances, the true 'frivolity', is identical to that which Nietzsche claimed for himself and attributed to the Greeks, a 'frivolity through sheer profundity': 'To see one's existence as it is, in a transfiguring mirror, and to defend oneself with this mirror against the Medusa – that was the brilliant strategy of the Hellenic "Will", so as to be able simply to live.'[22] It is also the strategy of the dandy, of the poet who is prey to an experience of the petrification of life. Nietzsche's head of the Medusa and Baudelaire's 'world gripped by corpse-like rigidity' are one and the same thing.

But is the Medusa's look not essentially the look of a feminine so overwhelming [*médusant*] that the bodyless Jokanaan flees from Salome, while Baudelaire, obsessed with images and bodies, makes continual but vain attempts to appropriate it? For the ambivalence is quite inescapable: pleasure and terror, hysterical *furia* and melancholic withdrawal, organize the rhythm of the relationship to the feminine. On the side of nature, desire of a woman or procreation, there is pure hatred: 'Woman is *natural*, that is, abominable.' But on the side of artifice, images or 'anti-nature' (prostitutes, lesbians), there is fascination or even androgynous identification with the Other, as Butor and Bersani have shown.

This ambivalence has something to do with Baudelaire's fantastic and phantasmic scenario of love for 'a Mother who is abyss', deadly chasm. His own psychic theatre is thus directly linked to the theatre of the soma which is staged in allegories. The body is by turns divested of affect – phantasized as fragment, mannequin, machine, skeleton – and then overinvested with the fascination of lyrical proximity. As object of love and terror, it constantly fractures the wholeness of the poetic and narcissistic Ego. More precisely, it is the body of the Other, of an overly maternal feminine which vampirizes and attracts. The erotic for Baudelaire is a permanent reconstruction of that 'new primal scene' (Joyce Macdougall) which is so clearly expressed in the 'morality of the toy': the cult of the partial object, of derealizing and disillusioning play. Desire, however ardent it may be, is therefore nothing but its own metonymy: the 'sonorous jewels' of the 'beloved' naked woman, the severed head of Jokanaan, all those captivating horrors.

Seeing and non-seeing, representing and non-representing: this returns us to the age-old bodily encounter with the mother, who in this case denies to Baudelaire the desire of another desiring-desire, of a genuine otherness of the feminine. For the poet-dandy was first of all a precocious-dandy: 'The precocious taste for women. I confused the odour of fur with the odour of woman. I remember. . . . In the end I loved my mother for her elegance. I was therefore a precocious dandy.'[23] Perfume, fur and then hair, elegant appearances, memory as the mystification of seeming: everything has that apotropaic charm through which the theatre of the feminine paradoxically ends up fusing with the theatre of the dandy. Baudelaire, who lives his life in front of a mirror, looks and always wishes to see beyond his look – so much so that he eventually identifies the Beautiful with a woman's face, mysterious, voluptuous, weary and melancholic. The feminine becomes his reservoir of the imagination, the site of a baroque modern erotics: 'Woman is fatally suggestive: she lives a different life from her own; she lives spiritually in the imaginations that she haunts and fecundates.'[24]

It is thus the poetic experience of big-city crowds which concentrates with the greatest intensity this *realization of the new*, this invasion of the Other into the Ego, this 'modern' temporality of the precarious and fleeting, this captivation by the image. 'The pleasure of being in crowds is a mysterious experience of sensual pleasure [*jouissance*] in the multiplication of number.'[25] It is pleasure in a completely quantitative otherness which prostitutes me in and through the other and carries me into a hysterical pantheistic whirlpool: 'Religious intoxication of big cities. – Pantheism. I am all, all is I.'[26] In this crowd of *déclassés*, the poet as baroque man tries to find a body for himself: 'Like those lost souls which wander in search of a body to inhabit, he can enter the personality of anyone else, whenever he likes.'[27] His own vacancy or empty passivity authorizes him to practise the cult of multiple sensation, with its intoxication of number, newness and the commodity.

This imaginary *corps à corps* of the modern therefore has some analogy with that of the baroque. There is the same loss, the same absent or forbidden body, the same aesthetic of multiplied and then fragmented otherness. Hence the eroticization of the new takes place through a sudden movement: through *apparition* or *disappearance*, as in Salome.

Apparition is the 'holy prostitution of the soul which gives itself entirely, poetry and charity, to the unforeseen, to the passing stranger'. In his famous poem *À une passante*, to which Benjamin returns time and again, Baudelaire freezes this experience of the shock of love in which a beauty 'in black mourning' is fleetingly encountered. As he looks in the other's eye, the poet feels a sexual commotion, 'that gentleness which bewitches, that pleasure which destroys'.

Un éclair . . . puis la nuit! – Fugitive beauté
Dont le regard m'a fait soudainement renaître,
Ne te verrai-je plus que dans l'éternité?

Ailleurs, bien loin d'ici! trop tard! *jamais* peut-être!
Car j'ignore où tu fuis, tu ne sais où je vais,
Ô toi que j'eusse aimée, ô toi qui le savais![28]

A flash – vanishing, sudden, never: the look captures the temporality of the modern, its poetry of the unforeseen, the impossible, the detailed, its baroque values. For it is precisely this 'completely new' which is already a 'never more', an ancient, which Baudelaire loved in the baroque architecture of the Église de Saint-Loup in Namur: 'Saint-Loup. Sinister and gallant wonder. Saint-Loup is unlike anything I have seen by the Jesuits. The interior, a catafalque embellished with *black*, *pink* and *silver*. Confessionals all in a varied style, subtle, refined, baroque – a *new antiquity*.'[29] This 'delightful catafalque', this 'sinister and gallant wonder', this whole metaphor of the extremes of desire, concerns the structure of seeing as the unconscious poetic experience. We can therefore say with John E. Jackson 'that Baudelaire's relation to the baroque now becomes the gauge of his relationship to this dialectic of the "terrible" and the "delightful"' – or, in other words, of his relationship to the uncanny, to strangeness so familiar that it bewitches.

But the 'never more' governs disappearance just as much as it does the sudden appearance. In 'Le Cygne', Baudelaire's Paris is a city opened up to Haussmann's modernization, a waning, withering, vanishing city. Benjamin remarks that it is as if Baudelaire had 'a premonition of the distinctive precariousness of city centres'. The ancient and the modern, loss and melancholy, allegorize the architecture of stone blocks:

Le vieux Paris n'est plus (la forme d'une ville
Change plus vite, hélas! que le coeur d'un mortel) . . .

Paris change! mais rien dans sa mélancolie
N'a bougé! palais neufs, échafaudages, blocs,
Vieux faubourgs, tout pour moi devient allégorie,
Et mes chers souvenirs sont plus lourds que des rocs.[30]

The allegories, whether of woman or the city, of appearance or disappearance, are always allegories of present or absent bodies, fragile living bodies which are also frozen body-memories. This is why the child is the one who looks most accurately at the new, with the eye closest to that of the poet: 'The child sees everything as new; he is always intoxicated.' But the poet, like Oedipus, can recover the native language of correspondences and delight only at the price of a quite different journey into the bottomless depths, into the archaic which bewitches and terrifies, into the instant which aims to interrupt time. It is a journey into the non-human or inhuman which dwells within us as it does within history:

Plonger au fond du gouffre, Enfer ou Ciel, qu'importe?
Au fond de l'Inconnu pour trouver du *nouveau*![31]

Faced with this gulf of the Unknown – which recalls the *Urwald* or 'primeval forest' where Benjamin wandered as in a dream – we may end here our journey into the arcana of Western history and take leave of our guide, the Angelus Novus, the baroque angel of opposites, of progress and the storm, of 'the storm of progress'. For the baroque reason lodged within the modern – the reason of the Angel, the androgyne, the 'demonic' Salome – was nothing other than this journey in all its detours and labyrinths. Baudelaire, Salome, Benjamin, Musil have been so many crossroads, arcades or levels in this theatre where body-reason, woman-reason lies hidden.

It is a theatre of the impossible – of excess, illusion and disillusion

– like Quevedo's *sueño* with which we began. 'Something' is always returning there, a sense of the abyss which motivates thought to persevere. 'Tirelessly the process of thinking makes new beginnings, returning in a roundabout way to its original object.'[32] Let us leave it to Octavio Paz, a poet as modern-baroque as Baudelaire, to say the closing words on 'the original object', on those correspondences or oxymorons of desire in which the star is always black, the invisible visible, and where Salome is always present – Presence itself.

> The city unfolds
> its face is the face of my love
> its legs are the legs of a woman
> Towers plazas columns bridges streets
> river belt of drowned landscapes
> City or Woman Presence . . .
> But your sex is unnameable
> the other face of being
> the other face of time
> the reverse of life
> Here every speech ends
> here beauty is illegible
> here presence becomes awesome
> folded into itself Presence is empty
> the visible is invisible
> Here the invisible becomes visible
> here the star is black
> light is shadow and shadow light
> Here time stops
> the four points of the compass meet
> it is the lonely place and the meeting place
>
> City Woman Presence
> time ends here
> here it begins.[33]

Notes

1. Benjamin, *GS* V, p. 72.
2. Ibid., p. 513.
3. Ibid., p. 62.
4. John E. Jackson, *La Mort Baudelaire*, pp. 13, 62.
5. Baudelaire, 'Le Salon de 1859', in *Oeuvres complètes*, vol. 2, p. 621.
6. Ibid., p. 623.
7. See 'Logologische Fragmente II', in Novalis, *Schriften*, vol. 2, Stuttgart: W. Kohlkammer 1965, pp. 533–6 and 558–9.
8. 'Les Paradis artificiels', in *Oeuvres complètes*, vol. 2, p. 430.
9. 'Réflexions sur quelques-uns de mes contemporains', p. 137.

10. Baudelaire, 'The Jester and the Venus', in *The Poems in Prose*, edited and translated by Francis Scarfe, London: Anvil 1989, p. 43.
11. Freud, 'The "Uncanny"', p. 244.
12. See Jean-Michel Rey, *Des mots à l'oeuvre*, Paris: Aubier-Montaigne 1979.
13. *Oeuvres complètes*, vol. 2, p. 695.
14. Ibid., p. 696.
15. Benjamin, 'Paris – the Capital of the Nineteenth Century', p. 166.
16. *GS* V, p. 115.
17. Ibid., p. 461.
18. *The Complete Verse*, pp. 177–9.
19. 'The Eighteenth Brumaire of Louis Bonaparte', in Karl Marx, *Surveys from Exile*, Harmondsworth: New Left Review/Pelican 1973, p. 146.
20. 'Exposition universelle (1855)', in *Oeuvres complètes*, vol. 2, pp. 578ff.
21. *GS* V, p. 178.
22. Friedrich Nietzsche, 'Die dionysische Weltanschauung', in *Nachgelassene Schriften 1870–1873: Nietzsche Werke* III, p. 52.
23. 'Journaux intimes: Fusées', in *Oeuvres complètes*, vol. 1, p. 661.
24. 'Les Paradis artificiels', p. 399.
25. 'Journaux intimes: Fusées', p. 661.
26. Ibid., p. 651.
27. 'Crowds', in *The Poems in Prose*, p. 59.
28. 'A flash of light – then darkness. O vanishing beauty, whose glance brought me suddenly to life again, shall I never see you once more except in eternity? Elsewhere, far from here, too late or perhaps never? For whither you fled I know not, nor do you know whither I am bound – O you whom I could have loved, O you who knew it!' 'À une passante', in *The Complete Verse*, p. 186.
29. 'Sur la Belgique', in *Oeuvres complètes*, pp. 951–2.
30. 'The Paris of old is there no more – a city's pattern changes, alas, more swiftly than a human heart. . . Paris is changing, but naught in my melancholy has moved. These new palaces and scaffoldings, blocks of stone, old suburbs – everything for me is turned to allegory, and my memories are heavier than rocks.' 'Le Cygne', in *The Complete Verse*, pp. 174–6.
31. 'Dive into the gulf's depths, and – what matters if it is heaven, or hell? – into the depths of the Unknown, in quest of something *new*.' 'Le Voyage', in *The Complete Verse*, p. 247.
32. Benjamin, *The Origin of German Tragic Drama*, p. 28.
33. Octavio Paz, 'Clear Night', in *The Collected Poems 1957–1987*, translated by Eliot Weinberger, Manchester: Carcanet 1988, p. 101.

INDEX